DUNS SCOTUS

GREAT MEDIEVAL THINKERS

Series Editor
Brian Davies
Blackfriars, University of Oxford,
and Fordham University

DUNS SCOTUS
Richard Cross

BERNARD OF CLAIRVAUX
Gillian R. Evans

DUNS SCOTUS

Richard Cross

NEW YORK   OXFORD
OXFORD UNIVERSITY PRESS
1999

Oxford University Press

Oxford   New York

Athens   Auckland   Bangkok   Bogotá   Buenos Aires   Calcutta
Cape Town   Chennai   Dar es Salaam   Delhi   Florence   Hong Kong   Istanbul
Karachi   Kuala Lumpur   Madrid   Melbourne   Mexico City   Mumbai
Nairobi   Paris   São Paulo   Singapore   Taipei   Tokyo   Toronto   Warsaw

and associated companies in
Berlin   Ibadan

Copyright © 1999 by Richard Cross

Published by Oxford University Press, Inc.
198 Madison Avenue, New York, New York 10016

Oxford is a registered trademark of Oxford University Press

Library of Congress Cataloging-in-Publication Data
Cross, Richard.
Duns Scotus / Richard Cross.
p.   cm.—(Great medieval thinkers)
Includes bibliographical references and indexes.
ISBN 0-19-512552-5; ISBN 0-19-512553-3 (pbk.)
1. Duns Scotus, John, ca. 1266–1308.   2. Theology—History—Middle
Ages, 600–1500.   3. Philosophical theology—History.   4. Philosophy,
Medieval.   I. Title.   II. Series
B765.D74C75   1999
189.4—dc21   98-25710

1 3 5 7 9 8 6 4 2

Printed in the United States of America
on acid-free paper

FOR ESSAKA

SERIES FOREWORD

Many people would be surprised to be told that there *were* any great medieval thinkers. If a *great* thinker is one from whom we can learn today and if *medieval* serves as an adjective for describing anything that existed from (roughly) A.D. 600 to 1500, then—so it is often supposed—medieval thinkers cannot be called "great."

But why not? One answer often given appeals to ways in which medieval authors with a taste for argument and speculation tend to invoke "authorities," especially religious ones. Such invocation of authority is not the stuff of which great thought is made—so it is often said today. It is also frequently said that greatness is not to be found in the thinking of those who lived before the rise of modern science, not to mention that of modern philosophy and theology. Students of science nowadays are hardly ever referred to literature originating earlier than the seventeenth century. Students of philosophy in the twentieth century have often been taught nothing about the history of ideas between Aristotle (384–22 B.C.) and Descartes (1596–1650). Modern students of theology have often been frequently encouraged to believe that significant theological thinking is a product of the nineteenth century.

Yet the origins of modern science lie in the conviction that the world is open to rational investigation and is orderly rather than chaotic—a conviction which came fully to birth, and was systematically explored and developed, during the Middle Ages. And it is in medieval thinking that we find some of the most sophisticated and rigorous discussions in the areas of philosophy and theology ever offered for human consumption. This is, perhaps, not surprising if we note that medieval philosophers and theologians, like their modern counterparts, were mostly university teachers, participating in an ongoing debate with contributors from different countries and—unlike many seventeenth-, eighteenth-, and even nineteenth-century philosophers and theologians—did not work in relative isolation from the community of teachers and students with whom they were regularly involved. As for the question of appeal to authority: It is certainly true that many medieval thinkers believed in authority (especially religious authority) as a serious court of appeal; and it is true that most people today would say that they cannot do this. Yet authority is as much an ingredient in our thinking as it was for medieval thinkers. For most of what we take ourselves to know derives from the trust we have reposed in our various teachers, colleagues, friends, and general contacts. When it comes to reliance on authority, the main difference between us and medieval thinkers lies in the fact that their reliance on authority (insofar as they had it) was often more focused and explicitly acknowledged than is ours. It does not lie in the fact that it was uncritical and naive in a way that our reliance on authority is not.

In recent years, such truths have come to be increasingly recognized at what we might call the "academic" level. No longer disposed to think of the Middle Ages as "dark" (meaning "lacking in intellectual richness"), many university departments (and many publishers of books and journals) now devote a lot of their energy to the study of medieval thinking. And they do so not simply on the assumption that it is historically significant. They do so in the light of the increasingly developing insight that it is full of things with which to dialogue and from which to learn. Following a long period in which medieval thinking was thought to be of only antiquarian interest, we are now witnessing its revival as a contemporary voice—one to converse with, one from which we might learn.

The Great Medieval Thinkers series reflects and is part of this exciting revival. Written by a distinguished team of experts, it aims to provide substantial introductions to a range of medieval authors. And it does so on the assumption that they are as worth reading today as they were when they wrote. Students of medieval "literature" (e.g., the writings of Chaucer or Dante) are currently well supplied (if not over-supplied) with second-ary works to aid them when reading the objects of their concern. But those with an interest in medieval philosophy and theology are by no means so fortunate when it comes to reliable and accessible volumes to help them. The Great Medieval Thinkers series therefore aspires to help remedy that deficiency by offering solid overviews of the lives and thought of medi-eval philosophers and theologians, coupled with modern reflection on what they had to say. Taken individually, volumes in the series will pro-vide valuable treatments of single thinkers, many of whom are not cur-rently covered by any comparable volumes. Taken together, they will constitute a rich and distinguished history and discussion of medieval philosophy and theology considered as a whole. With an eye on college and university students, and with an eye on the general reader, authors of volumes in the series write in a clear and accessible manner so that even readers without previous knowledge can learn something about these medieval thinkers. Each contributor to the series will also strive to in-form, engage, and generally entertain even those with specialist knowl-edge in the area of medieval thinking. So, as well as surveying and intro-ducing, volumes in the series will advance the state of medieval studies both at the historical and the speculative level.

In this respect, the present volume is typical. John Duns Scotus (c. 1266–1308), the "Subtle Doctor," is arguably the second most signifi-cant medieval philosopher theologian—the first (by fairly universal con-sent, whether from friends or foes) being Thomas Aquinas (c. 1225–74), with whom Scotus interestingly disagreed on a number of important issues. Nevertheless, there is not currently in English an introduction to and study of the thought of Duns Scotus—one which covers Scotus's thinking as a whole, not just the few philosophical theories commonly associated with him. Richard Cross's book is precisely such an introduc-tion. But it also provides a sustained critical reaction to Scotus, one which considers him as a theologian as well as a philosopher. Unlike those of Aquinas, many of Scotus's writings still await translation into English. And, though contemporary writers have begun to treat Scotus seriously as someone with whom to engage, evaluative discussions of his thinking, especially among analytical philosophers, have not always taken into ac-count as much as might be noted in his thinking when it comes to evalu-ating it. In his book, however, Cross discusses the thinking of Scotus with a firm command of the entire Scotus corpus behind him. And he does so as someone with a good knowledge of contemporary philosophy and with much intellectual dexterity. The result is something that nobody seriously concerned with medieval thinking can afford to ignore, and I am delighted to commend it to readers as the inaugural volume in the Great Medieval Thinkers series.

BRIAN DAVIES

PREFACE

The importance of John Duns Scotus (c. 1266–1308) in the history of Western thought is well known, and over the past few years studies of both his philosophy and theology have begun to appear. There is, however, nothing to give the English-speaking reader that provides a general overview of Scotus's theology—construing 'theology' broadly to include both natural theology (metaphysics) and revealed theology. This work represents a preliminary attempt at rectifying this lack. Deciding whether to write for the absolute theological and philosophical beginner or for the more specialist theologian or philosopher was not easy. I opted for the latter course. It is not for nothing that Scotus's contemporaries called him the "subtle" doctor, and it seems to me that an attempt to present Scotus in the simplest possible terms is likely to fail to capture what is most distinctive in his thought. Scotus *is* a complex and difficult thinker, not the least when making his own innovative contributions to the debates. The most rewarding approach is to confront this complexity head-on, trying, at least, to avoid some of the worst excesses of Scotist jargon. This is what I have attempted to do here. Understanding Scotus is always a provisional matter; opaque and obscure passages can suddenly yield meanings that constrain a reader to revise his or her view of a whole topic in Scotus. So I expect that an attempt to give a general picture of Scotus's thought, be it his philosophy or (as in this case) his theology, will generate debate. Writing on the history of ideas would be a sorry and (indeed) thankless task if this were not the case. I hope at least to show that Scotus has a profound and highly distinctive theological vision, and that it still has much to offer to the contemporary theologian. I have also tried to show where I think Scotus has gone wrong. I do so on the presupposition that the sort of theological opinions he espouses are broadly correct. There would, of course, be much of a theological nature that theologians today, of all denominations, would want to disagree with. I do not enter into that sort of debate, which seems a step removed from the historical and exegetical work I am tackling here.

Several people have helped me in various ways. Chapter 2 was discussed at some length at the philosophy of religion seminar at King's College, London, and at a class at the Studium of the Oxford Blackfriars. Rory Fox kindly read early drafts of what would become chapters 1–3, and conversations with Thomas Williams helped me greatly with chapter 7. Needless to say, the views here are mine, as are the mistakes. Finally, thanks, as always, to Dr. Essaka Joshua.

Oriel College   R. A. C.
Oxford
January 1999

CONTENTS

Abbreviations   xvii

1   Duns Scotus, Philosophy, and Theology   3

    1. *Duns Scotus: Life and works*   3
    2. *Philosophy and the scope of theology*   6
    3. *The nature of theology*   8
    4. *Theology and reason*   10
    5. *Duns Scotus: Theologian and philosopher*   13

2   God: Existence, Unicity, and Simplicity   15

    1. *The existence of a first agent*   16
    2. *The existence of an ultimate goal of activity*   23
    3. *The existence of a maximally excellent being*   23
    4. *The coextensiveness of these three properties*   25
    5. *The infinity of the first agent*   26
    6. *Divine unicity*   27
    7. *Divine simplicity*   29

3   God: Perfection, Infinity, and Religious Language   31

    1. *Perfect-being theology*   31
    2. *The univocity theory of religious language*   33

3. *Divine infinity*   39
4. *Divine simplicity and the divine attributes*   42

4   God: Knowledge and Agency   47

1. *Divine intellect and will*   47
2. *Divine knowledge*   48
3. *Divine agency*   56

5   God the Trinity   61

1. *The divine processions*   62
2. *The constitution of the divine persons*   65
3. *The unity of the divine essence*   67
4. *The unity of God's external action*   70

6   Humanity: Body, Soul, and Immortality   73

1. *Matter, form, and the human soul*   73
2. *The immortality of the soul*   77
3. *The resurrection of the body*   78

7   Humanity: Freedom, Ethics, and Sin   83

1. *Intellect, will, and freedom*   83
2. *Ethics*   89
3. *Sin*   95
4. *Original sin*   96

8   Humanity: Predestination, Merit, and Grace   101

1. *Predestination*   101
2. *Merit*   103
3. *Grace and the remission of sins*   107

9   Jesus: God and Man   113

1. *The relation between Christ's human nature and the Word*   114
2. *Christ's human nature*   117
3. *Grace, knowledge, and will*   122

4. *The incarnate divine person*   124
5. *The communication of properties*   125

10   Jesus: Predestination and Merit   127

1. *The motive for the incarnation*   127
2. *Redemption*   129
3. *Mary*   132

11   Sacraments   135

1. *Sacramental causality*   136
2. *Grace and character*   138
3. *Eucharist: Transubstantiation and sacrifice*   139

Appendix   147

1. *Metaphysics and the transcendental attributes*   147
2. *The formal distinction*   149
3. *The beatific vision*   149

Notes   153

Bibliography   215

Manuscripts   215
Printed primary sources   215
Secondary sources   218

Index Locorum   227

General Index   240

ABBREVIATIONS

Alexander of Hales, School of
Sum. Fr. Alex.   *Summa Fratris Alexandri*

Anselm
CDH   *Cur Deus Homo*
De Casu Diab.   *De Casu Diaboli*
De Conc. Virg.   *De Conceptu Virginali*
Monol.   *Monologion*
Pros.   *Proslogion*

Aquinas
De Car.   *Quaestio Disputata de Caritate*
Quae. Quod.   *Quaestiones Quodlibetales*
Script. Sent.   *Scriptum super Libros Sententiarum*
ST   *Summa Theologiae*

Aristotle
An. post.   *Analytica posteriora*
Cael.   *De caelo*

Cat.	*Categoriae*
De an.	*De anima*
Eth. Nic.	*Ethica Nicomachea*
Int.	*De interpretatione*
Metaph.	*Metaphysica*
Ph.	*Physica*
Soph. el.	*Sophistici elenchi*
Top.	*Topica*

Augustine
Contra Max.	*Contra Maximinum*
De Civ. Dei	*De Civitate Dei*
De Div. Qu.	*De Diversis Quaestionibus*
De Gen.	*De Genesi ad Litteram*
De Trin.	*De Trinitate*
Enarr. in Ps.	*Enarrationes in Psalmos*

Basil of Caesarea
Ep.	*Epistulae*

Boethius
De Per.	*De Persona et Duabus Naturis*

Bonaventure
Comm. Sent.	*Commentaria in Quatuor Libros Sententiarum*
De Myst. Trin.	*De Mysterio Trinitatis*

Calvin
Inst.	*Christianae Religionis Institutio*

Dionysius the Pseudo-Areopagite
De Div. Nom.	*De Divinis Nominibus*

Duns Scotus
Add. Mag.	*Additiones Magnae*
DPP	*De Primo Principio*
In Metaph.	*Quaestiones super libros Metaphysicorum*
Lect.	*Lectura*

Ord.	*Ordinatio*
Quod.	*Quodlibetum*
Rep.	*Reportatio Parisiensis*
Super Praed.	*Quaestiones super Praedicamenta*

Henry of Ghent
Quodlib.	*Quodlibeta*
SQ	*Summa Quaestionum Ordinariarum*

John of Damascus
De Fide Orth.	*De Fide Orthodoxa*

Peter Lombard
Sent.	*Sententiae in Quatuor Libris Distinctae*

Richard of St. Victor
Trin.	*De Trinitate*

Rupert of Deutz
De Glor.	*De Gloria et honore filii hominis super Mattheum*

William of Auxerre
Sum. Aur.	*Summa Aurea*

William of Ockham
Quod. Sept.	*Quodlibeta Septem*
Rep.	*Reportatio*

William of Ware
In Sent.	*In Sententias*

VERSIONS AND TRANSLATIONS

AW	Duns Scotus, *God and Creatures: The Quodlibetal Questions*, ed. and trans. Felix Alluntis and Allan B. Wolter (Princeton, N.J., and London: Princeton University Press, 1975)
DS	Henricus Denzinger and Adolfus Schönmetzer (eds.), *Enchiridion Symbolorum, Definitionum et Declarationum*

de Rebus Fidei et Morum, 36th ed. (Barcelona, Freiburg, and Rome: Herder, 1976)

FK   William of Ockham, *Quodlibetal Questions*, trans. Alfred J. Freddoso and Francis E. Kelley, Yale Library of Medieval Philosophy, 2 vols. (New Haven and London: Yale University Press, 1991)

FW   *Duns Scotus, Metaphysician*, ed. and trans. William A. Frank and Allan B. Wolter, Purdue University Press Series in the History of Philosophy (West Lafayette, Ind.: Purdue University Press, 1995)

OT   William of Ockham, *Opera Theologica*, ed. Iuvenalis Lalor and others, 10 vols. (St. Bonaventure, N.Y.: St. Bonaventure University, 1967–86)

PW   Duns Scotus, *Philosophical Writings: A Selection*, ed. and trans. Allan B. Wolter (Indianapolis, Ind., and Cambridge: Hackett, 1987)

Spade   Paul Vincent Spade (ed. and trans.), *Five Texts on the Mediaeval Problem of Universals: Porphyry, Boethius, Abelard, Duns Scotus, Ockham* (Indianapolis, Ind., and Cambridge: Hackett, 1994)

Tanner   Norman Tanner (ed.), *Decrees of the Ecumenical Councils*, 2 vols. (London: Sheed and Ward; Washington, D.C.: Georgetown University Press, 1990)

Vatican   Duns Scotus, John, *Opera Omnia*, ed. C Balić and others (Vatican City: Typis Polyglottis Vaticanis, 1950–)

Vos   Duns Scotus, *Contingency and Freedom: Lectura I 39*, ed. A. Vos Jaczn. and others, The New Synthese Historical Library, 42 (Dordrecht, Boston, and London: Kluwer, 1994)

WA   "Duns Scotus' Parisian Proof for the Existence of God," ed. and trans. Allan B. Wolter and Marilyn McCord Adams, *Franciscan Studies*, 42 (1982): 248–321

Wadding   Duns Scotus, John, *Opera Omnia*, ed. Luke Wadding, 12 vols. (Lyons: Durand, 1639)

WFS   "Duns Scotus on the Necessity of Revealed Knowledge" [*Ordinatio*, prol.1], trans. Allan B. Wolter, *Franciscan Studies*, 11 (1951): 231–72

WM   *Duns Scotus on the Will and Morality*, ed. and trans. Allan
               B. Wolter (Washington, D.C.: The Catholic University
               of America Press, 1986)

SERIES

BGPTM   Beiträge zur Geschichte der Philosophie und Theologie
               des Mittelalters
CCCM   Corpus Christianorum Continuatio Mediaevalis
CCSL   Corpus Christianorum Series Latina
CSEL   Corpus Scriptorum Ecclesiasticorum Latinorum
PG   Patrologia Graeca, ed. J.-P. Migne
PL   Patrologia Latina, ed. J.-P. Migne
STGM   Studien und Texte zur Geistesgeschichte des Mittelalters

MANUSCRIPT SIGLA

MS A   Assisi, Biblioteca Communale, MS 137
MS V   Vienna, Österreichische Nationalbibliothek, MS 1453

DUNS SCOTUS

DUNS SCOTUS,
PHILOSOPHY, AND THEOLOGY

1. Duns Scotus: Life and works

Duns Scotus is, along with Thomas Aquinas, perhaps the greatest of the medieval theologians and certainly the one who inspired the most interest in the centuries after his death.[1] But we know nothing of his life other than a few bare facts.[2] Scotus was a Franciscan friar and, thus, a member of one of the two most intellectually active orders of the time (the other, of course, being the Dominicans). One of the few definite dates we have for Scotus's life is his ordination: 17 March 1291, at St. Andrew's Priory, Northampton, which like Oxford was in the diocese of Lincoln. But this date allows us to hazard reasonably secure estimates for other dates, too. The minimum canonical age for ordination was twenty-five, so Scotus must have been born before 17 March 1266. And we know that the bishop of Lincoln conducted an ordination on 23 December 1290, at Wycombe. Assuming that Scotus would have been ordained at the earliest opportunity allowed by canon law, he must have not yet turned twenty-five by the time of the December ordination. This places his birth late in 1265 or early in 1266. We learn from John Major's *History of Greater Britain* that Duns, just north of the border into Scotland, was the place of his birth.[3]

Another definite date allows us to infer another fact. We know that Scotus was in Oxford in 1300, because his name appears in a letter, dated

3

26 July, as one of twenty-two friars presented to the bishop of Lincoln for a license to hear confessions. The list of names includes Philip Bridlington as the incoming Franciscan regent master in theology. And we know that Scotus took part in a disputation under Bridlington during his time as a "formed bachelor," one whose lecturing duties are over. This would mean that Scotus's studies in Oxford ended in June 1301, and thus—because the course was thirteen years' duration—must have begun in October 1288. Equally, allowing for the normal statutory arrangements, we can infer that Scotus commented on the *Sentences* of Peter Lombard between October 1298 and June 1299. Two books of this early *Lectura* survive, work that would form the basis for Scotus's edited version of his Oxford lectures—the *Ordinatio*.

We have two other firm dates that allow us to reconstruct most of the years between 1300 and 1307. First, a very early manuscript of Scotus's Parisian commentary on the *Sentences* has Scotus lecturing in Paris from 1302 to 1303. Scotus was forced to leave France, along with some eighty other pro-papal friars, during June 1303. The expelled students were allowed to return to Paris after April 1304, where Scotus must have completed his lectures on the *Sentences*. (The commentary on book 4 mentions papal documents that appeared in early 1304.)

We know that on 18 November 1304—our third firm date—the minister general of the Franciscan order appointed Scotus as the Franciscan regent master in theology at Paris, and Scotus presumably took up this post in 1305. One of Scotus's duties as regent master was to conduct disputations, and we have from this period Scotus's great set of quodlibetal questions, disputed probably in Advent 1306 or Lent 1307.

One final date allows us to reconstruct the last year of Scotus's life. We know that he was in Cologne on 20 February 1308, and that he was lector at the Franciscan studium there, a post he presumably took up in October 1307. Scotus died in 1308, on a date traditionally held to be 8 November. One further fact that we have comes from Scotus himself: his testimony that he spent some time in Cambridge.[4] Possible dates include 1301–1302, or (perhaps less likely) 1303–1304.

Scotus was thus living and working just a little less than two generations after Aquinas and Bonaventure, his greatest theological predecessors. But theologically a lot happened between these two mid-thirteenth-century thinkers and Duns Scotus. The important secular theologian Henry of Ghent (c. 1217–93) in many ways reshaped and deepened the theological agenda in Paris after Aquinas. (Henry came to theology late, and clearly belongs theologically to the years after Aquinas.) So the theological debate had moved on from Aquinas and Bonaventure, and very often we find Scotus engaging not with these earlier schoolmen but with his nearer contemporaries, thinkers from the 1280s and 1290s.[5]

This is not to say that Scotus ignored the work of the earlier schoolmen. Wherever possible in what follows, I try to relate what Scotus says to ideas we find in Aquinas, and this procedure is not entirely lacking in precedent in Scotus's own writings. (My reason for doing this is pedagogic rather than historical: I am assuming that most people interested in Scotus will already know something about Aquinas, and perhaps know very little about—say—Henry of Ghent.) On the other hand, I try to locate the topics I discuss in Scotus plausibly within their context in the history of ideas. And this sometimes involves discussion of Scotus's lesser-known immediate predecessors.

One conclusion that should, I hope, emerge fairly clearly to anyone who knows much about the thought of Scotus's eminent Franciscan predecessor Bonaventure is that we cannot talk of a Franciscan tradition of theology that would embrace both Bonaventure and Scotus, the two most significant Franciscan theologians of the middle ages. Scotus disagrees with Bonaventure almost as much as he disagrees with the Dominican Aquinas. On the other hand, much Franciscan theology *after* Scotus was driven by the agenda set by Scotus. Perhaps the clearest example of this is William of Ockham, who—at least in the earlier part of his life, when he was still writing theology—agreed with very many aspects of Scotus's theology (while disagreeing with Scotus on very many aspects of philosophy).

In fact, Scotus's influence on succeeding thinkers is great. There are some clear links between Scotus's thought and that of the Reformers. Perhaps the most obvious one is Scotus's merely forensic account of the remission of sins. There are some important features of sacramental teaching that have some links with later Protestant views: Scotus's intellectual preference for consubstantiation over transubstantiation, for example, or his denial of real supernatural powers to the ministers of the sacraments. On the Catholic side, Scotus's defense of the immaculate conception of Mary was crucial in the development of this dogma. Philosophically, too, Scotus is extremely important. As we shall see, Leibniz's 'possible worlds', so central to much modern metaphysics and philosophical logic, owe their existence to innovations made by Scotus. Scotus's famous account of individuation is still the starting point for modern discussions of the question. And his account of freedom of the will is the first serious attempt to defend an account of what philosophers today call "contra-causal" freedom. Scotus's discussions in the philosophy of religion, it perhaps goes without saying, are cited frequently in the modern literature.[6]

Scotus's written output includes the usual sorts of production of a scholastic theologian. It is not always easy to date these various works—though it is important to do so, since Scotus's dynamic thought underwent many changes. By far the most important set of works for understanding Scotus's theology are his lectures on the *Sentences*. The early *Lectura*,[7] as we have seen, dates probably from 1298 to 1299. Scotus appears to have begun correcting the earlier parts of his still-incomplete *Ordinatio* by 1300.[8] But it does not look as though he revised all of the *Ordinatio* as we have it before leaving for Paris where, as we have seen, Scotus began a new set of lectures, which we have in the form of *reportatio examinata* or student lecture notes checked by Scotus himself.[9] It is usually felt that Scotus's *Reportatio Parisiensis* was completed by 1305. (We have earlier, unexamined versions of these Parisian lectures too, but I will not use these less-reliable versions here.) The *Additiones Magnae* assembled by Scotus's student William of Alnwick supplement the Oxford commentary with material from the Paris lectures.[10]

I have already mentioned Scotus's Parisian *Quodlibetal Questions*.[11] Probably from this late period we also have the *De Primo Principio*, a version of Scotus's proof for God's existence perhaps compiled with the help of an assistant.[12] Scotus also produced some important questions on various Aristotelian works: the *Metaphysics* (books 1–9),[13] *On the Soul*, *Categories*, *On Interpretation*, and *Sophistical Refutations*.[14] Apart from the last books of the questions on the *Metaphysics*, these are felt to be early works, certainly dating from before 1300. But at least the last book of the *Metaphysics* questions postdates book four of the *Ordinatio*.[15]

2. Philosophy and the scope of theology

The role that reason has to play in theology is not a subject on which theologians have ever reached any consensus. Denominational differences and varieties of philosophical presuppositions have contributed to this lack of agreement. In the rest of this chapter, I want to examine the way in which Scotus delineates the engagement between philosophy and theology, or reason and revelation. I hope to show that Scotus makes a clear distinction between philosophy and theology, and that Scotus is deeply convinced of the rationality of theology.

Scotus distinguishes between *theologia in se* (theology in itself) and *theologia nostra* (our theology). The first refers to all possible knowledge about God: all those things which are naturally known by *God* about himself.[16] The second refers to the understanding possible for *us* to have in this life.[17] The 'theology' of interest throughout the rest of this chapter is *theologia nostra*. This theology is the study of those facts about God that we can only know via *revelation*. According to Scotus, the most important such fact is that God is a Trinity. We cannot know this fact by our natural reason. Scotus talks about God's Trinitarian nature as the subject of theology: God "in his essence" (*ut haec essentia*, lit. "as this essence").[18] God in his essence cannot be known naturally by material creatures like us.[19] We might put the claim as follows: God in his essence can only be known by his self-revelation. Scotus attempts to show that this is the case.[20] First, we cannot prove that God is a Trinity. We infer God's existence by our natural reason on the grounds that God is necessary to explain certain facts in the world around us. But we do not need to postulate that God is a Trinity in order to explain any of these empirical facts.[21] Secondly, Scotus argues that he can show that we can only have knowledge of God in his essence if God decides to reveal himself to us. His reason is that we can show that any relationship between a creature and God's essence is contingent, dependent upon the divine will.[22] (This does not, of course, prevent us from proving God's existence and his possession of certain attributes.)

Where, according to Scotus, can we learn about the contents of God's self-revelation? According to some of his contemporaries, there are two sources for revealed truths: the Bible and tradition.[23] Scotus sometimes argues for the more old-fashioned view that the Bible is the unique source for revealed truths. What we know about God in his essence is limited to what God reveals to us about himself in the Bible, and what we can deduce from the propositions contained in the Bible.[24] (This does not mean, of course, that *everything* in the Bible counts as theology; doubtless Scotus would have found plenty of metaphysics and natural science in it too.) On the other hand, Scotus's treatment of some doctrinal issues in theology involves appeal to tradition as a source of theology. Christ's descent into hell is not found in the Bible. But the Holy Spirit taught the apostles much that is not in the Bible; they handed it on in turn to us *per consuetudinem* (by custom).[25] The doctrines of sacramental character and transubstantiation are taught not in the Bible, but, according to Scotus, by Pope Innocent III; they are to be accepted merely because of the authority of the Roman Church.[26]

In accord with the majority thirteenth-century view, Scotus expressly notes that it is impossible to know and believe one and the same thing at the same time.[27] Given that theology is the science of things we ascertain by revelation—the science of "things believed"—I take it that our theology does not include things we know naturally. Certainly, none of the principles or axioms of theology are shared by any other kind of study: metaphysics or natural science, for example.[28] And I take it that none of the conclusions of our properly theological science are shared by any of these disciplines. So nothing that we can know about God by natural reason belongs to the study of theology.[29] The science responsible for yielding conclusions about the existence and attributes of God without appeal to revelation is *metaphysics*.[30] Theology for Scotus is thus rather more restricted in scope than it is for us. For example, the material that I cover in chapters 2–4 counts not as theology but as metaphysics. (Much of the rest of the material counts as theology.) On the other hand, theology, for Scotus, includes much more than is included in Aquinas's *sacra doctrina*. The reason is that the amount of material concerning God and humanity that according to Aquinas can be known naturally is far wider than the amount that Scotus holds to be known naturally. Aquinas, for example, believes that we can prove the incorruptibility of the soul. Scotus disagrees.[31] So human immortality is a philosophical truth for Aquinas, and a theological one for Scotus.

3. The nature of theology

Like Aquinas and most medieval thinkers after him, Scotus holds that theology is a science.[32] By 'science' today we mean a discipline that proceeds by induction, formulating hypotheses to explain data and verifying these hypotheses by experiment. It would certainly be odd to label theology a science in this sense. But Scotus means something different by 'science'. His model is the standard thirteenth- and fourteenth-century one, derived from Aristotle. On this model, a science is an axiomatized *deductive* system, consisting of basic propositions or axioms from which we infer conclusions or theorems.[33] The point of labeling theology a science is to bring out its character as a deductive system. The closest modern equivalent to an Aristotelian science would be pure mathematics. Pure mathematics is what Aristotle would label a *theoretical* science (one broadly said to do with things) not a *practical* science (said to do with actions).[34] The majority non-Franciscan view in the late thirteenth and early fourteenth centuries is that theology is a theoretical science, or at least primarily a theoretical science. As Aquinas puts it,

> It [sacred doctrine] is more theoretical than practical, since it is mainly concerned with the divine things which are, rather than with things human beings do.[35]

A different, broadly Franciscan, view is that theology is neither theoretical nor practical but rather affective or contemplative.[36] Scotus, on the other hand, reasons that theology is a *practical* science, not at all theoretical. Its aim is to issue in right action[37]—what Scotus labels 'praxis':[38]

> The intellect perfected by the habit of theology apprehends God as one who should be loved, and according to rules from which praxis can be elicited. Therefore, the habit of theology is practical.[39]

The argument, I take it, shows that theology is a practical science. But it does not yet show that theology is *merely* a practical science, and not at all theoretical. Scotus, however, provides a further argument to show that theology is not at all theoretical. He reasons that every item in the science of theology is, or can be, action-directing, because the more we know about theology, the more we might be disposed to love God. And Scotus proposes a distinctive description of a merely practical science that theology thus described would satisfy: "Every science that deals with theoretical items in no greater detail than is necessary for praxis is practical and not theoretical."[40] Theology on Scotus's account will necessarily satisfy this description, since any putatively theoretical item that theology covers increases, or can increase, our disposition to love God. Scotus does not hold that it is necessary that any of the propositions in the theological science *actually* have action-directing force. For any science to be practical it is necessary merely that the contents of the science *could* have action-directing force.[41]

I do not think that Scotus's account of theology here is remarkably different from Aquinas's. On Scotus's definition of a practical science, theology as described by Aquinas is such a science. In fact, it is worth noting that on this account of the distinction between a theoretical science and a practical one, it would be impossible for theology *not* to be a practical science.[42]

4. Theology and reason

The rationality of theology

Unlike Aquinas and, later, Ockham, Scotus does not expressly address the question of the rationality of theology. But as we shall see when we come to look in detail at certain of Scotus's theological claims and the ways in which he defends them, the philosophical *coherence* of these claims is always of extreme importance for him. On the other hand, in his account of transubstantiation, Scotus is prepared to accept what he sees as a needlessly complex account over a simpler and (for this reason) intellectually preferable account just because he thinks that the Church teaches it. But neither of these, of course, is at all the same as accepting an account that is known to be philosophically incoherent, as Ockham was later happy to do.[43]

Can we show that theology is necessary?

In the very first question of the prologue to the *Ordinatio*, Scotus asks whether or not we need revealed doctrine. The question clearly has a number of different possible senses. For example: Do we need revealed doctrine in order to be saved? Or: Can we show that there are some things that we cannot know by natural reason? Scotus sets up the debate as an argument between the "theologians" and the "philosophers." According to the theologians, we can prove that there are some facts that we cannot prove by our natural powers.[44] The reason for this is that we can show that the enjoyment of God is our final goal and that the relevant knowledge required to allow us to achieve this goal is beyond our natural cognitive powers.[45] On this account, unsurprisingly, a positive answer to the first question means that we must give a positive answer to the second. Philosophy, on this view, points beyond itself to theology.

According to the philosophers, a negative answer should be given to the second question. But the philosophers hold a stronger view than this. They claim that we can show that there is nothing that we cannot know by means of our natural powers (i.e., that theology is impossible). Scotus notes:

> The philosophers, then, would say that no supernatural knowledge is necessary for man in his present state, but that all the knowledge he needs could be acquired by the action of natural causes.[46]

Scotus, as we shall see, supposes that this view is adequately refuted in terms of the existence of *facts* about which philosophy cannot tell us; the point being that Scotus understands the view of the philosophers to relate to the second question, not the first.

Scotus's answer to the first question (Do we need revealed doctrine in order to be saved?) is a resounding "No." He reasons that it would be possible for God to save someone without the gift of faith, and a fortiori without any theological knowledge.[47] So Scotus clearly disagrees with the theologians. He also disagrees with the philosophers, because—as we have seen—he holds that there are some facts that we cannot know by natural reason. But he does not offer an unequivocal answer to the second question (Can we show that there are some things which we cannot know by natural reason?). His first proposed answer is that we can prove neither that there are some facts inaccessible to our natural reason, nor that there fail to be such facts.[48] This claim is extremely agnostic. Its result is that theology "will get nowhere with heathen philosophers."[49]

But Scotus is sometimes less ambivalent:

> Natural reason merely shows us that it is necessary for us to know definitely one part of this contradiction: "The enjoyment [of God] is [our] end; this enjoyment is not our end."[50]

This gives us Scotus's second answer. We can demonstrate that we need revelation to show us which disjunct is in fact true. On this position, we can show that the philosophers are mistaken. But the position is not quite the same as the view of the theologians. According to the theologians, we know that our goal is supernatural, and it is for this reason that we need revelation and the consequent theological science. According to Scotus, we know that we cannot know whether our goal is supernatural or not. Philosophy, for Scotus, points beyond itself rather more tentatively than it does according to the "theologians."

Should we believe the scriptures?

Scotus, as noted above, clearly holds that theology extends merely to those things that cannot be known by natural reason. Scotus thinks, however, that there are some good reasons why we should believe the scriptures: The scriptures are confirmed by the fulfillment, in the New Testament, of Old Testament prophecies; the scriptures are internally concordant; the scriptures were written by authoritative writers who were prepared to die for the truth of their faith; the scriptures are believed by a "famous and honest community" (i.e., the Church); the contents of the scriptures are eminently reasonable; and the scriptures contain accounts of miracles attested to by God. Further, non-Christian religious claims are easily shown to be irrational; non-Christian religions are ephemeral, and will not endure; non-Christians (Josephus, and the Sibyl) attest to the truth of the scriptures; and Christians experience that God will be present to those who ask for him.[51] Presumably, Scotus does not think that these reasons have any probative force. If they did, we could demonstrate the truth of all Christian doctrines by our natural reason. Scotus describes these arguments as "rationally convincing."[52] What Scotus is getting at is that Christianity is coherent and that there are good (non-demonstrative) reasons for believing it to be true.

The interest of the arguments lies fundamentally in the light they cast on what Scotus would count as good evidence for the truth of some claim that cannot be demonstrated deductively. The arguments themselves are fairly standard apologetic arguments that would be unlikely to convince anyone with a modern critical sensitivity to textual and historiographical issues. Whatever we make of the arguments, it is clear that Scotus is quite optimistic with regard to the good sense in believing in the Bible—and hence in supernatural revelation. Scotus is therefore optimistic with regard to the good sense of doing theology. This attitude is, of course, wholly consistent with Scotus's claim that supernatural revelation is necessary for us.

5. Duns Scotus:
Theologian and philosopher

Throughout the twentieth century, historians of scholasticism have debated the extent to which there was ever a scholastic *philosophy* at all, independent of theology; and, as a result, whether the major schoolmen—all of whom were trained theologians—could really be counted as philosophers as well as theologians. It seems to me that Scotus, like Aquinas, has a clear conception of the differences between philosophy and theology. As I have begun to try to show elsewhere, Scotus never relies merely on theological arguments when *ex professo* discussing philosophical matters.[53] Scotus is thus interested in giving a coherent account of the world independently of revelation. Scotus should therefore be counted as a philosopher with a philosophical agenda.

The discussion in this chapter has, I hope, made it clear that Scotus has a clearly theological agenda as well, an agenda with a distinct role: the understanding of revealed truth. As I hope we shall see in the rest of this study, the correct way of trying to understand revealed truth, for Scotus, necessarily involves a defense of what we would call the philosophical coherence of such truth. Theology, for Scotus, is a deeply rational exercise.

GOD: EXISTENCE, UNICITY, AND SIMPLICITY

The philosophical discipline responsible for proving God's existence is *metaphysics*. God's existence is the goal of metaphysics; so there is a crucial sense in which someone doing metaphysics is, for Scotus, doing natural theology.[1] Scotus's natural theology—what we can know of God *without* revelation, and consequently outside theological science—is sophisticated and of considerable complexity. Scotus clearly holds that God's existence can be rationally proved. In some ways, Scotus's natural theology is not unlike that of Aquinas. Like Aquinas, Scotus first attempts to show that there is some kind of entity that is prior to everything else; he then attempts to show that this entity has certain attributes in virtue of which we can label it 'God'.[2]

Before we look at the proof itself, we need to be clear about its overall structure. The structure is not exactly the same in the four different versions Scotus gives;[3] in the following discussion, I do not rely entirely on any one version. I hope, however, that my somewhat idealized account of the argument brings out clearly the points that Scotus is trying to make. Roughly, the argument runs like this:

    (i) There is a first agent.
    (ii) There is an ultimate goal of activity.
    (iii) There is a maximally excellent being.

(iv) These three properties are coextensive (i.e., any being which exhibits one of these properties will exhibit the other two as well).

(v) A being exhibiting any of these properties must be infinite.

(vi) There can be at most numerically one God.

(vii) God must be simple.

I shall describe Scotus's argument, keeping closely to this plan. As we proceed, it will, I hope, become clear how the different stages fit together.

1. The existence of a first agent

Central to Scotus's proof is the argument from efficient causation. In all of Scotus's versions of his proof, the argument exists in two forms, either one of which would, if successful, be sufficient to show the existence of a first efficient cause. I shall label the two versions the 'non-modal argument' and the 'modal argument', respectively. In many ways the two versions are very similar. The non-modal argument is simpler, so I shall use this version to get the basic structure clear. First, however, I shall discuss efficient causation.

Efficient causation

Crucial for understanding either argument is an idea of what Scotus means by 'efficient causation'. Central to the concept of efficient causation is the idea that a cause is in some sense *sufficient* for its effect. Scotus—like Aristotle and all the medievals—talks about substances causing effects, where possible effects include the properties of objects and the existence of objects. (I shall refer to such substances as 'agents'.) In line with this, Scotus would add to the sufficiency claim that agents have 'causal powers' in virtue of which they produce their effects. As we shall see in chapter 4, the presence or absence of such causal powers is used by Scotus to distinguish causal from various sorts of non-causal sufficiency (e.g., logical entailment).[4]

Cause-effect relationships can exist in ordered series (where a series consists of three or more members). Not all such series will share the same properties. Consider the following two favorite medieval examples: a hand (in virtue of its motion) moving a stick to move a ball; the series father-son-grandson.[5] In the first example, the hand, in virtue of its motion, brings about the motion of the stick, which in turn brings about the motion of the ball. On this account, the motion of the hand is in some sense sufficient for the motion of the ball. In the second example, the parents and their procreative actions are sufficient for the existence of their son, but they are *not* in any sense sufficient for the procreative actions of their son. The existence of the grandson requires *further* explanation.

Scotus labels these series 'essentially ordered' and 'accidentally ordered', respectively. I shall label an essentially ordered series an 'E-series', and an accidentally ordered series an 'A-series'. Scotus picks out three features that distinguish the two series:

> The first difference is that in essentially ordered causes, the second depends upon the first precisely in the act of causing. In accidentally ordered causes this is not the case, though the second may depend upon the first for its existence or in some other way.
>
> The second difference is that in essentially ordered causes the causality is of another nature and order, inasmuch as the higher is the more perfect, which is not the case with accidentally ordered causes. This second difference is a consequence of the first, since no cause in the exercise of its causality is essentially dependent upon a cause of the same nature as itself, for to produce anything one cause of a given kind suffices.
>
> A third difference follows, namely, that all essentially ordered causes are [temporally] simultaneously required to produce the effect, for otherwise some causality essential to the effect would be wanting. In accidentally ordered causes this simultaneity is not required.[6]

As Scotus presents these differences, the first is explanatory of the other two. What the first feature of an E-series amounts to can be captured as follows: some agent x brings it about that some item y has some property F, such that y's being F brings it about that some other item z has some property G. This is in accord with Scotus's claim that, in an E-series, "the second depends upon the first precisely in its act of causing." The causal relations in an E-series are thus transitive: x's bringing it about that y is F is *sufficient* for z's being G.[7]

An A-series will not fit this criterion. In an A-series, the initial agent x brings it about that some effect y exists, or has some property F, such that y's existing, or having F, is *not* sufficient for any further effect z.[8] On this showing, of course, there is no difficulty in y's being an agent; but the action of x will not be sufficient for y's bringing about z. We should note that, in both series, the fact that there are earlier causes (not necessarily temporally earlier, but logically prior) is *logically necessary* for there being later causes. This is a matter of definition; if there are later causes, then of course there will be earlier causes. Scotus will exploit this claim in his proof of the existence of a first agent.

The non-modal argument

The non-modal argument starts from the empirically evident claim that there exists something that is an effect.[9] Scotus correctly holds that no effect can produce itself, that (definitionally) no effect can be produced by just nothing at all, and that a circle of causes is impossible. Granted these claims, it follows that an effect must be produced by something else. Let us label this cause 'c'. Scotus reasonably notes that we can ask whether or not c is an effect. If it is, then we can ask the same about its cause c_1:

> And so we shall either go on ad infinitum so that each thing in reference to what precedes it in the series will be second; or we shall reach something that has nothing prior to it. However an infinity in the ascending order is impossible; hence a primacy is necessary.[10]

Causes, here, are agents and the powers in virtue of which these agents bring about effects. So the claim that there is a first cause amounts to the claim that there is a first agent.

This argument for a first agent explaining the existence of any effect relies on the impossibility of an infinite series of causes. Scotus attempts to justify this by appealing to his distinction between an E-series of causes and an A-series of causes. Rather like Aquinas, Scotus has no objection to an infinite A-series. But he does have an objection, which I shall outline in a moment, to an infinite E-series. He also believes that he can show that there can be no A-series unless there is an E-series. (This point is important, because if there can be an infinite A-series and no E-series, Scotus will not be able to argue successfully that there must be a first agent.)

Scotus tries to show that each of the three distinguishing features of an E-series is sufficient to block the possibility of an infinite E-series. Again, it is the first feature of an E-series that is most interesting. Scotus's suggestions here are rather puzzling and seem to me to be inconclusive. In the late *Reportatio* (closely paralleled in the *Ordinatio*) Scotus argues from the following premise: "In essentially ordered causes . . . each second cause, in so far as it is causing, depends upon a first."[11] Put in this way, it follows straightforwardly that there must be a first member of an E-series. But the premise is question-begging, and I can see no reason for wanting to accept it. It requires that a first cause is necessary as well as sufficient for any effect in an E-series. But this is not so. I noted above that in any causal series there is a sense in which the existence of earlier causes is necessary for the existence of later causes. But we cannot infer from this that a *first* cause is necessary for some effect. There are sometimes many different ways in which the same effect can be produced.

Taking account of this objection, we could loosely reformulate the premise as follows: "In essentially ordered causes, any later cause, in so far as it is causing, depends upon an earlier cause." Put thus, the premise looks wholly plausible. But there would be no problem with an infinite E-series thus construed. Howsoever many prior causes there were, any one of them would be logically sufficient for any later effect.[12]

As I noted above, Scotus, just like Aquinas, is happy with the claim that there could be an infinite A-series. The reason is that, however long or short an A-series is, its various stages will *always* require further explanation outside the series. An infinitely long A-series is no more problematic or explanatorily insufficient than a finite series. And no A-series could exist without one or more E-series to support its various stages.[13]

I have indicated where I think that there are problems with Scotus's non-modal argument. If effective, Scotus would thus far have demonstrated that any E-series will have a first member (i.e., that there will be a first efficient cause of the series). This might not look like a strong conclusion, but it is an important stage on Scotus's route towards God's existence.

The modal argument

We might be forgiven for imagining that Scotus might by now believe himself to have demonstrated the first conclusion mentioned above, namely, that there is a first agent. But Scotus does not think that the argument as it stands is strong enough to count as an (Aristotelian) *demonstration*:

> I have no demonstration when I argue: "Some nature is produced or
> effected, hence something is producing or effecting it," etc., since I
> start out with contingent terms.[14]

For a strict demonstration, according to Aristotle, the premises must be
necessarily true (i.e., such that they cannot be false).[15] A demonstration
that fails to satisfy this condition will not fail to be such that its premises
entail its conclusion, but it will yield a conclusion that is, like its premises,
at best contingently true.[16]

The modal argument is like the non-modal argument in many important respects. For example, it crucially relies on the impossibility of
an infinite series of E-causes. Scotus spells out the whole modal argument
only in *De Primo Principio*. As we shall see, the changes made to the non-
modal argument do not present any further logical difficulties.

The modal premise from which Scotus starts is

   (1) It is possible that something is caused.[17]

The truth of (1) is not contingent; it is logically necessary. Premise (1)
entails

   (2) It is possible that something is an agent;[18]

from which, reasoning from the impossibility of an infinite E-series just
as in the non-modal argument, Scotus further infers

   (3) It is possible that something is a first agent.[19]

Further still, Scotus holds that (3) entails

   (3*) Something can be a first agent.

The argument from (3) to (3*) offered by Scotus is extremely interesting. He reasons that something that is a first agent will be essentially
uncaused (i.e., such that it is impossible for it to be caused). Adopting a
very weak version of the principle of sufficient reason, Scotus suggests
that anything that is essentially uncaused is a necessary existent (i.e., one
whose non-existence is logically impossible). (I will return to this Scotist
principle in a moment.) The following claim will capture this position:

(4) If it is possible that something is an essentially uncaused being, then it is necessary that something is an essentially uncaused being.[20]

Scotus presupposes that any first agent is essentially uncaused. (Labeling it a 'first agent' entails that it has certain active causal powers, not that it actually exercises these powers. Scotus, as we shall see in chapter 4, wants to hold that the universe is radically contingent.) So:

(5) If it is possible that something is a first agent, then it is necessary that something is a first agent.

Coupling (5) with

(3) It is possible that something is a first agent,

we can infer

(6) It is necessary that something is a first agent.

This entails

(3*) Something can be a first agent.[21]

What should we make of the crucial premise (4) (Scotus's weak version of the principle of sufficient reason)? Clearly, it is not open to many of the objections that can be made against stronger versions of the principle. It does not commit Scotus to the claim that nothing can exist merely randomly (i.e., be both contingent and uncaused). And Scotus's principle has some prima facie plausibility. It is difficult to see how something essentially uncaused could fail to be a necessary existent.

The modal cosmological argument clearly bears out the claim that the study of basic metaphysical concepts—in this case, causation and necessity/contingency—yields as its result or object the existence of God.[22] The empirical input is minimal, and according to Scotus unnecessary for either the truth or the validity of the argument. The argument as Scotus puts it relies on his (failed) attempt to show the impossibility of an infinite E-series. The crucial premise (3) is clearly entailed by (2) if we suppose that an infinite E-series is impossible. But are there other ways of deriving (3)? Timothy O'Connor locates an argument in Scotus that will serve to demonstrate (3) without appealing to the impossibility of an infinite E-series. The argument can be laid out as follows:

(7) It is not necessarily the case that a being possessing a causal power C possesses C in an imperfect way

entails

(8) It is possible that C is possessed without imperfection by some item.

But if we couple (8) with

(9) If it is not possible for any item to possess C without dependence on some prior item, then it is not possible that there is any item which possesses C without imperfection,

we can infer

(10) It is possible that some item possesses C without dependence on some prior item.

Proposition (10) along with

(11) Any item possessing C without dependence on some prior item is a first agent

entails

(3) It is possible that something is a first agent.

('Being an agent' and 'possessing a causal power' are of course synonyms.)[23] And we have already seen that (3) entails (3*).

The argument here will clearly push Scotus's proof for the existence of a first agent further in the direction of the ontological argument. There seem to be no problems with the validity of this argument. And assuming that *necessary existence* is possibly a property, there may be little problem with the truth of the premises either. So the argument clearly represents a significant contribution to natural theology.

2. The existence of an ultimate goal of activity

The proof for the existence of ultimate goal(s) of activity is not spelled out by Scotus in much detail, since he regards his argument as closely analogous to the proof for the existence of a first efficient cause. Scotus reasons that at least some actions are goal-directed. On standard Aristotelian accounts of action, goals have some kind of *explanatory* role in action (hence Aristotle labels them 'final causes'). Clearly, it is possible to have a series of such causes: I wish to do *a* in order to gain *b*, and I wish to gain *b* in order to achieve *c*, and so on. Granted a sense in which a goal explains an action, Scotus argues that we could not have an infinite series of such goals: if we could, the teleological explanation would never get off the ground.[24] What Scotus wants to argue is that God is the ultimate goal of all actions. We normally think of goals as states of affairs, not as substances.[25] But clearly, goals can be subsistent entities too: objects of our love. This is the sort of goal Scotus has in mind. The series of entities that we love for the sake of something else must be finite, headed by something that we love for its own sake.

3. The existence of a maximally excellent being

The last step in the first part of Scotus's argument is to show that there must be some being or beings more excellent than any other beings. The argument is found most clearly in the *Reportatio*. Again, the argument relies on an analysis of the disjunctive transcendentals: in this case, necessary-or-contingent, infinite-or-finite, and exceeding-or-exceeded. Scotus supposes that all things can be objectively graded on some hierarchy of excellence. This claim is not as implausible as it might at first glance seem. Many of our ethical judgments, for example, are made presupposing such a hierarchy. As we saw above, Scotus holds that one of the features of an E-series is that a cause is always more perfect than its effect. Since, according to Scotus, we can show that for any E-series there is a first member, we can also show that there is a most perfect member.[26]

Scotus oddly claims that this supports the thesis that there is a "simply unexcelled" being, by which he means one that cannot be excelled—a maximally excellent being. Scotus is presumably supposing that a first agent is more perfect than any of its *possible* effects. Granted that, of our list of first causes, there is at least one than which no other is more perfect, it will follow that some agent is more excellent than any possible effect. And this is a property closely related to that of being maximally excellent.

Elsewhere, however, Scotus gives an intriguing modal argument that would, if successful, yield the required conclusion far more elegantly. The argument is in fact more or less indistinguishable from that provided by Anselm in chapter 3 of the *Proslogion*.[27] Scotus's argument—found most clearly in the *Reportatio*—presupposes that anything that is essentially uncaused must be a necessary existent; thus:

(4) If it is possible that something is an essentially uncaused being, then it is necessary that something is an essentially uncaused being.

But being essentially uncaused is a great-making property. So any maximally excellent being will be uncaused. Hence:

(12) If it is possible that something is maximally excellent, then it is necessary that something is maximally excellent.

If we couple this conclusion with

(13) It is possible that something is maximally excellent,

we can infer

(14) It is necessary that something is maximally excellent.[28]

Scotus spends some time justifying (13). The possible problem that he sees with it is that a maximally excellent being will be *infinite*; and Scotus sees a need to show that the existence of an infinite being is possible. I will discuss this argument in section 5 of this chapter.

The argument is even more clearly "ontological" in its basic thrust than the argument to a first agent.[29] The difficult premise is (13), which entails that all great-making properties are compatible with each other. Scotus never seriously addresses the problem of the possible incompatibility of great-making properties. But if (13) can be shown to be true, Scotus's argument will look fairly compelling.

4. The coextensiveness of these three properties

According to Scotus, any being that exhibits any of the three properties (viz., being a first agent, being an ultimate goal, and being maximally excellent) will exhibit the other two as well. Agents act for the sake of goals. But there is nothing for the sake of which the ultimate goal could be produced. So the ultimate goal is uncaused, and thus is the first agent.[30] Since being a first agent is a great-making property, any maximally excellent being will be a first agent. Equally, by the second property of an E-series, a first agent will be more excellent than any of its possible effects.[31]

Because Scotus holds that the three primacies are coextensive, his argument for God's existence will not require for its success the success of any more than *one* of the arguments outlined in the three steps just described. Furthermore, any one of the three arguments will, if Scotus is correct, allow us to infer directly the remaining two primacies. Thus, any one of the arguments, according to Scotus, will allow us to infer quite a lot about the God whose existence Scotus is attempting to demonstrate.

Scotus also shows that only one *kind* of being can exhibit the three properties.[32] This does not mean that there will be just one first agent. We could on this account still have a pantheon of first agents. The crucial feature will be that the members of our putative pantheon will all be the same sort of thing. The point of this step in the argument is that, supposing the three primacies to be properties necessarily exhibited by any God-like being, there can be at most one *kind* of God-like being. The step adds nothing in fact to Scotus's overall argument, since it is not necessary for any of the later stages. Equally, it is (probably) entailed by the claim—which Scotus attempts to prove later—that there can be at most *numerically one* first agent.

5. The infinity of the first agent

Central to Scotus's understanding of the divine nature is its infinity. I shall spend some time in chapter 3 showing precisely how Scotus understands infinity. But it will, I hope, become clear even in the present chapter that the concept of divine infinity is structurally important in Scotus's argument. Roughly, Scotus uses the idea of divine infinity to demonstrate divine unicity and simplicity. His procedure is thus the opposite to that of Aquinas, who takes divine simplicity as basic, and thence infers infinity and unicity.[33] Scotus expressly rejects Aquinas's attempt to derive divine infinity from divine simplicity.[34] Part of the reason for this lies in the radically different conceptions of divine infinity that the two thinkers have. I will describe these different conceptions in chapter 3.

Scotus attempts to prove the infinity of the first agent by arguing from its knowledge,[35] from the nature of a first agent,[36] from the nature of an ultimate goal,[37] and from the nature of a maximally excellent being. The last of these is the most interesting. A maximally excellent being must be infinite, since what is finite can be excelled.[38] It is in his attempt to prove that a maximally excellent being must be infinite that Scotus spells out his modal argument for the existence of a maximally excellent being, which I described above. As I noted there, Scotus devotes some space to a discussion of the claim that infinity is compatible with actual existence. He argues that the complex concept '(an) infinite being' is logically coherent, and therefore possibly exemplified. The concept is logically coherent since 'being' and 'infinite' are not logically contradictory.[39] And this yields the premise "It is possible that some being is maximally excellent," which is one of the premises that Scotus needs for the truth of his modal argument for a simply unexcelled being.

In *De Primo Principio*, Scotus refrains from labeling the first principle 'God' until he has shown that the first principle is infinite. This is a clear sign of the importance Scotus attaches to divine infinity. As he points out in *Ordinatio*, the existence of an infinite being is "the last conclusion to be established."[40] I shall follow Scotus in using the term 'God' from now on.

6. Divine unicity

Scotus offers six arguments for divine unicity (i.e., for the claim that there can be at most numerically one God), "any one of which, if proved, entails the initial thesis."[41] All but one start from the claim that God is infinite in some respect or another. The remaining argument attempts to infer divine unicity from divine necessity. Scotus offers a seventh argument from divine omnipotence. He does not believe that this argument has any probative force, because he does not believe that natural reason can demonstrate God to be omnipotent. (I discuss this claim in chapter 4.)

It seems to me that at least two of Scotus's seven arguments—that from infinite power and that from omnipotence—are successful. The first attempts to demonstrate that there cannot be two infinitely powerful agents.[42] As Scotus understands infinite power, an agent is infinitely powerful if and only if it is has the capacity to bring about any possible effect. Omnipotence adds a further qualification: an agent is omnipotent if and only if it has the capacity to bring about any possible effect *immediately* (i.e., without the activity of any causal chain between the agent and any of its effects).[43] On these definitions, an infinitely powerful agent might be able to bring about some of its effects only mediately, via a causal chain; whereas an omnipotent agent could bring about any effect directly.[44] As Scotus understands infinite power, it entails that the action of an agent that has the capacity to bring about any *possible* effect will be both necessary and sufficient for any *actual* effect. The action of an infinitely powerful but not omnipotent agent will be sufficient for any actual effect in the sense that such an agent is the first member of every E-series. (Scotus makes the point in the second sentence of the following quotation.)

Scotus's argument runs as follows:

> Two causes of the same order cannot both be the total cause of the same effect. But an infinite power is the total primary cause of every single effect that exists. Therefore, no other power can be the total primary cause of any effect. Consequently, no other cause is infinite in power. My proof of the first proposition [viz., two causes of the same order cannot both be the total cause of the same effect]: If this proposition did not hold, then a thing could be the cause of something that does not depend on it. Proof: Nothing depends essentially on anything

if it could exist even when this other is non-existent. But if C has two total causes, A and B, each of which is in the same order, then either could be non-existent and still C would continue to exist in virtue of the other. For if A were non-existent, C would still exist by reason of B, and if B were non-existent, C would exist by reason of A.[45]

The basic point of this passage is that there cannot be two causes of an effect, each of which is, independently of the other, causally both necessary and sufficient for the effect. The reason is that either one alone is causally sufficient: and that the other one therefore cannot be causally necessary.[46] Now, a cause of infinite power is both necessary and sufficient for any actual effect. There cannot therefore be two such causes. (Scotus is rejecting the possibility of what we might today label 'causal overdetermination'.)

Scotus's second successful argument for divine unicity is, as noted above, not one that he himself regarded as having probative force. Just like the argument from infinite power, this argument has some important modern versions.[47] Basically, Scotus argues that, if there were two omnipotent gods, G_1 and G_2, it would look as though each would be able to frustrate the will of the other, entailing—absurdly—that neither was omnipotent.[48]

Scotus suggests an objection to this argument. Could not the two agents "voluntarily agree on a common way of acting through some sort of pact?"[49] Scotus knows of two possible responses here. First, two omnipotent agents, even if they both agreed on how to act, would each be causally necessary and sufficient for any actual effect. This involves just the same contradiction as was highlighted in the argument from infinite power outlined above. Secondly, irrespective of what an omnipotent agent actually decides to do, it is only omnipotent if in principle its actions are not necessitated in any way. On the proposed scenario, G_1's actions are not necessitated by G_2, or vice versa. Hence the wills of G_1 and G_2 *could* still conflict, which is sufficient to generate the contradiction.[50] To block the contradiction, the two Gods would have to be in agreement necessarily. And Scotus would regard this as in conflict with divine freedom.

As Scotus presents his argument, its conclusion is entailed by the premise that God has the capacity to bring about any possible effect immediately. It is, I think, obvious that, thus construed, there could not be two omnipotent beings, for just the reason that Scotus gives. Can Scotus's argument be made to work with weaker premises? Not according to

Scotus, who expressly denies that the argument could work without his theological understanding of omnipotence. On Scotus's understanding of an infinitely powerful—but not omnipotent—agent, however, such an agent will have the capacity to produce any possible effect. This power could be frustrated by another infinitely powerful agent just as effectively as it could be frustrated by an omnipotent agent. So I do not see why Scotus should believe his argument to presuppose a theological premise.

7. Divine simplicity

Scotus clearly regards the demonstration of divine simplicity as an integral part of a proof for God's existence, including a discussion of it in his *De Primo Principio*. Furthermore, in this late work he makes it clear that every claim about divine simplicity can be sufficiently demonstrated from divine infinity.[51] Neither of these facts emerges so clearly in the *Ordinatio* and *Reportatio* accounts. This is no doubt partly a result of the structure imposed on these two works by the order in Peter Lombard's *Sentences*. In addition to the arguments for simplicity from infinity, Scotus also presents a proof for simplicity from God's necessary existence.[52]

Scotus's account of divine simplicity is far less ambitious than the account we find in Aquinas. Aquinas and Scotus both agree that God is simple in the sense of (i) lacking spatial parts, (ii) lacking temporal parts, (iii) lacking composition from form and matter,[53] and (iv) lacking accidental modifications. But there are two ways in which Scotus disagrees with Aquinas. According to Aquinas, God is (v) identical with his attributes, and (vi) such that his attributes are all identical with each other.[54] Scotus does not believe God to be simple in either of these ways. I deal with these two claims in chapter 3, and I examine Scotus's claim that God lacks temporal parts in chapter 4.

In *De Primo Principio*, Scotus places his basic argument from infinity first, and he evidently regards it as the most important. He reasons that a complex (non-simple) entity must be made up of parts, each of which will be less than the whole of which it is a part. The parts cannot themselves be infinite, since something that is infinite cannot be less that anything else. Neither can the parts be finite, since they then could not compose something infinite. So an infinite being cannot be made up of parts.[55]

A lot depends here on the kinds of part that Scotus has in mind. If Scotus is right that something infinite cannot be less than anything else, then his argument would be effective against the claim that God has *spatial* parts. Scotus, however, intends the argument to be effective against other kinds of complexity as well. Presumably, matter and form as putative component parts of a substance are each in some sense *less* than the whole of which they are parts. Equally, something infinite cannot be the subject of accidental modifications. Something that is subject to accidental modifications can gain and lose attributes; and according to Scotus the infinite cannot gain or lose anything.[56] In fact, however, Scotus's supposition that something infinite cannot be less than anything else is probably false.[57] If this is right, then the argument will not be effective even against the claim that God cannot have spatial parts.

Scotus has a further argument to show that God cannot be composed of matter and form. The unity of matter and form in a composite requires explanation. But this unity cannot be caused by the composite itself, since the composite would then be self-caused, which is impossible. It must therefore be caused by some other agent. The first agent therefore cannot be a composite of matter and form.[58]

As we shall see in the next chapter, Scotus holds that some kind of distinctions in God are consistent with the doctrine of divine simplicity. For example, as I have suggested, Scotus holds that God is distinct in some way from his attributes, and that his attributes are distinct in some way from each other. Equally, as I shall show in chapter 5, Scotus believes the Christian doctrine of the Trinity to entail some sort of complexity and distinction in God. Thus, Scotus's arguments for divine simplicity are not intended to exclude every sort of complexity. We shall see in some detail in the next chapter exactly what Scotus's position here amounts to.

Scotus offers a challenging and subtle proof for God's existence. Given that Scotus believes the proof of God's existence to be the goal of metaphysics, the success of his proof will be important for the success of his whole conception of the philosophical endeavor. It is Scotus the *philosopher*, not Scotus the *theologian*, who has a great deal invested in the existence of God.

GOD: PERFECTION, INFINITY,
AND RELIGIOUS LANGUAGE

We customarily talk about God in terms derived from our talk about creatures. In this chapter, I discuss Scotus's account of religious language. Scotus claims that some words, when applied to God and creatures, have exactly the same meaning or sense in both cases. Such a word is *univocal* when applied to God and creatures. The view that Scotus opposes holds that words applied to God and creatures have at best analogical senses. Scotus's view has some quite striking consequences for his account of divine simplicity. But before I discuss these questions, I shall look briefly at the sorts of attributes that Scotus thinks God has.

1. Perfect-being theology

As we have seen, Scotus holds that God is maximally excellent. This property entails that of being maximally *perfect*.[1] The claim that God is maximally perfect provides a way for us to infer a whole range of divine attributes. This way of constructing a concept of God has recently been labeled 'perfect-being theology',[2] and it seems to capture exactly an important feature of Scotus's philosophical theology. The method, as Scotus notes, is derived from Anselm. Scotus draws on his account of the pure perfections to spell out the implications of the method. A 'pure perfection' is anything that it is better to have than not to have. Borrowing an argument from Anselm,[3] Scotus holds that since God is maximally perfect, he will have these pure perfections:

> With regard to everything except relations, whatever is unconditionally better than something which is not it, must be attributed to God, even as everything not of this kind must be denied of him. According to Anselm, then, we first know something to be a pure perfection and secondly we attribute this perfection to God.[4]

What are these pure perfections exhibited by God? Scotus gives a list from Anselm:

> "[The substance of the supreme nature] is not a body, then," he says, "nor any of those things which bodily senses perceive. . . . It must be living, wise, omnipotent, true, just, eternal, and anything, absolutely speaking, that it is better to be than not to be."[5]

Setting aside "omnipotent" and "eternal," all of these are perfections that creatures can exhibit. But "powerful" is the root concept behind "omnipotent," and this is certainly a creaturely perfection. Equally, Scotus makes it clear that the root concept behind "eternal" is "alive";[6] another creaturely perfection. Scotus elsewhere adds more perfections to the list: intellect and will,[7] and, from Augustine, beauty and spirit.[8] In addition to these attributes, Scotus argues that God, like everything else, will exhibit the transcendental attribute of *being*, and those attributes that are straightforwardly coextensive with being—namely, unity, truth, and goodness (in the sense of desirability).[9]

God, as we shall see, has these attributes in an infinite degree; and, as Scotus notes, the crucial feature of all of these perfections is that they do not in themselves entail any kind of limit. Each perfection is in this sense compatible with its being exemplified to an infinite degree by some being.[10] God has some attributes that creatures do not have. But all of these—or at least all of those about which we can have knowledge apart from revelation—can be constructed from the list of creaturely attributes along with an additional "divine" modification. In the next section I discuss how we can go about constructing such divine perfections.[11]

2. The univocity theory of religious language

The meaning of these perfection terms is clearly derived in some sense from their application to creatures. Does this mean that God is, for example, wise in just the sense in which we might hope to be? Or good, or powerful, in the ways that we might be good, or powerful? If it does, then God will look like some kind of (large-scale) human person. If not, on the other hand, it will be difficult to see just what it *does* mean to claim that God is wise, or good, or powerful. Scotus defends something like the first of these two opinions. To understand his view, we need to get clear on some terminology.

Some definitions

We often use one and the same word in many different contexts. Sometimes we will be using the word in the *same* sense in these different contexts, and sometimes we will be using the word in *different* senses in these different contexts. If we are using the word in the same sense, we could say that we are using it *univocally*. If we are using it in wholly different and unrelated senses, we could say that we are using it *equivocally*. But we sometimes use a word in different but related or similar senses. In this case, we could say that we are using the word *analogically*.

By "the same sense," I mean that the word has the same *lexical definition* in both cases. In what follows, I shall presuppose that (only) univocal terms will satisfy this criterion. Furthermore, I take it that we can talk of a word's having two (or more) *similar* senses only if there is *something in common* between the two senses. But the senses can have something in common only if the attributes signified by the terms themselves have something in common. The attributes, presumably, include some more basic property that they have in common. If they did not, it would be difficult to see how we could claim that they were *similar* (rather than wholly different). For example, we could not claim that light blue and dark blue were similar colors unless they both had a feature in common—in this case blueness—in virtue of which they could be said to be similar to each other. Now, we can presumably find, or invent, a term to signify any common basic attribute. And this term will be univocal: it will be used in the same sense in all statements.

Given these definitions, we can assess Scotus's theory, and the theory that he opposes. Roughly, Scotus wants to argue that if we are to avoid the claim that all theological statements are equivocal, we will have to claim that at least some are univocal (in the sense just outlined). I shall label this claim the 'univocity theory'. Accepting the univocity theory does not commit Scotus to the claim that *all* theological statements are univocal. In fact, Scotus wants to defend the claim that most theological statements are analogical. But he does not think that analogy is possible without univocity. I shall label the theories that Scotus opposes 'non-univocity theories'. Such theories defend the claim that *no* terms are applied to God and creatures univocally.

Non-univocity theories

Scotus's arguments are expressly directed against the theory of Henry of Ghent. According to Henry of Ghent, there are no concepts that are univocal when applied to God and creatures.[12] He holds that there is, for example, one *irreducible* concept of wisdom—call it 'wisdom$_1$'—that applies to creatures, and another irreducible concept—wisdom$_2$—that applies to God. Each of these two concepts, according to Henry, is irreducible to any other concept. Each, in medieval terminology, is *simple*, not composed of other more basic concepts.[13] Henry claims that these two concepts are analogous (i.e., *like* each other) and that the basis for this likeness is the likeness between cause and effect.[14] On this account, there can be no concepts univocal to God and creatures, although concepts applying to God and creatures can be similar to each other. Henry proposes a cognitive method for discovering the sense of the concept as it is applied to God.[15] William A. Frank and Allan B. Wolter helpfully describe it as follows:

> If one looks long and hard at the abstract concept of [for example] "good," the mind eventually discovers the twofold interpretation that can be given to it. Thus the seemingly simple concept, whether it be that of "good" or "being," is really not simple at all in what it may mean. Each word has a twofold sense. . . . Henry regards the two meanings as diverse concepts—that is, they are both simple concepts, having nothing conceptually in common.[16]

Henry's account is extremely puzzling. Claiming that the two concepts are simple, and therefore irreducible to any common feature, en-

tails that they have nothing in common at all. In this case, it will be difficult to see how they could possibly be like each other in any respect. So
Henry's theory seems to amount to the position that all theological statements are equivocal. Scotus's criticisms of it, as we shall see, draw on
precisely this worry.

The best-known defender of a non-univocity theory is Aquinas.
Aquinas argues that any given term, when applied to God and creatures,
must have at best analogous senses. A sense here is what the term *means*:
its lexical definition. One term has two analogous meanings when applied
respectively to God and creatures.[17] Speaking of the *meanings* of terms is
much the same as speaking of concepts. So Aquinas's analogy of terms is
not prima facie much different from Henry's analogy of concepts.[18] Now,
if it is true of *every* term that we could possibly apply to God that its sense
is at best analogous to the relevant creaturely senses, then it seems to me
that Aquinas's account will amount to Henry's (i.e., it will in fact amount
to the claim that all theological statements are equivocal). The reason is
that if the terms we use to refer to *simple* attributes (i.e., attributes that
are irreducible to any more basic features) fail to be univocal, then they
will *necessarily* be equivocal, since simple attributes, by definition, cannot have more basic common features in virtue of which they could be
similar.[19]

Scotus's arguments against
non-univocity theories

As I have suggested, Scotus thinks that non-univocity theories will
amount to the claim that all theological statements are equivocal. I shall
label this claim the 'equivocation theory'. On the definitions offered, to
show that the univocity theory is true, Scotus has to show that the equivocation theory is false. In line with his opponents, Scotus refers to the
equivocation theory he is rejecting as 'analogy'.[20] But what Scotus is rejecting is not that some theological discourse will use analogy, just that
no theological claims are univocal. And, as I have suggested, this latter
claim is taken by Scotus as entailing the equivocation theory.

Scotus argues that, if the equivocation theory is true, then a number
of undesirable consequences follow. In a margin note in his *Ordinatio*,
Scotus notes that there are no fewer than ten arguments available to show
this.[21] The most interesting two of these can be found in more modern

form in William Alston's discussion of Aquinas on theological predication. I shall discuss these two arguments and a third that specifically addresses Henry's position.

Alston picks out two problems with the theory that I have labeled the equivocation theory. If the theory is true, then theological statements "(1) lack determinate truth conditions and (2) cannot figure in reasoning in the ways they are supposed to in Thomistic, and other, theology."[22] Scotus was aware of both of these problems. In his first argument against the equivocation theory, Scotus clearly presupposes the first of these. He notes that on the proposed scenario, there would be "no certitude about any concept" that is applied to God;[23] we could not tell whether a theological statement were true or false. Scotus makes the second criticism as follows:

> If you maintain that . . . the formal concept of what pertains to God is another notion, a disconcerting consequence ensues; namely that from the proper notion of anything found in creatures nothing at all can be inferred about God, for the notion of what is in each is wholly different.[24]

The idea is that, on the equivocation theory, we cannot use creaturely perfections to make inferences about the divine nature, since the creaturely perfection is "wholly different" from the cognate divine perfection. The argument appears more clearly in Scotus's early *Lectura*:

> Unless 'being' implies one univocal intention [i.e., concept], theology would simply perish. For theologians prove that the divine Word proceeds and is begotten by way of intellect, and the Holy Spirit proceeds by way of will. But if intellect and will were found in us and in God equivocally, there would be no evidence at all that, since a word is begotten in us in such and such a fashion, it is so in God—and likewise with regard to love in us—because then intellect and will in these two cases would be of a wholly different kind [*ratio*].[25]

(This passage makes it quite clear that Scotus regards Henry's analogy theory as effectively reducible to an equivocation theory.) Scotus's argument is that the failure of the univocity theory would render the whole Anselmian method—perfect-being theology—useless.

A third argument centers on Henry's claim that we have a cognitive process to allow us to form simple concepts, proper to God, which are analogous to the corresponding creaturely perfections. Scotus denies that there is any such process. According to standard medieval abstractive theories of cognition, we know a concept by abstracting it from sense data. The concept thus abstracted will be one of two things: either a concept of the *essence* of the object found in the sense datum (labeled by Scotus a 'proper' concept) or a concept of a necessary *property* of the object. Since no other abstractive cognitive process is available, there is no in-built mechanism for forming simple concepts of God that are *analogous* to those found in creatures.[26] Scotus does not deny that we can form proper concepts of God from our sense knowledge. But, as we shall see in a moment, this process relies on our having some *univocal* concepts that can provide a basis for the process. It is not a case of trying to devise, from our knowledge of creatures, some analogous simple concept applicable to God.

Scotus's univocity theory

The three Scotist arguments against the equivocation theory seem to me to be reasonable enough, and seem to provide sufficient grounds for adopting the univocity theory. Scotus describes the crucial features of his univocity theory in ways that tie in neatly to the first two proposed refutations of the equivocation theory just outlined. Scotus proposes two conditions that will be satisfied if a concept (i.e., the sense of a term) is univocal. He states:

> [First,] I designate that concept univocal which possesses sufficient unity in itself, so that to affirm and deny it of one and the same thing would be a contradiction. [Second,] [i]t also has sufficient unity to serve as the middle term of a syllogism, so that wherever two extremes are united by a middle term that is one in this way, we may conclude to the union of the two extremes among themselves.[27]

It is important to understand that Scotus does not regard the satisfaction of these two conditions as *entailing* that the univocity theory is true. They merely describe properties that a univocal concept will have. Equally, these two descriptions do not sufficiently demarcate univocal concepts from analogous or equivocal ones, although of course satisfying the two descriptions will be *necessary* for univocity.[28]

Scotus's theory, then, does not provide a set of conditions for distinguishing between univocal and equivocal concepts. The point, rather, is that we can give an account of analogy only if we accept that *some* concepts we apply to God and creatures are univocal. These univocal concepts correspond to attributes common in some sense to God and creatures.[29] These attributes are those in virtue of which we can claim that two analogous concepts are similar. In fact, the basic common attributes will count as a subset of the class of 'transcendental attributes', attributes that are either "indifferent to finite or infinite [being], or proper to infinite being."[30] Scotus argues that we can add to these univocal concepts certain further qualifications. By doing this, we can form complex concepts that are not shared by God and creatures.

From a simple univocal concept, then, Scotus believes that we can derive different complex concepts proper, respectively, to God and creatures. The process has several stages. First, we consider the complex concept of a creaturely perfection. Such a concept will include the simple perfection together with the fact that the perfection is limited or imperfect. For example, the concept of creaturely wisdom—which I have labeled 'wisdom$_1$'—will include a perfection—which I shall label 'wisdom$_0$'—along with the fact that the perfection exists only in a limited way in the creature. Second, we remove the limitation associated with the creaturely instantiations of the perfection. This yields the simple concept, in itself indifferent to finite or infinite. In my example, this process will yield the concept of wisdom$_0$. Third, we add the notion of the most perfect degree to the simple concept. This yields a complex concept that is proper to God (i.e., the concept that I have labeled 'wisdom$_2$'). Scotus gives an example:

> Take, for example, the formal notion of "wisdom," or "intellect," or "will." Such a notion is considered first of all simply in itself and absolutely. Because this notion includes formally no imperfection or limitation, the imperfections associated with it in creatures are removed. Retaining this same notion of "wisdom" and "will," we attribute these to God—but in a most perfect degree. Consequently, every inquiry regarding God is based upon the supposition that the intellect has the same univocal concept which it obtains from creatures.[31]

An important feature about this account is that the two complex concepts—creaturely and divine—are *analogous* to each other.[32] In my example, wisdom$_1$ and wisdom$_2$ are analogous to each other. But these analogies, for reasons given, are always spelled out in terms of some really common univocal concept. In my example, the common univocal concept in virtue of which wisdom$_1$ and wisdom$_2$ are similar to each other is wisdom$_0$.

In what sense are the attributes common to God and creatures really "common"? One possible account would be that such attributes are genera of which the divine and creaturely attributes are species. Thus, wisdom$_0$, for example, would be the genus of which wisdom$_1$ and wisdom$_2$ are species. But Scotus rejects this, arguing that God and creatures "share in no reality."[33] A complex attribute such as wisdom$_2$ (divine wisdom) is less composite than a species is. Scotus is happy to talk of a complex divine attribute as "One reality perfectly and imperfectly conceived."[34] The fact that the complex attribute is only *one* reality explains why no element of it can in any sense be *shared* by creatures. On the other hand, this does not, according to Scotus, exclude all commonality. He notes that the idea (*ratio*) of a *simple* transcendental attribute (i.e., the attribute considered without its intrinsic modes) is common "as a transcendental is."[35] The account is not very explanatory, since Scotus offers no further account of what it is for a transcendental to be common. But it is clear that Scotus does not want to deny all commonality. (If he did, of course, his own univocity theory could not be sustained.)

The theological result of all this is that the doctrine of divine ineffability, so strongly stressed by Aquinas and (to a lesser extent) by Henry of Ghent, is greatly weakened in Scotus's account. He holds that we can know quite a lot about God, "in a descriptive sort of way," as he puts it.[36] (We will see below what Scotus understands the implications of his theory to be for the doctrine of divine simplicity.) The difference between God and creatures, at least with regard to God's possession of the pure perfections, is ultimately one of degree. Specifically, the perfections exist in an infinite degree in God, and in a finite degree in creatures. How Scotus spells out the meaning of 'infinite' is the topic to which I now turn.

3. Divine infinity

In the previous chapter, I gave some of Scotus's arguments in favor of divine infinity. Here, I want to show more precisely how Scotus understands the concept of infinity. Scotus's account marks a radical departure from earlier views of divine infinity.[37] His target is Aquinas. According to Aquinas, finiteness and infinity are *relational* properties. A thing is finite if it has a relation to a *limiting* entity. Aquinas gives matter and form as his examples; there is a sense in which form limits matter (it limits matter's *potentiality* for being just anything); and there is a sense in which matter limits form (it renders a form non-repeatable, i.e., such that it cannot be shared). Equally, a thing is infinite if it *fails* to have such a relation to a limiting entity.[38] Aquinas's account of God's simplicity entails that God is a pure form. As such, his nature is not limited by matter, and is therefore infinite. Simplicity, for Aquinas, entails infinity just because infinity is defined as the lack of a relation to a limiting entity.

In the earliest part of his *Metaphysics* questions, Scotus seems to have agreed with this account of infinity.[39] Scotus's mature account of infinity is, however, very different. We can get a good idea of its basic outline by looking at his attempts to refute Aquinas's position. Scotus claims that Aquinas's argument for divine infinity commits an elementary error. We cannot infer from "[b]eing limited by matter entails being finite," that "[n]ot being limited by matter entails being infinite." Aquinas's argument commits the fallacy of 'affirming the consequent'.[40] Scotus claims instead,

> If an entity is finite or infinite, it is so not by reason of something incidental to it, but because it has its own intrinsic degree of finite or infinite perfection respectively.[41]

On this showing, divine simplicity is not sufficient to allow us to infer divine infinity.

What is this "intrinsic degree" to which Scotus refers? The basic model is quantitative: we abstract the concept of infinity from that of spatial extension, and then apply it to our concept of being (or good, or true, or whatever perfection we are attending to). In the *Quodlibetal Questions*, Scotus gives a detailed account of how we go about, first, constructing a concept of infinite spatial extension, and then abstracting from this a concept of infinity applicable to God.[42] Scotus's standard understanding of infinite spatial extension is taken from Aristotle. According to Aristotle, any spatial extension is only ever *potentially* infinite, not *actually* infinite; for any magnitude we have, we can in principle always get a larger magnitude by adding more.[43] Scotus then makes two moves. First, he asks us to imagine this potentially infinite magnitude all actualized at once:

> We might imagine that all the parts . . . remained in existence simultaneously. If this could be done we would have an infinite quantity, because it would be as great in actuality as it was potentially. And all

those parts which in infinite succession would be actualized and would have being one after the other would be conceived as actualized all at once.[44]

Secondly, Scotus asks us to apply this model, derived from *extension*, to an *intensive* amount of something: being, or goodness, or truth, or whatever perfection we are attending to.[45] As Frank and Wolter point out, this second move is analogous to one we frequently make in our daily existence. We frequently grade things as, say, better or worse, and we have no difficulty conceiving these grades as in some sense quantitative, as more or less of something.[46] Scotus is asking us to make just this cognitive move, from quantity to qualitative perfection—where the quantity in question is an actually infinite magnitude, and the qualitative perfection in question is of an actually infinite degree.

Involved in this cognitive move is a rather surprising step. The end result of the cognitive move is a concept of something infinite in *perfection*. Such a thing cannot be imperfect in any way. But a *quantitative* actual infinite—if it could exist in reality—would be imperfect. The reason for this is that such an infinite would be made up of parts, each of which would be less than the whole. Such parts would therefore be less *perfect* than the whole, and consequently the whole would be made up of imperfect parts. But something that is infinitely perfect could not be made up of imperfect parts. If it could, it would be less perfect than something made up of perfect parts: "An infinite being is perfect in such a way that neither it nor any of its parts is missing anything."[47] Since on this showing, any parts that an infinitely perfect being had would be no less than the whole, we would have to conclude that such a perfect being could not be composed of parts at all.[48]

In chapter 2, I showed how central the concept of divine infinity is in Scotus's natural theology. Scotus holds that if we conceive all the pure perfections on the highest degree, we obtain the most perfect concept of God available to us without revelation. But we can get a simpler concept that entails every more perfect and complex concept of God. The simpler concept is 'infinite being'.[49] The concept is central to Scotus's metaphysical project in the sense that it entails all other divine perfections. It is also central to Scotus's account of God in that infinity is taken by Scotus as the basic qualifying term distinguishing divine attributes from creaturely ones.

4. Divine simplicity and
the divine attributes

Scotus's account of divine infinity and his univocity theory of religious language have some striking implications for his doctrine of divine simplicity. As I suggested in chapter 2, Scotus denies both that God's attributes are all identical with each other, and that God is identical with his attributes. The account of divine infinity entails a third sort of complexity in God: God's attributes are themselves composites of pure perfection and its intrinsic degree (infinity). In the rest of this chapter, I want to look at these three sorts of complexity in Scotus's God, beginning with the composition between pure perfection and intrinsic degree.

The distinction between a divine
attribute and its mode

As we have seen, Scotus differs from Aquinas in his assertion that a degree of a perfection—such as finiteness or infinity—is a *real property* of a thing, not just a relational property (or, in the case of infinity, the *negation* of such a relational property). A degree of a perfection belongs to that set of properties labeled 'intrinsic modes'.[50] Such properties are *modes* of some attribute in the sense that they determine the *way* in which that attribute is instantiated. They are *intrinsic* to the attribute in that the attribute could never be instantiated without such a property. For example, a shade of a color is an intrinsic mode of that color. The shade determines the precise way in which the color is instantiated; and no color can be instantiated without being some shade or other. On this showing, an attribute and its intrinsic mode will be *formally distinct*.[51] The attribute is defined without reference to its mode, but its instantiations are in no sense really separable from their intrinsic modes.[52]

On Scotus's account, infinity when applied to God is just this sort of property. And this is quite distinct from Aquinas's view that infinity is just a negation. Clearly, allowing that a property like 'infinity' is in some sense distinct from the attribute that it modifies will entail that God has formally distinct properties; at the least, the *intrinsic mode* of any divine attribute, or of the divine essence, will be formally distinct from both the attribute and the divine essence.[53]

The formal distinction between
the divine attributes

As we saw in chapter 2, all of God's attributes are essential to him: he is inseparable from any of them, and they are inseparable from each other. But his attributes are nevertheless *different* attributes, and they satisfy Scotus's criteria for a *formal* distinction:

> There is therefore there [viz., among the divine attributes] a distinction that is in every way prior to the [operation of] the intellect, and it is this: that wisdom actually exists naturally, and goodness actually exists naturally, and actual wisdom is formally not actual goodness.[54]

The fact that the attributes are different from each other is entailed by—though perhaps not explained by—Scotus's univocity theory. According to this theory, the basic lexical definitions of some of the terms applied to God are exactly the same as the lexical definitions of those terms when applied to creatures. Now, the lexical definitions of many such terms, when applied to creatures, are different from each other. And Scotus's main criterion for a formal distinction between different attributes is, roughly, that the attributes admit of different lexical definitions.[55] So different divine attributes will be formally distinct from each other.[56] Scotus makes the point by arguing that, if these different attributes were not distinct in God, then (given his univocity theory) they would not be distinct in creatures either.[57]

So univocity, as understood by Scotus, entails a weak account of divine simplicity, according to which the divine attributes are distinct from each other. On Scotus's account, divine simplicity is consistent with God's having several formally distinct transcendental attributes. As Scotus puts it, "This formal non-identity is compatible with God's simplicity."[58] Simplicity, for Scotus, entails no more than that a simple being cannot have *really* distinct parts, as outlined in the previous chapter.[59] He suggests that his account just shows that a formal distinction does not entail any kind of limitation (i.e., that a formal distinction does not entail having parts).[60]

The formal distinction between God's
substance and his attributes

God's attributes are really identical with, and formally distinct from, each other. What is the relation of God's attributes to his substance? Scotus raises the question by means of the following objection:

It seems that divine simplicity is not preserved, because from the fact that the essence is put forward as a kind of subject, and these [attributes] as circumstances of the essence, it seems that these [attributes] are related to the divine essence as acts and forms.[61]

What the objection is getting at is that if we are to attribute a property to something, then that property must be something *really* distinct from the thing. It must be a form *instantiated* by the thing. Here, 'divine essence' refers to the concrete divine existent, something which we might want to label God's *substance*.[62] So, the question is: Does God *have* attributes, or is he just in every respect identical with his attributes?

Scotus replies by noting that an instantiated property does not have to be *really* distinct from its subject. A thing's *necessary* or *essential* properties, for example, are properties that it cannot exist without. But on Scotus's separability condition for real distinction,[63] properties that something cannot be without cannot be really distinct from it. (A thing's *accidental* properties, for Scotus, are really distinct from it, since it can exist without such properties.) Many of the transcendental attributes of a thing are essential properties of that thing, properties that it cannot be without. All of God's properties are essential properties. And Scotus seems to imply that God is the subject of his essential properties (i.e., the divine attributes) in much the same way as any substance, on his account, is the subject of its essential properties.[64] On this showing, there will be a formal distinction between God and his attributes. God and his attributes are inseparable, but the definition of no divine attribute will fully encompass the divine substance. Equally, Scotus holds that God's substance or essence is somehow *explanatory* of his attributes.[65] It is worth keeping in mind in this context Scotus's claim, noted in chapter 1, that we cannot have knowledge of the divine essence apart from revelation. All that our philosophical investigation into God can yield is a knowledge of his *attributes*, which are formally distinct from the divine essence.

How does Scotus's account here relate to that of Aquinas? Aquinas would agree, I think, with the claim that the univocity entails a weak account of simplicity. He expressly claims that God's simplicity prevents words we apply to God having the same sense that they have when we apply them to creatures. And Aquinas accepts a strong account of divine simplicity, according to which there are no distinctions at all between the divine attributes. For example, Aquinas holds that God's wisdom is in every respect identical with his goodness.[66] In fact, Aquinas holds that these attributes are in every respect identical with the divine essence, and that this essence is in turn identical with God's existence. On this account all divine attributes are just identical with existence. (Simplicity, again, is the controlling idea at the heart of Aquinas's philosophical theology.) In line with this, Aquinas accepts an analogy theory of religious language. On such a theory, Aquinas can appeal to the possibility of analogous definitions of 'existence'. What Aquinas wants to affirm about God's existence, for example, is that, as opposed to creaturely existence, it is such that its *richness* precludes further specification. I take it that anyone committed to a strong account of divine simplicity will have to reject the univocity theory of religious language.[67] Furthermore, because on Aquinas's theory we have no way of knowing the *content* of terms such as 'existence', 'wisdom', and 'goodness' when applied to God, Aquinas's theory will entail a strong *apophatic* (negative) theology: "We cannot know what God is, but only what he is not."[68] This is not to claim that we cannot make true assertions about God, only that the *sense* of such assertions is ultimately opaque to us.

Scotus's God is clearly far less simple than Aquinas's God. One reason for this is Scotus's univocity theory of religious language, itself grounded on a more fundamental metaphysical presupposition that there must be some sort of distinction between a thing's essential attributes even in the case of God. For Scotus, the crucial divine attribute, the one that explains all the ways in which God's attributes differ from creaturely attributes, is 'infinity'. An uncharitable account would be that Scotus's God is just a human person writ large. But it looks to me as though Scotus's account of religious language is necessary for the intelligibility and viability of the whole theological project. And I am inclined to agree with Scotus (and Aquinas) that the univocity theory of religious language will entail that God has distinct attributes. Equally, Scotus's appeal to divine infinity to explain the difference between created and uncreated transcendental attributes is a nicely explanatory way of giving an account of the difference between God and creatures. For these reasons it seems to me that Scotus's account of religious language and the divine attributes is important and worthy of serious consideration. In fact, it seems to me that a theory like Scotus's is required for theology—natural or revealed—even to get started.

GOD: KNOWLEDGE
AND AGENCY

1. Divine intellect and will

As we would expect, Scotus holds that God has intellect and will. He can
know things, and he can will them. Scotus's argument for this, however,
does not make use of the perfect-being methodology outlined at the beginning of chapter 3. Scotus does not believe that intellect and will are
demonstrably pure perfections.[1]

The argument for divine intellect presupposes that God has will.
Scotus offers several arguments for this latter claim, of which I will give
one. The argument is both the most interesting and the simplest: contingent causation exists; so the first agent causes contingently; so the first
agent causes freely.[2] For reasons that I will examine in chapter 7, Scotus
is convinced that the premise here ("contingent causation exists") is true.
In support of the inference to "the first agent causes contingently," Scotus
argues that necessity in God's actions is sufficient to block contingency
in our actions.[3] This does not seem obviously true. But, as we shall see
below, Scotus believes that God's causal concurrence is required for everything that happens—including our free actions. If two causes concur in
producing one effect, Scotus assumes that necessity in one of the causes
is sufficient to guarantee necessity in the effect. (I look at Scotus's discussion of God's causal concurrence below. In *De Primo Principio*, Scotus at

this point in his argument for God's will explicitly refers his readers to his discussion of God's causal concurrence.)[4] It is difficult to know what to make of Scotus's claim that necessity in one of two concurrent causes is sufficient for necessity in the effect. And—as I shall show below—the reason for this is that it is difficult to make any sense of Scotus's account of causal concurrence applied to free actions.

In favor of the second inference—from contingency to freedom— Scotus argues that all contingent events are brought about by free will.[5] Underlying this is an assumption, which I mention in chapter 7 (note 19), that genuine randomness is impossible. The argument in favor of divine intellect follows straightforwardly from this. No free agent can will something without knowing it. So God, as a free agent, must have intellect.[6]

2. Divine knowledge

Given that God has intellect, what can we say about his knowledge? Perhaps the most important feature of it is that none of God's knowledge is caused by anything external to himself. According to Scotus, God's simplicity entails that everything in God is in some sense identical with him; and God's necessity entails that he is immutable.[7] Each of these two claims—that everything in God is identical with him, and that God is immutable—entails that nothing external to God can be necessary for anything internal to him.[8] Suppose a creature were a necessary condition for the existence of something in God. On Scotus's simplicity claim, this would entail that a creature were a necessary condition for the existence of God's essence. And given that God is the first cause of everything, this is false. Equally, all creatures (as a matter of contingent fact) come into existence. So if a creature were a necessary condition for the existence of something in God, God would change.[9] Considerations like these lie behind the scholastic claim that God cannot be really related to any of his creatures. If God were really related to any of his creatures, something in God—his relation to his creatures—would require the existence of something external to him. So God cannot be really related to any of his creatures.[10]

The claim that nothing outside God is necessary for the existence of anything in God has some odd implications for God's knowledge. Put simply, it means that God's knowledge of creatures is not in any sense caused by the creatures themselves. To understand Scotus's position, we need to have a rough grasp of part of his philosophy of mind. According to Scotus—following Aristotle—our intellect has two "parts": the passive intellect (which Scotus prefers to call by the Augustinian term 'memory'), and the active intellect (to which Scotus often gives the Augustinian label 'intelligence'). The first of these is responsible for storing ideas, concepts, and so on (the items of my 'habitual knowledge'); the second (in Scotus's account, though not in most medieval accounts) is responsible for actually understanding them. The idea is that memory has a capacity to call habitual knowledge to mind, bringing about a state of actual understanding. The items in the memory are said to have 'intelligible existence', and to *represent* the extra-mental realities to which they correspond.[11] These intelligible objects are in some sense caused in our minds by the extramental realities they represent.[12] They are the means by which we know external reality.[13]

What happens when we have actual understanding of an object that we know habitually? The scholastics, perhaps following Aristotle, generally assumed that there is a universal mental language, and that we use this language when we *think*.[14] This notion of a mental language was used to spell out the difference between actual and habitual knowledge. According to Scotus, my memory along with the intelligible object it contains jointly cause actual knowledge in my intelligence.[15] This actual knowledge consists in a basic item in our mental language—a mental word—inhering in my intelligence.[16] Thus, a person x is in a state of having actual knowledge if a mental word inheres in x's intelligence. We might think of this mental word as a mental *act*. Scotus classifies it as a *quality* inhering in the intelligence.[17]

God's knowledge is different from this in at least two respects. First, God's knowledge is caused not by anything outside himself, but merely by his essence and (for some of his knowledge) his will. Secondly, although God does have actual knowledge produced from his memory and expressed in a mental word, he also has actual knowledge that is not so produced or expressed. I will look at this second feature in the next chapter.

Scotus discerns three sorts of objects of divine knowledge: the divine essence, necessary truths and all logical possibilities, and contingent truths. I shall label this second sort of object an 'N-object', and the third sort a 'C-object'. The set of N-objects includes all necessary truths, including the essences of things;[18] all possible combinations of contingent states of affairs (i.e., all logical possibilities);[19] and all possible individuals.[20] In line with post-Augustinian tradition, Scotus labels the common essences, as known by God, 'ideas'.[21] He does not label God's knowledge of logical possibilities and possible individuals 'ideas'.[22] But most of what he says about divine ideas is applicable to God's knowledge of possibilities and possible individuals. I use 'N-object' to refer to all such objects. I look at these three sorts of object—the divine essence, N-objects, and C-objects—and their relation to God's knowledge, in turn.

God's knowledge of his own essence

God knows his essence by a direct intuitive grasp of it as present to him.[23] Intuitive knowledge is knowledge of an individual object precisely as that object is *present* to the cognizer.[24] Furthermore, this knowledge is itself really identical with God's essence. God's self-love is necessary; so the self-knowledge required for this love must be necessary too.[25] And as we saw in chapter 3, necessary divine attributes are really identical with God's essence.

God's knowledge of necessary truths and logical possibilities

God's knowledge of N-objects is very different from this. Roughly, Scotus holds that all N-objects are somehow *caused* by God. Rival theories would make God's N-knowledge relate to concepts that are somehow "givens"—already there prior to God's thought. According to Bonaventure, for example, there are eternal relations in God to objects other than himself. God knows things other than himself only in virtue of these relations.[26] There is no suggestion in Bonaventure that these objects have any sort of *existence* outside God. But Henry of Ghent makes just such a claim: common and individual essences have some sort of existence outside God, and these essences are objects of God's knowledge.[27] Henry claims that such objects have *esse essentiae* (their essential existence) but not *esse existentiae* (their actual existence).

Scotus regards both of these theories as radically confused. The first, according to Scotus, entails that God's intellect is passive with regard to knowledge of N-objects. Its knowledge of such objects is somehow *caused* in it by the concepts that correspond to this knowledge, and this "demeans the divine intellect."[28] Against Henry's theory, Scotus draws attention to the unclear existential status of the extra-mental objects it posits. Extramental objects are indistinguishable from real material things. And in this case, real material things are everlasting and in some sense exist necessarily. Thus, as Scotus points out, no objects can be brought into existence;[29] or at best such objects will be merely altered somehow, getting actual existence in addition to their essential existence.[30]

Scotus reasons, therefore, that the N-objects of God's knowledge must be produced entirely by himself.[31] In fact, Scotus is convinced that knowing things in this way—by producing objects in intelligible existence— is a perfection.[32] Claiming that the N-objects of God's knowledge are produced by him does not mean that God could fail to produce them; it does not make them contingent. In fact, Scotus claims that God cannot fail but produce these N-objects. As Scotus puts it, God's intellect is a "merely natural cause" of the N-objects known by him.[33]

How does God produce N-objects? Scotus claims that God does so as a result of his intuitive grasp of his own essence. God's essence somehow contains the "entities" of all created things,[34] and God causes the N-objects by intuitively seeing his own essence. Thus, God, by seeing his essence, produces N-objects in intelligible existence. Scotus often refers to God's essence as the primary object of God's knowledge, and N-objects as the secondary objects of divine knowledge.[35] N-objects are, of course, the ideas of all possible essences and individuals. So Scotus holds that necessary truths, logical possibilities, and possible individuals are all brought into existence by God.[36]

Interestingly, Scotus also holds that God's knowledge of N-objects is really identical with his essence. The first agent necessarily possesses everything required for its causal activity. But without its knowledge of N-objects, it could not cause. So its knowledge of N-objects must be essential to it.[37]

God's knowledge
of contingent truths

Of course, God's knowledge of all logical possibilities does not tell him which of these contingent possibilities is *actual*. And this brings me onto the third sort of divine knowledge pinpointed by Scotus: knowledge of contingent actualities. Scotus is quite clear that God cannot know C-objects in the same way as he knows necessary truths and possibilities. Scotus's central presupposition in his discussion of God's knowledge of C-objects is that God's will is free. Suppose God's intellect could calculate which of all logically possible states of affairs should be actualized. God's free will could ignore this calculation, and thus (since God's intellect is always morally upright) possibly act badly. But of course God cannot act badly. Thus the actions of a free God could not be in any way dictated by his intellect.[38] So the divine intellect must gain its knowledge of C-objects in some other way. This way, Scotus reasons, must be by knowledge of the free decisions of the divine will. In short, God knows C-objects because he has freely caused them.[39]

These C-objects are not, of course, really existing things external to God. They are still objects merely in intelligible, mental, existence (though they presumably directly correspond to existing contingent things). As we saw above, Scotus holds that divine simplicity means that everything in God is identical with him. And Scotus is quite clear that all of God's knowledge is identical with his essence.[40] But this raises a problem. How could anything contingent—such as knowledge of a C-object—be identical with the divine essence?[41] Scotus does not really address this worry, although given his claims that everything in God is in some sense identical with God and that God's existence is necessary, Scotus certainly should do so. Perhaps the closest Scotus comes to a discussion of the problem is in distinction 39 of both *Lectura* and *Reportatio*. Scotus rejects the claim of Henry of Ghent that the divine intellect could gain knowledge of the determinations of the divine will directly from this will,[42] arguing instead that God's intellect knows the contingent decisions of the divine will by means of his essence. Scotus draws an analogy with human vision:

> If I were to have a constant act of vision, I now see a white thing and—if the white thing were removed—I would see something else as black without any change in the act of seeing; so the divine intellect sees the truth of some state of affairs [*complexionem*] made and brought about by the will (which truth his essence immediately presents to him).[43]

The idea seems to be that the numerical identity of God's act of understanding is not altered in any way by the *content* of this act—where the content is contingent upon the free decision of the divine will. And presumably it is this one act of understanding—irrespective of its content—that is identical with the divine essence. I am not sure, however, that this will go much of the way towards solving the contingency difficulty. After all, C-objects should be identical with the divine essence as much as God's knowledge of them is.

Accounting for God's knowledge of contingent truths in this way certainly safeguards the unconditioned nature of God; nothing outside God is required for him to have knowledge of contingent truths. But it seems to be open to an obvious objection. Scotus's account makes it look as though God's decision leaves no place for created freedom. Think about God's knowledge of future contingents, future events that may or may not come to pass, perhaps simply as a result of a human decision. If God knows these events—or even the C-objects necessarily corresponding to these events—by determining them, there seems to be no room for human freedom. And, as we shall see in chapter 7, Scotus is convinced that human beings are free in the strongest sense, with—like God—both the powers and the opportunities for determining their own actions. It is important to keep in mind, however, that Scotus believes himself to have overwhelming reasons for both of the following claims:

(1) God knows the future by determining it;
(2) Human beings are self-determining free agents.

We have already seen the crucial presupposition lying behind (1)—namely, that God is wholly unconditioned, and cannot gain knowledge from external causes. And in chapter 7 we shall look at Scotus's reasons for (2). Given that both (1) and (2) are true, Scotus concludes that a further claim must be true:

(3) A free creaturely action has two causes which are jointly necessary and sufficient: God and the creature.[44]

Scotus's argument, as Wolter and Frank have both pointed out, is not *explanatory*: it is a demonstration *that* (3) is true, not an explanation of *how* it is true, or of how (1) and (2) can be reconciled.[45]

Frank offers a useful summary of the sort of essentially ordered concurrent causality involved in this sort of divine-human cooperation (labeling it 'autonomous co-causality'):

> Although the two [autonomous partial co-]causes are ordered as superior to inferior according to their essential natures as active powers, the inferior's dependence on the superior in its act of causing is not a matter of participating in the other's fuller causality, nor does the superior otherwise move the inferior to exercise its causality. Rather, both superior and inferior causes act on behalf of the common effect with an independent, self-moving exercise of causality. To be sure, neither on its own effort suffices to cause the effect: neither is the total cause. In short, each cause independently exercises its causality, but only in cooperation do they bring about the effect.[46]

Scotus's standard example of such essentially ordered autonomous co-causes is "the concurrence of male and female in begetting offspring. . . . Neither mother nor father suffice independently of the other, and, further, the necessary contribution of each is rooted in an essential difference between their generative powers."[47] Divine and human causal concurrence is like this. Both causes are necessary, and they are jointly sufficient, for a free human action. And God knows the outcomes of free human actions as a result of his own causal role.

This account of God's knowledge of free human actions is subtle and intriguing. But it is not clear to me that it is ultimately coherent, or that Scotus's sophisticated account of autonomous co-causality is really applicable here. Scotus's claim is that God can know future contingents by being an autonomous co-cause of such events. Now, knowledge—by definition—cannot be false. So if God really knows creaturely actions, his casual activity must be *sufficient* for the events that he knows. If God's activity here is not sufficient, then there is no way that God can guarantee the outcome. On the theory of autonomous co-causality, God's action is—by contrast—necessary *but not sufficient* for the production of the effect. So it cannot be the case *both* that God knows free human actions, *and* that he is an autonomous co-cause of such actions. Scotus's doctrine, as it stands, is not just (as Wolter and Frank rightly point out) non-explanatory; it is straightforwardly incoherent. Scotus should take the contradictory nature of (3) as evidence that either (1) or (2) is false. And in fact it seems to me that his arguments in favor of (1) and (2) are—contrary to what Scotus supposes—far from overwhelming. As I shall show in chapter 7, Scotus does not have a good argument for (2). And the argument for (1) presupposes a doctrine of simplicity that we might consider far too strong.

God's knowledge of temporal truths

There is a further puzzle about divine knowledge. How can a timeless God—a God who exists outside time—have knowledge of time? As I have tried to show elsewhere, Scotus unequivocally accepts that God is timeless, lacking both temporal extension and temporal location.[48] A God who is timeless cannot have the sort of knowledge of time that requires of its subject temporal location (e.g., what time it is now, or what happens tomorrow). But there is no reason why a timeless God cannot have knowledge of those temporal facts that can be known without temporal location. We do not need, for example, to have temporal location to know that certain events occur before other events, or that such and such happened on, say, 8 November 1308.[49] Scotus is quite clear that God can have knowledge of this second sort of temporal fact. For example, when dealing with the problem of God's knowledge of the temporality of creaturely existence, Scotus claims:

> Just as [God] in eternity compares his will "as creative" to the soul of the Antichrist as possible for some time, so he in eternity compares his will "as creating" to the soul of the Antichrist as actually existing at that instant for which he wills to create that soul.[50]

Scotus also tries (unsuccessfully) to claim that God can have knowledge of the first sort of temporal fact (i.e., the sort of fact that requires its knower to have temporal location). An objector tries to argue that a timeless God cannot know such temporal facts—and hence that, since God can know such facts, he cannot be timeless.[51] Scotus tries to deflect the objection by reiterating that God can have knowledge of different times as outlined in the quotation above. So Scotus obviously—and mistakenly—supposes that his account is sufficient to allow God knowledge of the first sort of temporal fact as well. But this is not so, and Scotus's reply clearly fails to meet the objection. On the other hand, it seems to me right that a timeless God cannot know the first sort of temporal fact. The theist anxious to defend God's timelessness ought to devote his or her energies to showing why this divine "ignorance" does not have harmful consequences for divine omniscience.

3. Divine agency

Omnipotence and primary causation

According to the schoolmen, God is a partial cause of everything (other than himself) that exists and occurs. God is the *primary* cause; the created causes that act concurrently with God are *secondary* causes. Scotus generally spells out the relationship between primary and secondary causes as the relationship between the first member of an E-series and any subsequent member. (An exception to this, as we have just seen, is God's causal concurrence with our free actions. While God's action and our action are essentially ordered, they are also *autonomous*.) God is the primary cause of everything by being at the head of every E-series. As we saw in chapter 3, relationships of essential causality are transitive. This might seem to make creaturely concurrence superfluous. But Scotus does not think that it does. He draws a distinction between secondary causes and instrumental causes. *Secondary causes* have intrinsic causal powers. *Instrumental causes* do not have causal powers; or if they do, these powers are caused by the principal agent, and endure only for as long as the principal agent uses its instrument.[52] Scotus describes carefully the way in which a genuine secondary cause is activated by the primary cause:

> I believe that . . . a secondary cause . . . has a certain subordination of its active form [i.e., its causal power] to the active form of another. Through this subordination, when the prior cause becomes active in its order of causing, the second naturally becomes active in its order of causing. And thus the secondary [cause] is said to be a "moved mover," not because it receives its motion from the primary cause (through which it moves), but because in its motion it depends on another whose motion is naturally prior.[53]

On this account, a secondary cause is activated by the activation of its causal powers. That its causal powers function when they do is presumably the result of the causal activity of the primary cause. But a secondary cause—unlike an instrument—is a cause in the sense that the effect caused by its causal powers is not caused by the higher cause.[54]

As we saw in chapter 2, Scotus believes that God's infinite power can be demonstrated by natural reason. A being is infinitely powerful if it is capable of producing any effect. As we also saw, Scotus distinguishes infinite power from omnipotence. A being is omnipotent if it is capable of producing any effect without the causal concurrence of secondary causes. An omnipotent being, for example, would be able to burn something without fire, and quench someone's thirst without water. Scotus believes that God is omnipotent in this way.[55] But he does not believe that it is possible to demonstrate that God is omnipotent. We believe in God's omnipotence merely on the basis of revelation.[56] According to Scotus, there is a probable argument in favor of omnipotence:

> The active power of any secondary cause exists in the first cause in a more eminent way than in the second cause. Now what possesses the active power more eminently can cause the effect, it seems, without the intervention of what possesses it only in a lesser degree. To produce an effect no imperfection is required in the active power. For imperfection is not essential to acting, rather it is an impediment.[57]

But he thinks that we could plausibly accept the premise ("The active power of any secondary cause exists in the first cause in a more eminent way than in the second cause") while denying the conclusion. Aristotle could argue, for example, that the premise entails no more than "[a] cause with such eminent power can indeed produce the effect of such a power, but only in its own orderly way, which means it functions precisely as a higher and remote cause."[58] Furthermore, Scotus claims that we could plausibly hold that the power to cause effects immediately—the distinguishing mark of omnipotence—implies imperfection: "Where an essential order exists, nothing can be adjacent to the least perfect unless it is in some measure imperfect."[59]

Nevertheless, these arguments against omnipotence are not probative; if they were, of course, we could demonstrate the falsity of the Christian faith. And for Scotus the articles of the Christian faith are true.[60] We should also note that Scotus's claim that God is omnipotent does not entail occasionalism (i.e., that God actually exercises his omnipotence by causing everything in the universe directly). Scotus's claim is just that God *could* so act.

Divine freedom and timeless agency

Scotus offers a highly nuanced and original account of freedom. I examine it in detail in chapter 7. Scotus is quite clear that a free agent has a power to produce opposite effects in exactly the same circumstances. When I bring about effect *e*, for example, I could in exactly the same circumstances bring about not-*e*, or even do nothing at all. Scotus analyzes created freedom into three different sorts of indeterminacies: a created agent is free to produce opposite *acts*, it is free to will opposite *objects*, and it is free to cause opposite external *effects*.[61] According to Scotus, God's free will has the second and third of these indeterminacies, but not the first. Human beings need the first sort of indeterminacy—for producing opposite acts—because they bring about their effects piecemeal, and the first indeterminacy is what allows for some sort of *process* in created activity. Thus, creatures do one action at a time, and they necessarily perform one action after another. So the power to perform different acts is in fact an imperfection; it implies process and mutability. Thus it cannot be found in God.[62] God in fact has one timeless act. By means of this one act he freely wills different objects, and causes different effects.[63] God thus freely produces any state of affairs he wants, timelessly and without going through any process.

God's timelessness means that God has no "time" in which to make his free choice with regard to which effects to bring about. Scotus believes, however, that it is possible to make a free choice in an instant. He argues that, at exactly the same time as a free agent chooses to bring about effect *e*, it retains its power to bring about not-*e*.[64] Scotus argues that this power is necessary for genuine contingency in the will. (I discuss his reasoning in chapter 7, section 1.) Clearly, if Scotus is right about this, then he has a tool that will allow him to give an account of timeless freedom. Given that a free agent has a power for opposites in the same instant, it is logically possible that either of the opposites be brought about. If there were no such power in God, then he would not be able to bring about effects freely. (On any alternative account, freedom entails power for opposites *before*—but not during—the actualization of one of the opposites. On this account, free agency requires temporal succession.) Still, how would a timeless God have time to choose? Scotus sees no reason for God's choice to take time. All that matters for him is that there is a logical sequence in God's activity; the divine intellect presents all possibilities to the will logically prior to the will's choice of just one of these possible states of affairs.[65]

Scotus's claim that free agents have a power for opposites in the same instant—their synchronic power for opposites—revolutionized central aspects of both theology and metaphysics. In theology, Scotus's claim enables him to give an account of God's power as ranging over sets of compossible (i.e., compatible) states of affairs. Each compossible set is known by the divine intellect as logically possible; the divine will, in one timeless action, actualizes one of these sets. This account of divine power enables Scotus to provide a theoretical framework for the talk of the "two powers" of God that we find commonly from the thirteenth century.[66] The distinction is between God's "absolute power" and his "ordained power." The first of these picks out God's power to bring about any state of affairs, actual or possible (things that are and things that might have been); the second, his power to bring about those states of affairs that are actual. Of course, the distinction is not intended to suggest that God has more than one set of causal powers. It is just a convenient way of stating that God can do more than he has actually done. Scotus often talks about things God could have done by his absolute power, by which he means that some counterfactual state of affairs is not logically impossible. (I discuss some of these claims in later chapters.) Of course, Scotus is clear, anything that God *does* is brought about by his ordained power. It is a mistake to suppose that Scotus holds God's absolute power to be some kind of executive power capable of overruling the ordained power. Thus:

> God can act otherwise than is prescribed not only by a particular order, but also by a universal order or law of justice, and in doing so he could still act ordainedly, because what God could do by his absolute power that is either beyond or runs counter to the present order, he could do ordainedly.[67]

The point of this passage is that God's ordained power relates to whatever he actually chooses to do. There is nothing that God could bring about by his absolute power which, were he actually to bring it about, would not be brought about by his ordained power.[68]

By drawing attention to the realm of the non-actual as restricted by logical possibility, Scotus is able to make sense of the notion of God's absolute power in a way denied to his thirteenth-century predecessors.[69] Scotus's account of the synchronic power for opposites has some important metaphysical consequences too. Knuuttila puts the matter neatly:

> In Duns Scotus's modal theory modal notions are no longer understood as clarifying the states of the actual world at different times. The domain of possibility is accepted as an a priori area of conceptual

consistency which is then divided into different classes of compossible states of affairs, of which the actual world is one. Thus it was not Leibniz who invented the idea of a possible world; the idea is present in Duns Scotus' modal theory.[70]

And this move allows Scotus to distinguish logical possibility from the possible exercise of real causal powers.

Scotus's account of a synchronic power for opposites, as I have suggested, undergirds his account of God's timeless action. But there is an obvious objection to the idea of timeless action. How could a timeless God bring about different effects at different times? The crucial fact to keep in mind, I think, is that God as a disembodied omnipotent agent does not need to go through any *process* in order to act. (I discussed this aspect of Scotus's account of divine agency above. Briefly, God is free to will opposite objects and effects; but he does this through just *one* action. He is not free to will opposite actions.) Scotus capitalizes on this when trying to explain how a timeless God could bring about different effects at different times:

> A new effect can be made by an old act of the will without a change of will. Just as I, by means of my continuous volition—by which I will something to be done—will do it just for the "when" for which I will to do it, so God in eternity willed something other than himself to be for some time, and then created it for the "when" for which he willed it to be.[71]

The fact that a creature is created at time t does not entail that God has to do anything at t. All God has to do is to will (eternally) that the creature begins to exist at t.[72]

Scotus's discussion of God's knowledge and agency shows considerable similarity to modern discussions of the same topics. Perhaps the most distinctive feature is Scotus's bold attempt to give an account of God's knowledge of free human actions given both that God is wholly unconditioned and that determinism is false. And Scotus's explicit claim that divine power ranges over all logical possibilities—all states of affairs that do not include a contradiction—is of obvious importance in the history of ideas.

GOD THE TRINITY

According to orthodox Christianity, God is a Trinity of persons: Father, Son, and Holy Spirit. Traditionally, the Father is in some sense the source of the other two persons; the Son and the Holy Spirit are said to proceed from him. Central to all understandings of this doctrine is that the claim that there are three divine persons does not entail the further claim that there are three Gods. Not surprisingly, this doctrine has caused theologians some difficulty. Eastern Christianity, taking its cue from the great Cappadocian fathers (Basil of Caesarea, Gregory of Nyssa, and Gregory of Nazianzus), has tended to emphasize what are sometimes known as "social" models of the Trinity. The divine persons on this view are something like three individuals living in indivisible community with each other.[1] The West, following Augustine, has tended to see the three persons as something like three ways in which the one divine essence exists. On this admittedly rough analysis, the difficulty faced by those theologians who prefer social models of the Trinity is avoiding tritheism; the problem for the more "Augustinian" theologians is avoiding modalism, the belief that the three persons are just modes of divine self-presentation to us.

Scotus, like most of the scholastics, is located firmly within the Augustinian tradition on this question. In this chapter, I want to look in detail at Scotus's account of the Trinity, discussing his theory of the divine processions, the constitution of the divine persons, the unity of the divine essence, and the unity of God's external activity.[2]

1. The divine processions

Trinitarian orthodoxy is clear that the divine processions do not entail something's being brought into existence. Scotus argues that the productions of the Son and Spirit are necessary—voluntary, but not *freely* elicited. Thus, the productions exist whenever God exists. And God is timeless. So the productions of Son and Spirit are timeless too.[3]

Scotus's basic model for the divine processions is the production of acts of knowledge and love by the human mind. The background here is Augustine's *De Trinitate*. In this work, Augustine proposes a number of analogies, derived from human cognitive processes, for the Trinity.[4]

The generation of the Son

The post-Augustinian Western theological tradition tends to spell out the procession of the Son by drawing on an analogy from human cognition: specifically, the production of a mental word. I discussed this feature of human cognition at the beginning of chapter 4. Basically, a mental word is produced jointly by the memory and the intelligible object contained by the memory. Scotus uses this model to give an account of the procession of the Son—the "Word"—in God. Scotus holds that memory and the intelligible object, in the presence of the extra-mental object represented by the intelligible object, is naturally productive of a mental word. The divine essence is an intelligible object present to God's memory.[5] So the divine memory is naturally productive of a state of actual knowledge in God—the divine Word.[6]

According to Scotus, all three divine persons have the divine memory,[7] though of course only the Father has it in such a way that it produces the Word.[8] Scotus is clear that it is the Father who is responsible for this production. So it is specifically the divine memory as had by the Father that produces the Word. Equally, the Word of God is not simply identical with God's essential knowledge. All three persons have the divine intelligence and knowledge. And this knowledge is something distinct from the divine Word.[9]

The procession of the Holy Spirit

In a way analogous to that in which the Word is a state of actual knowledge produced by the divine memory, the Holy Spirit is a state of actual love produced by the divine will. Just as in the case of the generation of the Son, this 'notional'[10] act of love is distinct from God's essential act of love shared by all three persons. This notional act of love presupposes knowledge; nothing can be loved unless it is already known.[11] The object of God's love is his essence.[12] This last claim places Scotus at some distance from Augustine's position. According to Augustine, the Holy Spirit is the love the Father and Son share *for each other*: "The Holy Spirit is ... the common charity by which the Father and Son love each other";[13] or, in a passage cited by Scotus: "The Holy Spirit is something common to Father and Son, whatever it is, or is the consubstantial and coeternal commonness itself."[14] Scotus holds that the Holy Spirit's infinity results from the infinity of the object for which the Holy Spirit is an act of love. But the personal properties of the Father and Son are not infinite, since nothing other than the divine essence itself is infinite.[15] So it is the divine essence that is the object of divine love.[16] Scotus does not discuss the first of the two quotations from Augustine given above; but in line with his theory he expounds the second—that the Holy Spirit is the communion of Father and Son—to mean that the Holy Spirit is the shared love of Father and Son for the divine essence.[17]

The "filioque"

Augustine used his account of the mutual love of Father and Son to defend the view that the Holy Spirit proceeds from the Father *and* the Son.[18] Scotus is just as clear as Augustine that the so-called *filioque* ("and from the Son") is true. But his reasons are very different from Augustine's, because Augustine's defense of the *filioque* is not open to him. Scotus, in an unusual moment of historical sensitivity, cites a lengthy passage from Grosseteste outlining a possible difference of opinion between the Greeks and the Latins, the Greeks accepting that the Spirit proceeds from the Father through the Son, the Latins accepting that the Spirit proceeds from both Father and Son.[19] Scotus believes the Latin view to be the teaching of the Church, and he accordingly accepts it.[20] But he also believes that the Greek view is open to a fatal philosophical objection. The Son has the divine will prior (logically prior) to the production of the Spirit. But having the divine will logically prior to the production of the Spirit is causally both necessary and sufficient for being an agent responsible for the production of the Spirit. It is sufficient because, as we have seen, the divine will is automatically active in the production of a divine person. It is necessary since there can be only one will-originated production in God. Scotus concludes that the Father and Son jointly produce (and presumably cannot avoid producing) the Holy Spirit.[21] In fact, the divine will is not divided between the Father and Son in any way. So they produce the Holy Spirit "as one principle."[22] Scotus allows that there is a sense in which the Father, but not the Son, produces the Spirit from himself: the Son proceeds from the Father, and so receives from the Father his power for producing the Spirit—just as he receives the divine essence from the Father.[23]

So Scotus defends the Latins' *filioque* for reasons very different from those proposed by Augustine. Unlike many post-Augustinian Western theologians, however, Scotus does not accept that the *filioque* is required in order to allow for a distinction between the Son and the Spirit. Thomas Aquinas, for example, argues that, necessarily, the divine persons are distinguished by relations, and that there are no relations in God other than relations of origin. If there is no relation of origin between Son and Spirit, then Son and Spirit will not be in any sense distinct from each other.[24]

Scotus believes this to be false. He agrees that the persons are distinguished by their relations of origin. But he does not accept Thomas's inference that such a relation must obtain *between* the Son and the Spirit in order for them to be distinct. The property in virtue of which the Son is a person—and thus distinct from the other persons—is *filiation* (i.e., being a son). The Son is distinct from the Spirit in virtue of the fact that the personal property of the Spirit is different from that of the Son.[25]

The processions and the divine persons

Why should Scotus suppose that these productive acts result in persons? The items produced necessarily by the divine memory and will cannot be external to God, because, as we saw in the previous chapter, all of God's external acts are contingent.[26] God has no passive potentialities, so the items produced cannot perfect, or inhere in, the divine essence.[27] But the items produced are not in every way identical with the things that produce them, because nothing produces itself.[28] So the items produced will be persons: *instances of* the divine essence.[29] (I return to the relations between the divine persons and the divine essence in section 3 below.)

2. The constitution of the divine persons

As we have seen, Scotus believes the persons to be distinguished by their relations of origin. Unlike the majority of both Western and Eastern theologians, however, Scotus does not believe that there are any compelling reasons why this should be so. The persons, he argues, could just as well be distinguished by non-relational, or *absolute*, properties. The standard reason for holding that the persons are constituted by relations is that such a theory is necessary in order to avoid the heresy of *Arianism*—the belief that the Son is different in essence or kind from the Father, and hence less than the Father. Augustine, for example, held that the three persons are equal, and therefore the same in kind or *essence*.[30] Furthermore, there cannot, according to Augustine, be any accidental difference between the three persons, because accidents can be lost, and therefore cannot belong to the immutable God.[31] So there can be neither essential nor accidental differences between the divine persons. But the three persons can differ in their relations, since being related does not imply being changeable. Equally, the Father can be always related to the Son, and the Son always related to the Father, without this implying that the Father and Son differ in essence.[32]

Whatever the intrinsic strengths or weaknesses of this line of reasoning, there is no reason for Scotus to accept it. Scotus's ontology contains entities that are neither essential (in the sense of being both necessary and quidditative), accidental, nor relational. The individuating entity or 'haecceity' of a substance would be a good example.[33] In the *Lectura* and book 1 of the *Ordinatio*, Scotus seems to regard the claim that the divine persons are constituted by non-repeatable *absolute* (non-relational) properties as preferable to the claim that the divine persons are constituted by their relations to each other,[34] though he gives arguments on both sides of the question. For example, in favor of the standard Augustinian view—which I shall call the 'relation theory'—he suggests that the existence of both the divine essence and an absolute property in a divine person will entail that the divine person is composite,[35] and that the divine essence is divided into discrete individuals.[36] In these early texts, however, Scotus clearly regards these two arguments as unsound.[37] And it is easy to see that the premises do not obviously entail the conclusions. In favor of the opposing view, that the persons are constituted by absolute properties— the 'absolute-property theory'—Scotus argues that relations are always logically posterior to the absolute items they relate;[38] and that the proposed relational properties—paternity, sonship, and so on—look to be repeatable, and therefore not sufficient to distinguish one person from another.[39] These arguments, however, are according to Scotus likewise insufficient to establish the absolute-property theory, and he proposes some replies that the defender of the relation theory could offer. In reply to the first argument, he denies that it is necessarily the case that relations are in every case logically posterior to the absolute items they relate[40]—though it seems to me difficult to see how this could be the case. Scotus does not know a reply to the second argument; though, as he rightly points out, if the relation theory is true, the argument must be soluble.[41]

The overall view in these two early texts is that the issue must be decided not by appeal to argument but by appeal to authority. This remains Scotus's official line. But he became less sanguine about the absolute-property theory as he got older.[42] In *Ordinatio* 3, Scotus sees the absolute-property theory as less probable than the relation theory, on the grounds that his authorities—the Church Fathers—prefer the relation theory. He still believes, however, that there are no decisive *arguments* either way.[43] The text, however, has a reply to the second argument in favor of the absolute-property theory cited above—an argument to which the younger Scotus could find no reply. Relational properties are not univocal between God and creatures; so we cannot infer from the repeatability of such properties in creatures—paternity, sonship, and so on—that they are repeatable in God.[44]

The relative dates of *Ordinatio* 3 and book 1 of the *Reportatio* are not clear. But in the latter text, Scotus is even clearer about the preferability of the relation theory to the absolute-property theory.[45] Again, Scotus's official view is that the issue cannot be decided merely on the basis of argument, and that an appeal to authority is necessary. But he also proposes a new argument in favor of the relation theory. A created person—

indeed any independent substance—properly exhibits three features: existence per se, individual unity, and non-repeatability (incommunicability). It gets these three features not from its essence but from its 'ultimate actuality'—its haecceity. A divine person likewise exhibits these three features. But the first two features belong properly to the divine essence, and are had by a divine person merely in virtue of its having the divine essence. The third feature, however, belongs to a divine person in virtue of its personal property. This property must be generically distinct from the absolute divine essence, and so must be a relational property.[46] (The idea is that generic distinction entails a distinction in [Aristotelian] category; and the only category generically distinct from all absolute categories is the category of relation.) But Scotus does not abandon his claim that the issue must be decided by authority, so he perhaps did not regard this argument as very convincing.

According to standard versions of the relation theory, the relations that distinguish the divine persons are paternity, sonship, and passive spiration (i.e., being produced by will).[47] The relation theory, as understood by Scotus, entails that the *constitutive* properties—those properties in virtue of which the divine persons are distinct and non-repeatable—are the relations just listed. But, according to Scotus, the relation theory does not entail that the divine persons do not have any other properties. For example, the Father according to Scotus has the privative absolute property of being unbegotten.[48] If on the other hand we accept the absolute-property theory, none of the relational properties just listed is constitutive of a divine person (though, of course, these properties are still properties of a divine persons; they are just secondary or non-constitutive). But Scotus is clear that, if we accept the absolute-property theory, the sorts of properties that could constitute the divine persons cannot be just negative or privative. Being unbegotten, for example, could not be a constitutive property of the Father.[49] The reason is that every negation is repeatable,[50] and therefore cannot be sufficient to render a person non-repeatable.[51]

3. The unity of the divine essence

As we saw in chapter 3, Scotus claims that there can be only one God. So the three persons of the Trinity cannot be three Gods. Nevertheless,

Scotus holds that the three persons are three instances of the divine essence in a way that bears some relationship to the way in which three human beings are instances of human nature.

According to Lateran IV, the divine essence is *indivisible*.[52] Scotus is happy to cite the Council's claim here. The divine essence is not such that it can be divided up between three different discrete individuals (in the same way as human nature is divided up among its different instantiations).[53] The indivisibility of the divine essence follows straightforwardly from divine unicity.[54] But if the divine essence is indivisible, how can it be instantiated by three different persons? To explain how an indivisible essence could be so instantiated, Scotus distinguishes two crucial features of any created essence: repeatability (communicability) and divisibility.[55] An essence, according to Scotus, is repeated by the individuals that instantiate it, such that each of these individuals is really identical with it.[56] The idea is that, say, any human being instantiates every feature required to be human, and that no human being could fail to do this. So any human being is really identical with human nature. But no human being is *formally* identical with human nature; each human being includes an individuating haecceity, non-repeatable and formally distinct from human nature.[57] The divine essence is repeatable in this way; it is "communicable to many by identity."[58] Human nature is like this; but when human nature is repeated it is also divided up into numerically discrete individuals. The divine nature is not divisible; so it is repeatable without being divisible. It thus remains numerically one thing; it is "communicable without division."[59]

It is not clear prima facie how anything could be like this—repeatable without division. But Scotus believes that there are overwhelming considerations—theological in one case and metaphysical in the other— in favor of the claims that God is a Trinity of persons and that there is only one God. And given both these claims, Scotus could reasonably conclude that at least one essence is repeatable without division. So Scotus is certainly right to try to give an account of the different features of an instantiation relationship, to allow the tenability of a Trinitarian account of God.[60]

Scotus gives an example from the created order to try to explain what he has in mind. According to Scotus, the intellective soul—which is "in a certain way unlimited in perfecting its matter"[61]—exists such that the whole of it is in each part of the matter to which it is united. Thus, each part of a body (each bodily organ) has the whole of the body's soul—the soul is repeated in each organ—without the soul being itself divided into numerically discrete individuals.[62] The divine essence is—in this respect—like the soul of an organic body; repeatable, but not thereby divisible. Scotus claims likewise that the explanation for the divine essence being repeatable but not divisible is the unlimitedness—the *infinity*—of that essence.[63]

Just as in the case of a human being, Scotus's account of the Trinity entails a formal distinction between person and essence.[64] A divine person includes *both* the divine essence *and* the person's non-repeatable constitutive property.[65] Scotus appeals to the formal distinction between each divine person and the divine essence to block potentially damaging anti-Trinitarian arguments. For example, the identity of the Father with God, and of the Son with God, prima facie entails that the Father is identical with the Son. But Scotus believes that both Father and Son are formally distinct from the divine essence. And this allows him to conclude that the Father and Son are not formally identical—they are not in every respect the same.[66] Scotus claims that they have *essential* identity, but not *formal* or *hypostatic* identity—they are not the same person.[67] To try to explicate what he means, Scotus again draws on an example from the created order: two human beings, each of whom is really identical with—and formally distinct from—his or her human nature. Each of Socrates and Plato, for example, is really identical with human nature. But neither is formally identical with human nature, since each includes an individuating feature, a haecceity, which is not included in human nature as such. The relationship between divine persons and the divine essence is analogous to this.[68] But the relationship is not in all respects the same as that found in the created order. Socrates and Plato are really distinct in the sense that Socrates could exist without Plato, and Plato without Socrates. The divine persons are not really distinct in this way; they are not separable. Scotus sometimes talks of the divine persons as really distinct. But the sense of "really distinct" here is not Scotus's standard one of "separable." What Scotus means is that the Father is not a part of the Son; *not being the Father* is a necessary property of the Son. (It is not a necessary property of the divine essence; hence the Father is formally distinct from the divine essence, but really distinct [in the relevant sense] from the Son.)[69] Again, the indivisibility of the divine essence should be sufficient to alert us to the inseparability of the divine persons.

Scotus's formal distinction seems to me easy enough to grasp in the case of created items. We clearly need some way of distinguishing the different necessary properties—repeatable or non-repeatable—of a substance from each other, and the formal distinction seems to me a wholly coherent and metaphysically innocuous way of doing this. Whether or not the doctrine can be applied straightforwardly in the case of the Trinity is a harder question. The problem is not with the formal distinction itself, but with Scotus's claim that the divine essence is both repeatable and indivisible. On this account, each divine person is really identical with the numerically singular divine essence. And it is difficult to see how the divine persons could be really identical with numerically one item without themselves being numerically one.[70] So it is difficult to feel that Scotus's solution of the Trinitarian dilemma is wholly satisfactory, even though it represents a marked improvement over the very agnostic accounts of his predecessors.[71]

4. The unity of God's external action

According to Augustine, the unity of God's nature entails that all of God's external actions belong to all three persons.[72] Scotus agrees with this, and offers a series of arguments to support the inference. The thrust of all the arguments is that God's existence as a Trinity of persons is logically prior to his possession of any other causal power (e.g., the capacity for producing things external to himself). Scotus opposes his account to that of Henry of Ghent. According to Henry, God creates in virtue of the knowledge and love that are respectively the Son and the Spirit.[73] A consequence of Henry's view, according to Scotus, is that none of the three persons can properly be said to create. The Father cannot, since he does not possess the Son and Spirit as causal powers of his own.[74] Neither do the Son and Spirit create. On Henry's view, the Son and Spirit are themselves the causal powers used in creation, and we would not usually claim that the causal powers of an item x are the causes of x's effects. x—not x's causal power—is the cause of x's effects.[75]

Scotus argues instead that the causal powers God uses in creation belong equally to all three persons. In the *Ordinatio*, he suggests three arguments for this, of which I give two. (i) God's knowledge and love of his essence, in virtue of which the Son and Spirit are automatically produced, is prior to his knowledge and love of any other object. So Son and Spirit exist logically prior to God's having the actions—the knowledge and love of contingent objects—necessary for the production of things external to God. So all three persons act as one in any such production.[76] (ii) The instantiation of an essence is logically prior to the instantiation of the causal powers entailed by the essence. So all three divine persons have the divine essence logically prior to their having the causal power for creation. So all three divine persons act as one in creation.[77]

Unlike Augustine, Scotus is happy to allow that the three divine persons have individual properties beyond merely their relations to each other. So there is no reason why his Trinitarian ontology could not in principle allow for disunited external divine activity. In fact, it seems to me that there are good reasons for wanting to allow such activity. We only believe that God is a Trinity because of our prior perception of God's activity in the economy of salvation, and we certainly perceive different roles for the different divine persons. So it seems to me that there are in principle good reasons for wanting to prefer Henry's theology here.

Scotus's Trinitarian theology constitutes a powerful exposition of the Augustinian tradition, perhaps the most consistently rational exposition of this tradition that has ever been attempted. It seems to me that the problems Scotus encounters can be ascribed more to the tradition itself than to his account of it. Anyone interested in taking the Augustinian tradition seriously will need to examine Scotus's careful account of the indivisible repeatability of God's unique essence. Equally, Scotus's defense of the absolute-property theory will appeal to anyone who believes that there could not be such things as subsistent relations, or relations that are somehow properties of their subjects—rather than, say, things that somehow "hang between" two subjects.

HUMANITY: BODY, SOUL,
AND IMMORTALITY

1. Matter, form, and the human soul

The medievals, following Aristotle, analyze substances into two components: matter and form. Like Aristotle, they believe that an analysis of this sort is necessary to explain change. When one substance changes—through some process—into another, something remains constant over the change. This "something" is 'matter'. But matter is arranged in different ways—perhaps very different ways—before and after any change. The arrangement of matter is known as 'form', or more properly 'substantial form', though, as we shall see, not all forms are simply ways in which matter is arranged. Form is supposed to explain why a given substance is the sort of thing it is.[1] The medievals—again following Aristotle—label the forms of living things 'souls'. Thus, the form of Felix the cat could be called Felix's 'soul', for example. A soul is the sort of form in virtue of which a substance is alive.

For various reasons the medievals tend to see forms as discrete individuals. My form, for example, is *numerically distinct* from your form.[2] The individuality of form is presupposed to the medievals' defense of the immortality of the soul, for example. It is also presupposed to the various different medieval defenses of the doctrine of transubstantiation. (I examine two of these in chapter 11.)

One of the crucial points of the matter-form analysis is that it is supposed to explain how a material substance is (despite its various different parts) a *unity*. Some medievals, following Aristotle, believe this unity requirement to entail that no substance could have more than one substantial form. This view is particularly associated with Aquinas.[3] According to Aquinas, a living substance is a composite of matter and (the relevant sort of) soul. Soul is that in virtue of which matter is arranged to be a living body.[4]

Most of the scholastics believe that this straightforward analysis fits poorly with both empirical data and theological orthodoxy. On Aquinas's account, the death of a living being—Felix the cat, for example—involves the complete loss of one form (a cat-like form), and the complete gain of another (a carcass-like form). Given that the identity of a body's form is necessary for the identity of the body, Felix's body cannot be the same body dead as alive.[5] Neither can any of Felix's accidental (non-essential) properties (e.g., his color) remain numerically the same, given the claim (accepted by all the medievals) that accidents cannot naturally "migrate" from body to body. But this account of Felix's death looks immensely implausible. Empirical data certainly suggests that Felix's heart, or his paws, do remain numerically the same over his death. All that has happened to them is that they have stopped functioning in particular ways.[6]

Aquinas's view was believed to lead to theological unorthodoxy too, and indeed at the time Scotus was writing had been condemned as heretical on one occasion. Basically, if the identity of a body does not remain over death, Christ's body in the tomb after his crucifixion is not the same body as that which he had when alive.[7]

After 1277 most of the schoolmen—with the exception of convinced Thomists—believed that living substances have at least two essential forms: a bodily form (giving matter its physical arrangement) and a soul (giving to the substance certain biological and [where relevant] psychological functions).[8] On this view Felix the cat, for example, is composed of *body* (i.e., matter along with bodily form) and *soul*.

There is a formidable objection to this sort of view, clearly anticipated by Aquinas. Analyzing body into matter and form is supposed to allow us to explain the unity of that body. Organized matter, on the face of it, is as good a candidate for unity as anything. But this unity is lost if there is more than one essential form. Scotus provides a very sophisticated alternative account to this. He holds that it is simply not true that the presence of exactly one form is necessary for substantial unity.[9] So Scotus proposes instead a quite different criterion for substantial unity. A material substance is a unity if and only if some of its properties are such that they could not be had by any of its parts alone.[10]

These seemingly obscure and abstract discussions have some huge consequences for different thinkers' understandings of the relationship between the human soul and the human body. To understand these consequences, we need to look a bit more closely at a claim that all the schoolmen believed to be true: that thinking—the most characteristically human activity—is an immaterial process.[11] Scotus marshals an array of arguments in favor of this claim. The basic one is that the *object* of our knowledge is not in every case itself material: "We possess some knowledge of an object under an aspect that it could not have as an object of sense knowledge";[12] so we have some knowledge that is not mere sense knowledge. The idea is that "knowledge of an object under an aspect that it could not have as an object of sense knowledge" is knowledge of an immaterial object. And knowledge of an immaterial object cannot itself be material. What sorts of immaterial object does Scotus have in mind? He lists eight such objects: (i) universals (corresponding to natural kinds); (ii) qualities in general (whiteness, for example); (iii) relations between objects (even when these relations are not the sorts of things that could be directly perceived by the senses); (iv) distinctions between sensible and non-sensible things (stones and angels, for example); (v) relations between concepts; (vi) our own cognitive acts; (vii) first principles (e.g., the principle of non-contradiction); (viii) our own reasoning processes.[13] According to Scotus, we know by introspection that we have knowledge of such objects.[14]

The immateriality of our cognitive processes entails that the agent responsible for these processes must be immaterial as well. The objects of material agents are themselves material.[15] Furthermore, material agents are determined to certain classes of objects. But we know that we are free to choose as we want. So the agent of this choice cannot be material.[16]

On this view, the human soul is an immaterial substance responsible for our cognitive and appetitive activities. Clearly, this soul must have some way of interacting with the body. And it is when discussing this interaction that we see the vast gulf between the unitarian view of Aquinas and the pluralist view of Scotus. Aquinas's unitarian account is able to provide a very straightforward solution to the body-soul interaction problem. The human soul has two distinct functions: it is an immaterial agent that causes a human being's cognitive and appetitive processes; it is the *form* of that human being's body. On this view, soul interacts with body in virtue of *part* of the soul being *part* of the body. The soul moves the body by moving itself; and (presumably) the body affects the soul by affecting itself.[17]

Scotus's pluralist theory cannot provide such a neat account of the causal interactions of body and soul. As far as I can see, Scotus just assumes that the soul has certain causal powers in virtue of which it can move its human body in certain ways.[18] It might be thought that Scotus's account is indistinguishable from some sort of Platonism, according to which the soul has no intrinsic link with the body at all, but is rather something like an immaterial agent moving the body "from outside." On this sort of account, describing the soul as a *form* of a human being is at best vacuous. When discussing *ex professo* the unity of body and soul, Scotus seems simply to assume that the whole human composite is the ultimate subject of the soul's cognitive and appetitive processes.[19] But elsewhere he provides an argument against the sort of Platonism I have just been trying to describe. As we saw above, Scotus holds that a sufficient condition for substantial unity is the presence of one or more properties that could not be properties of any of the parts of the composite. And Scotus believes—following Aristotle—that a human being does have some such properties. Acts of *sensation* require the right sort of body (i.e., matter + bodily form of the relevant type) and soul, capable jointly of processing sense data.[20] Scotus also argues that being alive requires both a body and a soul. He does not believe that the soul alone is the cause of human life; soul and body together are such that, when united, the composite that they form is alive.[21] So a human person must be a substantial unit, and she or he must have body (matter and bodily form) and soul as parts.

Unlike Aquinas, Scotus does not believe that any human acts of knowledge require a body. Although according to Aquinas acts of knowledge are immaterial, the natural process leading to such acts has necessarily material components—for example sense data.[22] Scotus believes, however, that sense data are not necessary for acts of knowledge—or even for human beings to have knowledge of material things. He argues that an object can itself have a causal role in cognition just as easily as a sense datum can. Intellectual cognition requires the intellect and its object; there is no reason for the object to be present to the intellect as a sense datum.[23] This claim is, of course, a further move towards the sort of Platonism that Aquinas was so anxious to reject.

2. The immortality of the soul

Aquinas and Scotus both believe that the human soul is immortal, and thus that it can survive without the human body. Underlying this belief is a prior one: that the soul—unlike the substantial forms of non-human material substances—is created directly by God. Scotus argues that it is possible to show that the human soul is created. Presupposed to his argument is the claim that the soul is immaterial. The immaterial human soul is more noble than any bodily form. But a less noble form cannot be an active principle in the production of a more noble form. So the human soul cannot be produced in virtue of the power of a bodily form.[24] But neither can the human soul be produced by an immaterial form (e.g., another soul). An immaterial substance like the human soul does not include matter. So it has to be produced without anything changing into it. It has, in short, to be produced from nothing. And immaterial substances like the soul cannot produce things from nothing.[25]

As we have seen, Aquinas, unlike Scotus, believes that the human soul, in addition to being the causal subject of our cognitive experience, is also the form of the human body. Aquinas's unitarian view here makes it relatively hard for him to give an account of the immortality of the soul. Prima facie, it is extremely hard to see how something that is essentially the form of a body could survive without that body. Aquinas, however, argues that the soul's immateriality is sufficient for its immortality. To be immaterial is not to include matter. But a substance that does not include matter does not have separable parts in virtue of which it could be destroyed. (Felix, recall, is destroyed if his matter loses its cat-like form.)[26] Aquinas is aware that the immortality of the soul presents difficulties for his view that the soul is the form of the body. He resolves this by claiming not that the soul is essentially the form of the body, but that it is essential to the soul that it have an *inclination* to be the form of the body— it will be the form of the body unless prevented.[27]

Scotus is less sanguine than Aquinas about the possibility of proving the soul's immortality—though, like Aquinas, he is convinced that there is nothing incoherent about the idea of the soul existing apart from the body. In the *Ordinatio*, Scotus claims that there are some probable arguments in favor of the immortality of the soul.[28] The first—which derives from a claim Aristotle makes in *On the Soul*[29]—is that if the immaterial operations of the soul can exist without matter, then the soul itself can too.[30] In the *Ordinatio*, Scotus offers a reply to the argument, reasoning that immateriality does not entail separability from matter.[31] In the *Quodlibetal Questions*, however, Scotus seems happy to accept the argument as it stands, so he evidently is prepared to allow it some force.[32] More interesting, perhaps, are Scotus's attempts to reply to Aquinas's arguments in favor of immortality. Basically, Scotus simply denies that all natural destruction takes place through the separation of parts.[33] So he is not likely to be convinced by Aquinas's claim that lacking separable parts entails being indestructible.

None of this, of course, means that the soul cannot survive the body. Scotus in fact thinks that, in principle, any form could survive the demise of its body.[34] But no form other than the human soul can do so without a miracle. The survival of the soul, however, is not miraculous; hence Scotus's claim that the soul is, as a matter of fact, indestructible or incorruptible.

3. The resurrection of the body

The Christian tradition has never regarded the immortality of the soul as sufficient for a full account of the afterlife. The incarnation and bodily resurrection of Jesus have been taken by the Christian tradition to indicate that the body has a central place in the nature and destiny of humanity. So the Christian tradition, drawing on Jewish antecedents, has always wanted to spell out post-mortem human existence in terms somehow of the resurrection of the body. And Scotus is no exception here.[35]

The resurrection of the body—unlike the post-mortem survival of the soul—is according to Scotus something which has to be brought about directly by God. This is not because Scotus believes that it is in principle impossible for natural agents to bring the same object into existence at two different times. Scotus believes that a natural agent producing effects x and y of kind F at times t_1 and t_2 brings about numerically the same effect only if the *matter* of x and y is the same.[36] But the case of the resurrection of the body is a bit more complicated than this. Human bod-

ies are reconstructed from the same matter that they had when alive—
whatever form that matter is existing under at the time of the resurrection, and in whatever place it is existing. Natural agents can only produce effects in certain ways. And the matter from which resurrected
bodies will be reconstructed will exist as all sorts of substances, and under all sorts of forms. Most of these substances will not be suitable sorts
of things for a natural agent to produce a body from; some, as Scotus
points out, will be dust, and some ashes,[37] and some will be fire, air, or
water.[38] So no natural agent will be able to bring about the resurrection
of the body. Equally, once our bodies have been reconstructed, only God
will be able to reunite our souls to them, since only God can in any case
unite body and soul.[39]

   That our bodies can be resurrected only by a supernatural agent does
not mean that there is anything unnatural about the resurrection. Scotus
believes that there is demonstrably in the universe a passive potentiality
or liability for bodily reconstruction—so the resurrection does not do
violence to the created order.[40] Furthermore, the soul has a natural ten-
dency to be united to the body.[41] Aquinas believes that this natural ten-
dency is sufficient to allow for a proof of the future resurrection of the
body. According to Aquinas, following Aristotle, "nothing unnatural is
eternal"; but given that the soul has a natural inclination for union with
the body, its separation from the body is unnatural.[42] Scotus replies that
the union of the soul to the body is at best an accidental state of affairs,
and hence cannot be an essential perfection of the soul. And there is nothing unnatural about lacking an accidental perfection.[43] So we cannot
prove the resurrection of the body on merely philosophical grounds.

   The idea of resurrection seems in fact to be open to a powerful philosophical objection. We normally suppose that *persistence* is necessary for
identity over time: a substance x retains identity over time—say from
t_1 to t_2—only if x persists from t_1 to t_2. The resurrection of the body seems
to violate this persistence condition. Aquinas offers an ingenious solution to this problem. According to Aquinas, there is a crucial sense in
which the body gains its identity through the soul. It is the body it is because it is united to this soul, not that soul. And the human soul persists
even when its body has perished. So a resurrected body will be the same
as the earlier earthly body simply because of the identity of its soul.[44]

   Scotus rejects Aquinas's account for a mixture of authoritative and
philosophical reasons, and attempts instead to show that the persistence

condition is false. According to Augustine, the omnipotent God could recreate the universe even if everything were to be destroyed.[45] But there are some arguments for wanting to reject the persistence condition too. Suppose God were to destroy a substance. Nothing of that substance would then exist, just as before its creation. But "nothing" does not have any genuine properties, and hence no properties that could prevent the substance from being brought into existence. So there is nothing about it that will prevent the same thing being brought into existence again.[46] Equally, there is no reason to suppose that there is anything about an object between t_1 and t_2 that would have any effect on its identity at t_2.[47] So even if we accepted Aquinas's claim that the identity of a body is caused by its form, Scotus is convinced that we would not need to appeal to the persistence of the body's form in order to explain the possibility of its resurrection.

Scotus insists, however, that for the same body we would need to have the same matter. There is an obvious problem with this: as we live, we continually gain and lose matter, making it difficult to speak of the "same" matter at all. So Scotus spends some time discussing what this sameness requirement really entails. On one view, the resurrected body includes both those parts that it was born with and those parts that it gained early on in life; on another, the resurrected body includes both the parts it was born with and those parts that are most properly "intended by nature" to be parts of this body.[48] On both of these views, Scotus presumably believes that a parcel of matter does not need to have completely fixed parts for its identity.[49]

Scotus in fact believes in any case that it is false that a body's identity is caused by its form. Basically, he holds that a human body is something over and above its parts. So—pace Aquinas—there is no way in which its identity could be caused by any one of its parts.[50] On Scotus's view, then, Aquinas fails to demonstrate the possibility of bodily resurrection.

Scotus's talk of the reconstruction of the human body from the same matter might seem to do insufficient justice to the scriptural claims that the resurrected body is changed, related to the earthly body as a tree to a seed; a spirit-filled body, not a soul-filled body.[51] Doubtless in the front of Scotus's mind is that a necessary condition for numerical identity is being the same sort of body. But he is not wholly insensitive to the need for the resurrected body to have gifts that the earthly body lacks. Thus, according to the schoolmen, the resurrected body has *agility*, *clarity*, *subtlety*, and *impassibility*. The agility of the resurrected body will allow it to move from place to place freely, with no effort and without the use of bodily limbs.[52] This gift is in fact *natural*, not supernatural; God simply increases the strength of the soul's power to move the body, while at the same time decreasing the natural resistance to motion offered by the body's joints and nerves.[53] Clarity is a (supernatural?) gift whereby the body perfectly manifests itself through the most appropriate physical appearance.[54] Subtlety is the gift of existing in the same place as other bodies.[55] This gift, according to Scotus, is not the result of any intrinsic positive quality. Rather, God removes the natural powers that earthly bodies have to expel each other.[56] Equally, impassibility is not an intrinsic gift. Rather, God prevents things external to the resurrected body from harming it. He does this by failing to exercise the divine primary causal cooperation that is required for the production of any natural effect.[57] Scotus gives the example of the three boys in the furnace.[58] God failed to exercise the causal power required—in cooperation with the fire—for the fire to produce its natural effect.

In several ways, Scotus's view of the soul is more "Platonic" than Aquinas's: (i) he claims that the soul is united not to matter directly but to an already formed body; (ii) he rejects the claim that the soul can causally interact with the body by being a part of the body; (iii) he rejects the claim that we need sense data for knowledge of material things; and (iv) he explicitly rejects Aquinas's occasional claim that being the form of a body is an *essential property* of the soul. Despite this, however, Scotus does not believe that we can show the immortality of the soul, because he does not believe that the fourth item in this list of Platonist moves can actually be demonstrated. It is held by faith alone. Equally, he rejects any attempt to prove the resurrection of the body. On the other hand, as I have tried to show, he argues far more effectively than Aquinas that immortality and resurrection are coherent, and therefore possible.

HUMANITY: FREEDOM, ETHICS, AND SIN

In this chapter, I want to look at Scotus's account of human freedom, ethics, and sin (actual and original). Scotus's ethics lays great stress on the range of human actions that could be commanded by God. And his account of freedom is similarly voluntaristic: the will is radically indetermined, free to make its own choices. Scotus's account of freedom allows place for genuine wrong-doing or sin; not all of our bad actions are just mistakes. Scotus's account of original sin, however, is in every respect weaker than the standard Augustinian one accepted by most of his contemporaries. The supernatural gifts of unfallen humanity were minimal, and their loss has only the smallest effect on human existence.

1. Intellect, will, and freedom

Intellect and will

According to Thomas Aquinas, there is a real distinction between the soul and its powers of cognition and appetition—its intellect and will.[1] Scotus disagrees with this position, arguing instead that there is merely a *formal* distinction between the soul and its powers of intellect and will.[2] Scotus reasons that if there is a real distinction between the soul and its powers, it will follow (falsely) that a power, and not the soul, is the cause of any human action.[3] I think that we could plausibly take Scotus to be arguing against any rigorous sort of faculty-psychology here. Scotus holds that the soul, and not any of its powers, is the cause of its mental acts, which I take it means that the soul's powers are not in any strong sense *faculties* causing their own activities.[4] Scotus understands this to mean that the soul has two different ways of acting, and two corresponding causal powers. Thus, our souls have certain powers in virtue of which they can perform certain actions or operations. When assessing Scotus's claim here, we need to keep in mind that Scotus is not always very careful with his terminology. Thus he often talks of the soul's *powers* as causing effects. In fact, Scotus often talks about powers in general in this way. I am assuming, however, that this is a sloppy way of speaking, and that Scotus uses it just for convenience. Thus, when tackling the question directly (e.g., as we have seen, in attacking Aquinas's account of the relation between the soul and its powers), Scotus is far more careful. In what follows, I will often—like Scotus—speak of intellect and will as two different faculties, each causing its own actions. Like Scotus, I do this for semantic convenience merely—it is easier to talk about the intellect doing something than it is to talk of the soul doing something by means of the intellect. At no point does the argument rely on this way of talking.

Freedom

The operations of intellect and will are related in various ways. For example, I cannot consciously will actions unless I have some idea of what I hope to achieve or gain.[5] And I do seem to be able to exert some sort of control over my reasoning processes.[6] Many of the schoolmen hold that the will has a natural desire for the self-fulfillment that is found in *happiness*, such that, if the intellect presents an object as conducive to happiness, the will automatically sets in motion the relevant bodily processes to allow a person to achieve the good presented to the will. Aquinas accepts this sort of account.[7] Of course, the intellect can—for whatever reasons—be mistaken about what conduces to happiness; that is why we sometimes act wrongly.[8]

Presupposed to Aquinas's view is the belief that a correct understanding of the nature of happiness will entail acting morally. If we correctly see that happiness consists in the vision of God, we will (in order to achieve this goal) act morally well.[9] Achieving happiness and acting morally well on this view coincide, and moral decision-making is ultimately a matter of making the correct prudential calculations as to how best to achieve happiness.[10] This does not, of course, mean that we cannot act altruistically. Sometimes it will be necessary for us to act in such a way if we are to reach our goal.

There is much to be said in favor of a view such as Aquinas's. Scotus, however, strongly rejects almost every feature of this account. There seem to me to be two different but related motivations for Scotus's dissent. The first is that Aquinas's view does not do sufficient justice to human freedom. The second is that it does not take account of the nature of a *natural* power. (I will explain what this means in a moment.)

It is important to keep in mind that Aquinas's account does allow for contingency in human action. He believes that, under certain circumstances, the deliberations of the intellect are *contingent*, such that no one could predict in advance how they will turn out.[11] Scotus does not accept that the operation of the intellect could ever be like this. He believes that our cognitive processes are *determined*:

> The intellect falls under the heading of "nature," for it is of itself determined to understanding and it does not have it in its power both to understand and to not understand; or as regards propositional knowledge where contrary acts are possible, it does not have the power both to assent and dissent.[12]

On Scotus's view, then, Aquinas's account of the locus of contingency in human actions is simply false.

Scotus believes that there is good evidence to support the claim that human beings are free in the strongest possible sense. I shall discuss this evidence in a moment. Given that this contingency cannot arise in the functioning of the intellect, Scotus reasons that it must instead arise in the functioning of the *will*. Following a suggestion made by Aristotle,[13] Scotus posits a basic contrast between *free* powers and *natural* powers. Free powers (i.e., the will) have three features not shared with natural powers. The first of these features is being *indetermined*, being a power for opposites: "with no change in its nature, either [of two contraries or contradictories] falls equally under its power."[14] The will's indeterminism entails its remaining two features: that a free power is a self-mover, a sufficient cause of its own actions; and that a free power can refrain from acting even when all the conditions necessary for its acting obtain.[15]

We might think that the sort of indeterminism Scotus defends amounts to no more than randomness. But Scotus takes it to be empirically evident that we are free in his sense. We know this somehow introspectively; we know somehow that when we did action *a*, we could have done not-*a*, or refrained from acting altogether.[16] Scotus offers some other arguments as well. The will must be free, because if it were a merely natural power, it would act whenever there are no natural barriers to its activity.[17] Equally, all parties in the debate accept that the will can control itself via the intellect. So it should be able to control itself directly too.[18]

Given this, Scotus argues that the distinction between free and determined is both exhaustive and basic: "One can give no other reason why [a power] elicits its action in this way except that it is this sort of cause."[19] When trying to describe the sort of causation involved in being a free self-mover, Scotus is a bit more explicit. He argues that there is an indeterminacy of "superabundant sufficiency," and that something indeterminate in this sense "can determine itself."[20] Given that the will is free, this description is fair enough. But the arguments given above in favor of our being free in Scotus's sense are unsound. The first is viciously circular: we can only know that, when we did *a*, we could have done not-*a*, or refrained from acting altogether, if we know that we are free. The second relies on a particular and questionable understanding of what it is to be a natural power. The third does not look obviously true. I can do some things via a tool that I cannot do without it.

There is another objection to Scotus's account of free agency. We often think of *reasons* as explaining actions. If we think that reasons for actions are always overwhelming, Scotus's sort of account cannot allow for explanatory reasons lying behind actions. There is a further component of Scotus's theory, however, which allows him to overcome this objection. Scotus's account of the superabundant sufficiency of the human will ties in with a theory of what we might call the "moral psychology" of choice-making.

As we saw above, Aquinas, following Aristotle, gives an account of human actions as directed to our natural self-fulfillment in happiness. On the Aristotelian account defended by Aquinas, all events are goal-directed, tending towards the self-fulfillment of their agents. And all substances have a natural inclination to their self-fulfillment.

Scotus agrees with this sort of teleological account as a general account of the created order. But he does not believe that free agents are like this.

He holds that, in addition to its natural inclination to self-fulfillment, a free power (i.e., the will) has a further inclination: an inclination to justice. Scotus, following Anselm, calls these two inclinations, respectively, the *affectio commodi* (affection for the beneficial or advantageous) and the *affectio iustitiae* (the affection for justice).[21] The precise nature of the affection for justice is the subject of some debate. Perhaps the most plausible is the view that the affection for justice inclines the will to act in accordance with the moral law irrespective of its connection with our own happiness.[22] The idea is that these inclinations explain the fact that the will has two different modes of operation: one in which it seeks self-fulfillment in happiness, and one in which it seeks justice.

Scotus argues that the presence of both these inclinations is necessary for freedom. Suppose our will had just the affection for the beneficial. Our intellect could present to our will a number of different options—happiness, or justice, for example. But our will would only be able to will happiness. The reason is that the will would be like every other natural power: necessitated to its own self-fulfilment.[23] We know, however, that the will is not like this. As we have already seen, Scotus believes that we know by introspection that we are free. And he has another argument against the will's being a purely natural power. All accept that the will can exercise some sort of control over the intellect. But if the will automatically willed its own self-fulfillment in happiness, then it would automatically constrain the intellect to consider happiness all the time. And we know that it does not do this. So it cannot be the case that the will automatically wills happiness.[24]

As I have pointed out, Scotus is clear that human will does in fact have an inclination to its own self-fulfillment, the *affectio commodi*. We know that it has this since in an Aristotelian teleological universe everything has such an inclination:[25] "a nature could not remain a nature without seeking its own perfection."[26] But given that we are free, and that the will is not a purely natural power, it follows that the will must have some way of modifying its basic natural inclination. So it must have another way of acting as well. And this way of acting derives from the will's inclination to justice. Scotus sometimes calls this inclination the will's 'natural freedom':[27] it is that in virtue of which the will can determine itself to a different course of action from a slavish seeking after the natural goals of human existence.[28]

There is, I believe, a clear reason why Scotus associates freedom with the affection for justice. Natural powers are determined to their own self-fulfillment. And this determination entails that natural powers are auto-matically active (unless prevented), and that they are "maximal" seekers of their goals—they seek their goals with the full force available to them. This is just the nature of a natural power. Happiness is necessarily willed by the human will with the full force of the will's natural inclination.[29] So the inclination for justice is required—in some cases—in order for us to act well. Scotus makes the point with a vivid discussion of a case in which the inclination for justice failed to moderate the will's natural in-clination for happiness: the case of the fall of Satan. Satan desired happi-ness—the vision of God—immoderately, not in the way willed by God:

> There are three ways, however, in which a will, able to moderate itself as regards the happiness befitting it, could fail to do so. As to intensity, it might love it more passionately than it deserves. Or through pre-cipitance, it might want it sooner than is becoming. Or with disregard for the proper causal way to obtain it.[30]

So the presence of the inclination for justice is necessary, in at least some circumstances, to account for our being able to act well; and it is in these sorts of circumstances that we are genuinely free.[31]

The discussion of the fall of Satan makes it clear that Scotus's two inclinations allow him to give a radically un-Aristotelian solution to the problem of wrong-doing. Of course, the two-inclinations theory is not necessary to account for all wrong-doing. Ignorance can certainly account for many cases of wrong-doing, as on the traditional Aristotelian picture.[32] But, as St. Paul noticed, we can sin even when fully apprised of what we should do.[33] According to Scotus this happens when the inclination to jus-tice fails to temper the will's natural inclination to its own self-fulfillment. In such a case, self-fulfillment is of course rationally chosen (happiness is a natural goal of human existence, and can never be irrationally chosen), even though (in the way it is willed) morally wrong. And Scotus is quite clear that this sort of morally bad action can rationally be chosen even by a subject in full possession of all the information necessary to make a good choice.[34]

How could we will justice over and above happiness if it is the case that justice will perhaps fail to make us happy? Scotus argues that it is not possible for us to will to be miserable. But, he claims, we can fail to will happiness.[35] This is what is happening, presumably, when the incli-nation to justice tempers our natural desire for happiness. We will an action *a* because it issues in justice; and we refrain from willing an action not-*a* that will issue in immediate self-fulfillment.

As just hinted, the will's two inclinations can allow reason to explain our actions without its determining them. Our intellect can present different courses of action to the will—perhaps one leading to happiness and one leading to justice—and the will is then free to choose between them. There is of course a "reason" for each course of action; the essence of freedom lies in the will's self-determination to one or other of the proposed courses of action. In fact, Scotus is convinced that the reasons for actions play a vitally important causal role in the process of acting. He argues that a reason for an act of willing (act*a*) is a partial cause of *a*, where the other cause that with the reason is sufficient for *a* is the will itself.[36] Scotus argues that if the reason alone were sufficient, then the will would be purely passive;[37] and that if the will alone were sufficient, the will could will without any reason at all[38]—both of which are false.[39] But the self-determining component in the decision to perform *a* in Scotus's account derives solely from the will.

Scotus's account of the will is thus voluntaristic: the will is a radically free, self-determining cause. And Scotus's account of the will's two inclinations seems to accord well with experience. We do often knowingly act wrongly, and there is no reason to suppose that the best explanation for this is just emotional pressure. Scotus's claim that we can explain this wrong-doing in terms of an inordinate rational desire for our own immediate self-fulfillment seems immensely plausible.

2. Ethics

It is sometimes thought that Scotus's voluntarism extends to his ethics too, and that he accepts some sort of divine command theory. I shall argue that, although Scotus's theory shares important characteristics with divine command theories, it should not properly be seen as such a theory. Scotus's theory is not open to an objection that is fatal for divine command theories, and thus might prove appealing to those who share the sorts of motivations that lead to acceptance of a divine command ethic.

There seem to me to be two basic sorts of divine command ethics. On a strong divine command theory, God's command is both necessary and sufficient for an action to have moral value. On a weak divine command theory, God's command is necessary but not sufficient for an action to have moral value.[40] The motivation for accepting such a theory in either version is the preservation of divine *sovereignty*: there is nothing other than God for which God's existence is not a necessary condition. (We looked at Scotus's acceptance of this view in chapter 4.) Thus, moral values derive from God; they do not restrain him. Both versions of the divine command theory are, however, open to a fatal objection. What is the origin of the obligation to obey God? It cannot be a divine command, since the theory is then circular; it cannot, however, be anything other than a divine command, since on the theory no obligations derive from anything other than a divine command. The divine command theory also makes it difficult to give anything other than the thinnest account of God's goodness.

The most obvious alternative ethic is one according to which our moral actions are governed by natural law discerned by right reason.[41] On such a theory, we can deduce certain universally binding laws from the nature of created things. Both divine command theorists and natural law theorists accept that a divine command is *sufficient* for the moral value of certain actions—perhaps those that would, other than the divine command, be morally neutral. Scotus gives two useful examples of such parts of positive law: the obligation imposed on us by God to confess our sins to a priest,[42] and the obligation imposed on Adam and Eve not to eat the fruit of the tree of knowledge.[43]

Traditionally, Scotus has been thought to accept some sort of divine command theory. For example, Anthony Quinton characterizes Scotus's position as follows: "Things are good because God commands them and not vice versa, so moral truth is not accessible to natural reason."[44] In fact, it is easy to show that Scotus does not accept a divine command theory. On either version of the divine command theory, a divine command is *necessary* for an action to have moral value. Scotus is quite clear, however, that it is not the case that a divine command is necessary for an action to have moral value. Scotus talks of an action being morally good if it has all the features that are *conveniens* (appropriate) to it:[45] thus, it must be an appropriate sort of action for the agent and its object, in the relevant circumstances.[46] Furthermore, this *convenientia* is discernible by reason.[47] If an action is performed in accordance with a discernment of its *convenientia*, Scotus says that it is performed in accordance with *recta ratio* (right reason).[48]

Equally, we do not need to add any further component to these considerations for us to be able to tell that we are obliged to perform such and such an action:

> The first goodness seems to come from the circumstance of the end, for given the nature of the agent of the action, and of the object, one immediately concludes that such an action ought to be performed by this agent for such an end, and that it ought to be chosen and wanted for the sake of such an end.[49]

So Scotus does not believe that a divine command is necessary for obligation. I think we can conclude that, in the senses outlined at the beginning of this section, Scotus does not accept any sort of divine command ethic.[50]

As I have pointed out, Scotus clearly accepts that a divine command is sufficient for the moral goodness of some sorts of actions—confessing one's sins, or not eating certain sorts of fruit. What sorts of restriction does Scotus place on the domain of possible divine commands? As we might expect, there are some things that God cannot command. For example, he cannot command anyone to hate him. The reason is that according to Scotus it is necessarily true that "If God exists, he alone should be loved as God."[51] Elsewhere, Scotus argues similarly that "something must be loved most of all, and this is none other than the highest good."[52] Other principles that follow deductively from this one are also necessarily true: for example, "no irreverence should be shown to God."[53] These laws are true "antecedent to any decision of [God's] will."[54] And Scotus argues that these moral principles—since they are necessarily true—belong properly to natural law.[55] So these laws provide further evidence that Scotus does not accept any thorough-going divine command ethic. These laws are binding on God, since God is intrinsically just, and thus bound by duties expressed in necessarily true propositions.[56] Let us label this sort of justice 'justice$_1$'. Justice$_1$ binds God by inclining him *deterministically* ("in a quasi-natural manner") to render his own goodness what is due to it.[57]

So there are some clear restrictions on what God can command. All of the restrictions we have looked at so far have to do with the duties that all—including God—owe to the divine nature. Scotus holds, however, that there are no *other* constraints on what God can command. So no moral principles concerning actions whose objects are creatures are necessarily true. This does not mean that there are not many such moral principles that are contingently true, true unless God decides to command otherwise. Thus, as I have tried to show, a divine command is not necessary for the truth of these moral principles. They hold automatically unless God commands otherwise.

These principles are not strictly speaking part of natural law. The only precepts of natural law are those corresponding to necessarily true propositions. But Scotus believes that there is an extended sense of 'natural law' that includes those moral principles that are true but for a divine command:

> Something may be said in an extended sense to belong to the law of nature if it is a practical truth that is in harmony (*consonum*) with the principles and conclusions of the law of nature, in so far as it is immediately recognized by all to be in accordance (*convenire*) with such a law.[58]

God can, of course, command us to perform such actions—actions that would be morally good even without divine command. He did so command us, according to Scotus, when promulgating the second table of the decalogue.[59] And if he does this, he exhibits a certain sort of justice; he is "just to a creature."[60] Let us label this justice 'justice$_2$'. God exhibits justice$_2$ if he "makes one created thing correspond to another . . . because this created nature demands something suited to it."[61] Justice$_2$ is not strictly part of divine justice.[62] Nevertheless, Scotus claims that God's justice$_1$ somehow inclines him non-deterministically to exhibit justice$_2$:

> It could be said that this single justice, which determinately inclines the divine will only to its first act [viz., loving God], modifies each of these secondary acts, though not in a necessary manner, as though it could not also modify the opposite of each.[63]

And in this case, justice$_1$ is somehow inclining God to respect the intrinsic values of things.[64] So, according to Scotus, justice$_2$ is consonant with justice$_1$, and appropriate to the way creatures are.[65]

When talking about cases in which God could dispense us from the observance of the second table of the decalogue, Scotus often tries to relate God's actions to the preservation of justice (i.e., here justice$_2$). For example, when discussing God's allowing the Patriarchs after the Flood to marry bigamously, Scotus is careful to show that the divine dispensation here preserves justice by prioritizing the primary end of marriage—

procreation—over a secondary end—the sharing of male and female bodies on a one-to-one basis.[66] Here, Scotus unequivocally tries to show how God, in his dealings with humanity, respects the intrinsic values of things.

Scotus uses the Latin terms *iustum* (just) and *rectum* (right) to describe God's actions as they exhibit justice$_2$.[67] But he also uses *iustum* and *rectum* in a rather different sense. As we have seen, God does not have to exhibit justice$_2$, because for any act exhibiting justice$_2$, God could will the opposite of that act:

> Without contradiction the will could will the opposite, and thus it could justly will such; otherwise it could will something by its absolute power and not do so justly, which seems incongruous.[68]

Equally, God could put in place any set of contingent laws he wished; and since God has the power to set up moral laws, those laws will be just (*recta*).[69] It is by examining this sense of *iustum* and *rectum* that we shall see why Scotus believes that there are no restrictions—other than those outlined above—on what God can command his creatures to do.

Why should Scotus suppose this: that for any creature-directed action God commands, he can equally command the opposite?—or, equivalently, that no moral principles concerning actions whose objects are creatures are part of natural law? Scotus's reason is that God has no obligations to us; and he believes that if moral principles concerning actions whose objects were creatures were necessarily true (and therefore part of natural law), then God would have certain obligations to us that he would be bound to respect. Scotus has two arguments to show that God has no obligations to us.

The first argument in favor of this claim is that there is no commutative justice between God and creatures. Commutative justice is that justice that governs the exchange of goods, giving equal for equal.[70] If there were something that God *owed* to his creatures, there would be commutative justice between God and creatures. But according to Scotus, commutative justice requires equality between the two parties. God and his creatures are not equal, and thus there is no commutative justice between God and his creatures. So God does not owe his creatures anything, and has no obligations to them.[71]

The second argument is based on God's contingent willing of things other than himself. Scotus holds that God's will "tends to nothing other than himself except contingently."[72] What Scotus means is that God has libertarian freedom with respect to every action he does to his creatures. Now, if God has any obligations to his creatures, then there are some divine actions directed to creatures that fail to be brought about by God's libertarian freewill. So God has no obligations to his creatures.[73] I shall refer to this as the 'contingency argument'. (We have seen some other of Scotus's motivations for wanting to accept this argument in chapter 4.)

Of course, neither of these arguments is sufficient to show that there are no constraints at all on what God could command. The first could be accepted by someone who held an account defended recently by Thomas Morris, according to which, even though there are no duties that obligate God, God necessarily acts in accordance with "principles which would express duties for a moral agent in his relevant circumstances."[74] I have suggested that Scotus's God does sometimes so act;[75] but Scotus is unequivocal in denying that God *necessarily* so acts.

Allan Wolter has suggested a way of reading the second argument that places certain blocks on what God can command. According to Wolter, God can dispense from the commands in the second table of the decalogue "according to the dictates of right reason."[76] Little that Scotus says supports this sort of reading. In fact, the only prima facie plausible support is a text cited by Allan Wolter, which claims, "Whatever God has made, you know that he has made it with right reason."[77] For a creature to act with right reason, as we have seen, is for him or her to respect the intrinsic values of things. But, as we have seen, Scotus uses the words 'just' and 'right' in several different senses. In fact, Scotus's discussion of some concrete examples militates strongly against Wolter's reading. For example, the prohibition on lying belongs to the second table of the decalogue, and God can dispense us from this.[78] But lying can never accord with the intrinsic values of things:

> To lie by its very nature implies an intention which is bad, because it is an intention to deceive, and although some acts which do not include a bad intention could be good by reason of some good circumstance, nevertheless an act that includes a bad intention could never be good, because it formally includes a bad will; and so it is in the present case.[79]

Scotus argues similarly in the case of adultery. Adultery according to Scotus "cannot possibly be good" (i.e., presumably, cannot possibly be in accordance with the intrinsic values of things).[80] But God can of course

revoke the prohibition on adultery. Equally, when discussing God's command to Abraham to sacrifice Isaac, Scotus claims that God can make
human sacrifice licit or illicit at will, without any other change in circum-
stance.[81] On this account, there are no restrictions on what God could
command his creatures to do to each other. So we should interpret God's
'right reason' to be simply whatever God decides to do.[82]

How we assess Scotus's position will probably depend on how sympathetic we feel to the sorts of motivations lying behind the acceptance
of a divine command ethic. If we are sympathetic to these motivations,
we may well believe that Scotus's position is preferable to a divine command ethic. Scotus's position is not vulnerable to the fatal objection to
any divine command ethic that I outlined at the beginning of this section
(i.e., that the obligation to obey God must be somehow independent of
any divine command). Scotus's contingency argument, however, does not
entail anything more than Wolter's attempted reformulation of Scotus's
position. And someone who was unsympathetic to the motivations underlying an acceptance of a divine command ethic would, if he or she accepted
the contingency argument, probably want to accept not Scotus's position
but the one Wolter attributes to him.

3. Sin

Scotus's account of sin is wholly legal or forensic. Human sinfulness, according to Scotus, is not some kind of real quality inhering in the sinner.
Actual sin does not cause any lasting state in the sinner. Sin is just a lack
of rectitude in an *act*, not in a *person*.[83] Against Bonaventure, Scotus reasons that sin cannot affect the rectitude of a person's soul. The soul is
created by God; nothing created, therefore, can destroy its essential rectitude. Furthermore, the soul is a free cause of its sinful actions. But free
(and therefore contingent) effects do not alter their cause in any way.[84]
Against Aquinas, Scotus reasons that sin cannot consist in the lack of a
supernatural habit. Such a habit is created by God, and is a (part of) a
free cause of an act. So, for reasons analogous to those employed against
Bonaventure's view, sin cannot affect a supernatural habit.[85]

Furthermore, the guilt attaching to sin, according to Scotus, consists
merely in God's decision to punish a person for his or her sinful acts.[86]
Scotus argues on the basis of a passage in Augustine that, after a sinful

act is completed, the liability for punishment incurred cannot be any real property of the sinner. Commenting on Psalm 32.1, "Blessed is he whose unrighteousness is forgiven and whose sin is covered," Augustine claims that God's "turning his face from sin is the same as not holding a person to punishment."[87] Scotus understands this to mean that God can will not to punish someone without any concomitant change in the sinner. So "to remain in guilt [*reatus*] after a [sinful] act is just for [the sinner] to be ordered by God's will to a punishment equal to the sin."[88] Sinfulness is no more than liability for punishment; and this liability consists wholly in God's deciding to treat us in accordance with the moral difformity of our actions. Persons can certainly have morally bad qualities or habits; but *sinfulness* cannot be one of these.

4. Original sin

Thus far I have given an account of Scotus's ethics, including his discussion of wrong-doing and sin. But there is more to be said about human sinfulness than we find merely in the account of actual sin. It is traditionally thought by Christian theologians that our ability to act well is radically reduced—or even obliterated—by *original sin*: sinfulness that all humans seem to have innately.

The doctrine of original sin is most strongly associated, in the Western Church, with Augustine. According to Augustine, Adam in the garden of Eden lacked any sort of physical defect, and was blessed with perfect holiness and the ability not to sin. Adam's sin was infinitely bad, and its result was twofold: that human beings "suffer from a hereditary moral disease," and that they are "born subject to the inherited legal liability to judicial punishment for Adam's sin."[89] The first of these—the moral disease—consists in the concupiscence that dominates human activity. This concupiscence is original sin. It is passed from parent to child via the natural processes of procreation that it necessarily taints. The second feature is usually labeled 'original guilt'. According to Augustine, it is inherited by all from Adam on the grounds that all human beings were in some sense 'in' Adam when he committed to sin, and hence that all human beings were as guilty as Adam for the first sin.[90]

In the middle ages, Henry of Ghent defends the extreme Augustinian line. He holds that the prelapsarian state of original justice is *natural*, and that its loss is transmitted as a *physical* defect. Henry characterizes original justice as the 'natural rectitude' of the will, something like a natural quality belonging to the will. Henry, expanding on an Augustinian image, likens the will to a line. The will naturally has natural rectitude in the same way as a line is naturally straight; the will can, however, just like a line, curve in on itself and lose its natural rectitude.[91] By calling this quality 'natural', Henry makes it clear that it is the sort of quality that the will has unless prevented. Henry also believes that the effect of this natural justice is to allow the will to dominate the lower sense appetites.[92]

Scotus disagrees with both parts of this account of original justice. He reasons that if it were natural to us to have original justice, we should be able to know this by natural reason. And, as he points out, "The most excellent philosophers could not establish this."[93] Secondly, it cannot be the case that the effect of original justice is the domination of otherwise rebellious sense appetites. The will, Scotus argues, is greater in power than any natural quality; so if a natural quality (e.g., original justice) can dominate the sense appetites, a fortiori the will should be able to.[94] Neither argument here seems entirely successful. The first relies on a principle that Scotus elsewhere rejects.[95] The second seems simply mistaken: in principle, the will and a quality might be able jointly to bring about an effect that neither could bring about alone.

Scotus replaces Henry's Augustinian theory of original justice with a much less ambitious account. According to Scotus, original justice is a *supernatural* gift, a form or quality inhering in the will. Consistently with this, Scotus is clear that the Fall simply reduces us to our natural state.[96] Equally, the effect of original justice is not, as Henry supposes, to give the will the power to dominate the various sense appetites. Rather, original justice brings it about that the sense appetites do not need to be dominated; original justice brings it about that the sense appetites are not at war with the will and each other. They exist "in tranquillity."[97] To achieve this, Scotus reasons, original justice must entail that supernatural gifts are given to the sense appetites too, to allow them to perform in the way required.[98]

So according to Scotus the primary result of original justice is not an increase in will power, but mental tranquillity. Original justice has other effects too. One is immortality. Again, Scotus defends a much weaker account than the strong Augustinianism of some of the schoolmen. Aquinas, for example, argues that original justice preserves the body from all corruption.[99] Scotus rejects this. As he limpidly puts it:

> I do not see that that quality [viz., original justice] could bring it about
> that such a body could not be subjected to a contrary, and be subjected
> to such an extent that it died.[100]

Scotus argues instead that original justice does not preclude the natural
corruptibility of the body.[101] Neither is the body physically protected
against violence or deprivation (although in the state of innocence there
is no danger of such misfortunes actually occurring).[102] Nevertheless, in
the state of innocence, bodies (which naturally age and tend towards corruption) do not die. God intervenes in time, and carries them to paradise
and the beatific vision[103]—where presumably they gain the glorious gifts
belonging in the present order to resurrected bodies.[104]

Original justice also joins us naturally to God. An automatic consequence of the supernatural gift is that we tend to love God.[105] Scotus distinguishes original justice from 'sanctifying grace', that grace in virtue
of which we can perform meritorious actions:

> If there were [in prelapsarian humanity] a supernatural gift, it never-
> theless is not necessary that it is a principle of meriting; for it is related
> to grace (which is the principle) as both exceeding and exceeded.[106]

Furthermore, Scotus is clear that, in the prelapsarian state, it would have
been possible to have original justice but not sanctifying grace—though
not vice versa; the possession of sanctifying grace required the possession
of original justice.[107]

Scotus's dissociation of original justice and sanctifying grace raises two
questions, one factual, one counterfactual. The factual question is: Did
Adam, in the garden of Eden, possess sanctifying grace as well as original justice? According to Peter Lombard, he did not, and Scotus agrees
with him:

> Natural rectitude or original justice is separable from sanctifying
> grace, if the opposite (viz., original sin) does not pre-exist in [the
> person]. This is clear in the case of Adam, who, according to the Master
> [Peter Lombard], "although he had [that] whence he could remain,
> did not have [that] whence he could advance," because he did not then
> have sanctifying grace.[108]

Compared with the more Augustinian views of some of his contemporaries, Scotus's account considerably lessens Adam's prelapsarian state.
Aquinas, for example, holds that Adam was fully endowed with super-

natural gifts, including sanctifying grace.[109] Scotus's Adam was spiritually undeveloped, unable to perform meritorious actions.

The counterfactual question is more complicated: Would Adam have gained sanctifying grace if he had not fallen? Scotus never explicitly states that he would have. On the other hand, he often assumes that unfallen humanity would have been capable of meritorious actions.[110] Since sanctifying grace is required for meritorious actions, I think we should infer that Adam would have gained such grace if he had not sinned.

As I just mentioned, Scotus holds that Adam's sin lost him the gift of original justice.[111] Thus, he lost the tranquillity that reigned in his lower appetites. The idea is that God gave Adam a gift that Adam was commanded (by divine positive law) not to lose. Since Adam failed in one of his obligations, he earned punishment.[112] According to Catholic teaching, Adam's sin is somehow transmitted to his descendants. This transmitted sin is known as 'original sin'. Scotus's account of original sin is very different from the Augustinian one that I sketched briefly at the beginning of this section. According to the Augustinian account, the essence of original sin is *concupiscence*, the inordinate desire that seems necessarily to infect human bodies. Scotus believes there to be some insuperable difficulties with such a concupiscence theory. First, concupiscence belongs to the sense appetite, and therefore cannot count as sin; secondly, the inordinate desires of the sense appetite are natural—they are merely what is prevented by the presence of original justice.[113]

Of course, it is easy for a concupiscence theory to explain the transmission of original sin to Adam's descendants. Concupiscence is like a bodily infection, and, like some bodily infections, can be passed from parent to child.[114] Scotus's theory has no such straightforward account. On his theory, original sin is just a *privation*—the lack of original justice—and certainly not a positive quality, whether spiritual or bodily.[115] Scotus's theory of original sin derives fairly closely from that of Anselm. According to Anselm, God has decided that original justice is a gift that we all in some sense *should* have; thus Adam accepted the gift of original justice on behalf of the whole of humanity, such that, if he were to lose it, the whole of humanity would lose it with him.[116]

As it stands, this does not seem very satisfactory. How could Adam's accepting a gift on behalf of the whole of humanity entail that his loss of the gift is sufficient for our losing it too?[117] In the early *Lectura*, Scotus merely repeats Anselm's account. But in the *Ordinatio* he provides an ingenious attempt to make it more rigorous. This attempt develops the central feature of Anselm's account, that God has decreed that original justice is a gift that we in some sense *should* have. God's will for humanity with regard to original justice is expressed in two ordered divine decisions: that we should have original justice and that God will give it to us unless Adam places a barrier to this gift by sinning.[118] The second divine decision means that Adam's sin is sufficient for our not having original justice. These two divine decisions are, of course, contingent. But the first is prior to the second. This means that, even if Adam's sin prevents us from having original justice, this justice is still a quality that we are required (i.e., obliged) to have. By failing to have the gift, we are failing in one of our obligations to God.[119] It is this failure that Scotus identifies as original sin.

Scotus's position is evidently preferable to the Augustinian one. And he provides a necessary clarification to Anselm's theory. We might not find his claim that we can be obliged in a way that we cannot possibly satisfy very fair or just. But on Scotus's ethical theory God can impose obligations on us at will, and the divine imposition of such obligations is sufficient for their justice. So even though Scotus's Anselmian theory of original sin does not entail his ethical theory, there is a clear link between these two aspects of his thought.

There are links too between Scotus's account of human freedom and his doctrine of original sin. It is evident that his account of human freedom is supposed to be a description of postlapsarian human capacities. After all, Scotus's basic argument for his strongly libertarian account of freedom is empirical and introspective. So it will not surprise us that Scotus tries to minimize the effects of the Fall.

HUMANITY: PREDESTINATION,
MERIT, AND GRACE

1. Predestination

The Christian tradition has consistently held that God predestines some people to salvation: the enjoyment of everlasting life and the vision of God. Why does God predestine some people in this way? One answer is that God foresees the good works these people perform, and decides on this basis to save them. This answer allows God to differentiate justly between people, and does clear justice to the possibility of God's depriving some people of salvation.[1] Scotus believes, however, that this answer is demonstrably false. As we saw in chapter 4, God knows future contingents merely on the basis of the free determinations of his will. So his knowledge of our free actions derives solely from the fact that he has decided that we will act in certain ways. So our actions have no casual role in the genesis of God's knowledge of how we will act. Thus his decision about our salvation cannot in any sense be caused by our actions.[2]

Scotus therefore argues instead that God's decision to predestine some people to salvation is made prior to his knowledge of our actions.[3] Of course, Scotus's objection to the first view does not entail such a strong conclusion. On the objection, God could will our actions and then, on the basis of this, will our salvation. But Scotus proposes an argument for his stronger conclusion. God always wills in the most orderly manner. Someone who wills in this way chooses the goal before he chooses the means to the goal. So God first chooses salvation for a person, and then wills the means—grace, faith, merits, and good actions.[4] It is because a person is saved that he or she acts in such and such a (morally good) way. Thus, God necessarily wills salvation prior to foreseen merits.[5]

This does not entail, however, that God wills damnation for a person in a way analogous to his willing salvation. Scotus argues rather that God wills damnation for a person on the basis of that person's actions. It is because a person acts in such and such a (morally bad) way that he or she is damned. Damnation, according to Augustine, is only good if it is *just*;[6] and it can only be just if it is willed on the basis of someone's works.[7]

The point of this discussion is to avoid the sort of 'double predestination' view later defended by Calvin.[8] On this view, God wills both salvation and damnation prior to his knowledge of our actions. This seems to make God arbitrary and cruel. But Scotus's claim that God does not predestine the damned to damnation is open to at least two objections. If God's knowledge of the actions of, say, Judas (who along with Lucifer is a standard theological example of someone damned) is necessary for his decision to damn Judas—as Scotus's position seems to imply—does this not make Judas's actions a necessary condition for a divine decision, and thus violate the claim (discussed in chapter 4) that nothing external to God is necessary for anything internal to him? The solution is in fact straightforward. God's knowledge of Judas's actions is derived entirely from the determinations of his divine will. But this solution immediately raises a second problem for Scotus's theory. If God's knowledge of Judas's actions is caused by the determinations of the divine will, does this not entail that the actions on the basis of which Judas is damned are willed by God? And it is a short step from this to the claim that God predestines Judas to damnation.[9] Scotus believes that it is true that God wills the actions on the basis of which Judas is damned. But he does not accept the short step from this to the claim that God predestines Judas to damnation. To understand the argument, we need to recall that, for Scotus, God's predestination to salvation is necessarily (logically) prior to his knowledge of a person's actions. Thus, when willing salvation for someone, God first of all predestines that person to salvation, and then wills that person's actions necessary for the achievement of salvation. In the case of Judas, however, God's first move is to *refrain* from willing salvation; he next wills that Judas performs the actions of the basis of which God will—in the next logical moment—decide to damn him.[10] On this account, God does not predestine Judas to damnation.

I leave it to the reader to decide whether or not Scotus's careful account will allow him to avoid Calvinism here; though it seems to me that Scotus is clearly right to see that some work needs to be done to defend the Augustinian account against Calvinism. Scotus's account of predestination prior to foreseen merits does not mean that merit has no place in his system. In fact, as we have seen, Scotus holds that meritorious action is part of the *means* to the achievement of salvation. Nevertheless, as we shall see, Scotus does not hold that it is logically necessary for a person's salvation that he or she act meritoriously. In the next section, I will try to give an account of Scotus's views on merit, pinpointing exactly how they dovetail with his account of predestination.

2. Merit

Irrespective of their different views on predestination, the medievals all accept that human beings are capable of acting meritoriously, acting in such a way that God gives a *reward* for the action. For Scotus, this idea of God giving a reward is central to the idea of merit:

> The meritorious work is one acceptable to God in a special way, viz., as worthy of a reward. I say "in a special way" because God accepts all acts with a general acceptation. He loves them according to their goodness and orders them to himself as their last end. A meritorious act, however, he accepts with reference to some good which ought to be justly awarded it. "Meritorious," then, implies two additional relations in the act, one to the accepting will, the other to the award that the will has assigned to the act.[11]

God "accepts" our acts ("loves them according to their goodness and orders them to himself as their last end"), and any meritorious act he accepts additionally "with reference to some good which ought to be justly awarded it." As we shall see, Scotus supposes that if we have grace we can merit both the gift of eternal life and an increase in grace, and that although there is no sense in which we can merit the first gift of grace,[12] there is a sense in which we can merit the restoration of this grace after a fall, via the sacrament of penance. I will return to these various issues below.

s believes that any reward God gives to us is given freely. God is
ged to reward us; neither does he do so necessarily. Can the no-
merit survive this voluntaristic twist? It might, for example, be
ht that the notion of merit entails that God will necessarily reward
us. But I do not think that any of the medievals would agree with this.
Central to the major thirteenth-century accounts of the issue is the claim
that the meritoriousness of our actions is the result of a *divine decision* to
reward our actions.[13] Given this basic claim, the schoolmen distinguish
between two sorts of merit: *meritum de condigno* (condign merit) and
meritum de congruo (congruous merit). There are several ways of spelling out this distinction. That proposed by Bonaventure is typical. There
are two elements in Bonaventure's distinction. First, acts that merit condignly do so in virtue of some sort of justice—not equality, but a certain
'proportionality'—between the act and the reward. Acts that merit congruously exhibit no such justice. Secondly, given the divine decision to
reward certain actions, God has placed himself under an obligation to
reward condignly meritorious actions. But he has placed himself under
no such obligation to reward congruously meritorious actions.[14] Of these
distinctions, the first is, I think, supposed to be explanatory of the second. God decides to place himself under an obligation to reward certain
acts because these acts are in terms of justice proportional to the reward
they earn. This proportion is in turn explained by another feature of condignly meritorious acts. Such acts can only be performed by someone with
the supernatural gift of grace.[15] This grace places the acts in the supernatural realm; and this characteristic is necessary for any sort of proportion to a supernatural reward.

Scotus has a distinction between condign and congruous merit as well,
though it is in fact very different from the one just described. Central to
it is the idea that the creature cannot refuse the reward offered as a result of condign merit; whereas he or she can refuse the reward offered as
a result of congruous merit. So, as in Bonaventure, the notion of necessity does in some sense attach to condign merit, and not to congruous
merit; but the necessity, as we shall see, is the result not of any lack of
divine freedom, but of a lack of creaturely freedom. And Scotus never
claims—unlike Bonaventure—that the necessity attaching to the reward
of congruous merit is the result of any sort of obligation imposed on God,
whether by himself, freely, or otherwise. Underlying this is Scotus's insis-
tence that nothing outside God is sufficient for an external divine action.

So Scotus rejects Bonaventure's way of drawing the distinction between condign and congruous merit. But he does not reject all the features of Bonaventure's account. Like Bonaventure, he denies that there could ever be any equality between a human act and the reward assigned to it.[16] But he presumably wants to claim—like Bonaventure—that there is a proportion between the human act and the divine reward.[17]

Scotus's proposed replacement way of drawing the distinction between condign merit and congruous merit is quite complicated. Underlying it is the claim that the reward for condign merit is everlasting life, and that the reward for congruous merit is the gift of sanctifying grace (i.e., justification). Scotus's presupposition—which I will return to below—is that no human action can be sufficient for justification; although some human actions might be sufficient for a justified person to receive the reward of everlasting life.

Given all this, Scotus spells out his distinction as follows. In virtue of his or her meritorious actions, a person receives a reward from God. This reward is given at a particular time. Let us label this time 't'. Now, t is the temporal limit of the meritorious act, and it is an extrinsic limit. (In other words, the reception of the reward, although temporally immediately contiguous to the act, is *later* than the meritorious act.) Scotus argues that, at t, the recipient of a congruously merited reward can refuse the reward. At t, the person can instead begin to will in a demeritorious way. But things are different in the case of the recipient of a condignly merited reward. At t, this person is deprived of his or her opportunity for refusing the reward.[18] Why should this be? Scotus believes, as we shall see, that the reward given for condign merit is the beatific vision and everlasting life,[19] and that anyone enjoying this vision is impeccable.[20] Condign merit is thus—given God's decision to reward certain actions—*sufficient* at t for the reception of the reward. Congruous merit—the sort of merit that disposes for justification after confession—is not like this. It is not sufficient at t for the reception of its reward. In line with this, Scotus often refers to congruous merit as no more than a *disposition* for the reception of a reward.[21]

On the account thus far, condign merit gains eternal life, and congruous merit gains justification after confession. Scotus believes, however, that a person with sanctifying grace can, in addition to meriting eternal life, merit an increase in grace too. Although Scotus does not make this clear, I take it that this is another instance of condign merit. The reason is that—unlike congruous merit—an act meriting an increase in grace will be sufficient the reward (i.e., for the increase in grace). Scotus implies that the increase of grace is simultaneous with the whole (temporally extended) meritorious action.[22] The reward for a congruously meritorious action is not like this. Necessarily, it is given only at the very last instant of the meritorious action. It is for this reason that it is possible to fail to receive the reward for a congruously meritorious action; we can in the very last instant begin to act in a way that blocks the reception of the reward. But this is not possible if the reception of the reward is simultaneous with the meritorious action; for as long as we are acting meritoriously, we receive the reward. Condign merit is *sufficient* for its reward.

Scotus does not believe that meritorious actions are in every case necessary for the reception of sanctifying grace. Specifically, he believes that it is not possible to merit the very first gift of such grace (given standardly in the sacrament of baptism).[23] In fact, Scotus believes that we receive the very first gift of grace as a result of the merits of Christ.[24] (I discuss Christ's merits and their relation to our salvation in chapter 10.) For reasons that will become clear below, Scotus believes that we can lose sanctifying grace.[25] God can, however, return this grace to us. And he does so by means of the sacrament of penance. According to Catholic doctrine, sacramental confession requires some sort of sorrow for sins. Scotus, as we have seen, holds that some actions are congruously meritorious of sanctifying grace. These actions are those that merit the restoration of lost grace in the sacrament of penance. Scotus holds that such meritorious actions are (in the current dispensation) *necessary* for the restoration of grace.[26] The action he has in mind is sorrow for our past sins; specifically, sorrow performed with all the circumstances required for moral goodness.[27] This sorrow can take two forms, depending on whether or not it is performed by someone with sanctifying grace. The act of sorrow performed by someone without sanctifying grace is called 'attrition'; the same act performed by someone with sanctifying grace is called 'contrition'. Scotus is clear that attrition is congruously meritorious of grace.[28] This is not—as has sometimes been suggested—a form of Pelagianism. As I have tried to make clear, Scotus does not believe that a congruously meritorious action such as attrition could ever be *sufficient* for grace. At the instant at which grace is given, the sinner could fail to receive it. But the Pelagian claim is that the sinner can earn grace without divine aid; in other words, that the sinner's actions are *sufficient* for grace. So Scotus does not

accept the Pelagian heresy. Furthermore, this merit is done in cooperation with Christ. God has decreed that our cooperation is required if we
are to receive the reward, and that our cooperation, although not in any
sense equal to the reward, is meritorious.[29]

In fact, Scotus argues that there is a sense in which contrition is necessary for the restoration of grace. He explains this as follows. At the instant at which grace is given to the sinner, the act that was attrition becomes an act of contrition by the addition of grace. If contrition is not
present, however, the gift of grace is immediately lost.[30]

Scotus's teachings about congruous merit and attrition might seem to
be inconsistent with his belief in predestination prior to foreseen merits.
After all, it seems that, so long as I produce an act of attrition for a sufficient period of time, God will (unless I prevent him) restore grace to me.
Thus, I could merit the restoration of sanctifying grace. And having sanctifying grace at time t is sufficient for being saved at t. I think Scotus has
an answer to this, though he does not state it unequivocally. It seems to
me that what counts as a sufficient period of time for attrition is wholly
determined by God, such that someone whom God has not predestined
could never produce a sufficiently long act of attrition to merit the reward of sanctifying grace. Scotus states of the final instant of attrition that
it is something "which God has fixed that it should be the end term of
that motion of attrition," and that it is that "up to which God has determined that the attrition should last."[31] And there seems to me no reason
why we need to assume that the divinely determined period of attrition
need be the same for everyone. Some person's attrition might never be
such that God restores sanctifying grace to that person.

3. Grace and the remission of sins

What is it for a person to be justified? Scotus believes—following the
standard late thirteenth-century line—that a person is justified if and only
if a created quality—habitual grace—inheres in his or her soul.[32] This
doctrine owes a lot to an Aristotelian analysis of virtue. According to
Aristotle, virtues are 'habits'.[33] They are good habits, caused by our actions.[34] We learn from the *Categories* that a habit is a type of 'quality'.[35]
On this account, a virtue is an accidental form—a quality—belonging to
the soul. The medievals took over this account of virtue and applied it to

both grace and the theological virtues. Unlike natural human virtues, these supernatural virtues cannot be acquired by any merely human activity. They have to be created by God.[36] Scotus agrees with this account. Grace is a supernatural habit, created by God:

> The other requirement in an act [for it to be meritorious] is its relationship to a supernatural form which renders the person or operative power acceptable and is assumed to be grace or charity.[37]

This habit is—following the Aristotelian analysis—a quality.[38]

Given all this, of course, it is easy enough to see how grace could be lost. It is a "spiritual beauty" of the soul,[39] and it can be lost by demeritorious action.[40] The gain and loss of this spiritual quality are real changes in a person.

Scotus believes that sanctifying grace and the theological virtue of charity are one and the same.[41] He also identifies it with the infused supernatural virtue of justice.[42] Scotus holds that charity inheres in the will. His basic reason is that charity is *de potentia Dei ordinata* necessary for merit. Only free actions are meritorious. So if the habit is a necessary condition for merit, it must inhere in that power of the soul that is responsible for free action (i.e., the will).[43]

According to Aquinas, the presence of such a habit is (logically) necessary for justification.[44] Scotus, however, disagrees. He argues that there is no reason why God could not accept someone without a habit of grace. I will deal with this possibility in a moment. But first I want to look at some reasons Scotus gives as to why—*given that the Catholic teachings about justification and penance are in fact true*—we need to posit such a habit.[45] Scotus argues, first, that a change from injustice to justification can only occur if God brings about a real change in the sinner. The immutable God cannot simply begin to accept a sinner when previously he did not.[46] The idea is not that God could not save someone without a habit of grace. Rather, Scotus's claim is that, in such a scenario, a person is either *always* saved or *always* damned. Secondly, Scotus claims that a habit of grace is required for an orthodox (anti-Pelagian) account of merit. If we could merit without a supernatural habit, then we could merit justification merely in virtue of our natural powers. And the claim that we can merit merely in virtue of our natural powers is the error of Pelagius.[47]

I will return to the second of these claims below. The first—that the immutable God cannot begin to accept a sinner without a real change in the sinner—seems highly problematic. And the problem is one that Scotus himself notices. It is simply not true that a timeless God cannot simply will not-a at t_1 and a at t_2—for example, my not being justified at t_1 and my being justified at t_2—without any other change in the created order—for example, the creation of a habit of grace. (We looked at the notion of God's timeless willing in chapter 4 above.) Thus, God could will my beginning to be justified, even without the creation of a habit of grace.

In fact, Scotus recognizes a possibility exactly analogous to this when discussing the remission of sins (itself a necessary part of the process of justification). As we saw in chapter 7, Scotus's understanding of sinfulness is wholly forensic; we are sinners just if God decides to hold us liable to punishment. Scotus's understanding of the remission of sins is likewise forensic. The remission of sins does not involve the removal of any quality or real relation in the sinner. It consists merely of a divine decision not to punish the sinner.[48] Thus, God's one will-act involves willing punishment for a person at t_1 and non-punishment at t_2, without any corresponding real change in the person at all.[49] This does not mean that God does not usually require that we perform acts of penance in the process of the remission of post-baptismal sin. Scotus understands penance as the willing submission to a punishment, "regularly required for the removal of sin."[50] This penance does not, however, cause a real change in the sinner; it is merely a requirement contingently made by God for the remission of post-baptismal sin.[51]

On this account, the remission of sin involves essentially no more than God's willing non-punishment (sometimes but not always after a period of voluntary punishment). The remission of sins does not bring about any real change in the sinner. For the same reason, then, there seems nothing to prevent there being a change in status with regard to justification without the creation or destruction of a habit of grace. Scotus in fact recognizes this objection to his attempt to show that Catholic teaching requires the existence of habits of grace. His reply, however, is obscure and far from satisfactory:

> This argument does not support its conclusion, just as will be made clear in [book] 4 distinction 16, where it will be said that God remits the offense to the sinner naturally prior to giving him grace. So the arguments . . . are to be taken as about passive acceptation and the order or dignity to eternal life, which pertain to the justified person and not to the sinner. . . . [They are not to be taken] as about the remission of the offense alone, which is in itself less than being just.[52]

The gist of this is that the priority of the remission of sins over the infusion of grace means that the argument in favor of the possibility of the remission of sins without a real change in the sinner should not be taken as supporting the possibility of justification without a real change in the sinner. But it is difficult to see why this should be so. I do not see why the logical priority of the remission of sins over justification is sufficient to block the sort of inference Scotus's putative opponent wants to draw (i.e., that justification could take place without any real change in the sinner).

In addition to being the principle of merit, Scotus believes that the habit of grace performs other functions too. First, the habit increases the moral perfection of an action.[53] Secondly, it enables us to perform morally good actions "easily, pleasurably, expeditiously, and promptly,"[54] indeed, more so than if we did not have it.[55] Note, however, in connection with these two points, that more effort will allow us to perform a natural action that is just as morally perfect as any action performed with the habit of grace.[56]

Scotus is clear that a habit of grace is not necessary for justification:

> God by his absolute power could well have accepted—by the special acceptation mentioned above [viz., meritorious acceptation]—a beatifiable nature existing in its purely natural state; and similarly, he could have accepted as meritorious its action to which the inclination was merely natural. But it is not believed that he did dispose to accept pure nature or act, because for "an act from a purely natural state to be meritorious" approaches to the error of Pelagius.[57]

This need not surprise us. Scotus's stress on divine acceptation seems to make a habit of grace dispensable. Scotus's conclusion is that the divinely-chosen revealed scheme for justification is contingent. God could have chosen a different method of salvation altogether. He could, for example, have chosen the Pelagian way.[58] What seems less clear to me than it is to Scotus, however, is that Catholic teachings about justification and penance require the existence of habits of grace. (I outlined my reasons for this above.)

There is a second issue related to the non-necessity of the habit of grace for salvation. To what extent does the habit naturally make someone worthy of salvation? As far as I can tell, Scotus holds that the value of the habit of grace is in no sense anything *intrinsic* to it. Scotus holds that it has the value it does only "according to the divine laws"—laws that are contingent, not necessary.[59] I take it, then, that the worthy-making features of the habit of grace are contingent. God could in principle damn someone with the habit.

In Aquinas's theory of grace, a habit of grace is not sufficient for our being able to perform graced acts. Aquinas argues that we also need actual grace; God moving the will to act in certain meritorious ways.[60] Scotus is happy to talk about the Holy Spirit cooperating with the created will in the production of meritorious acts. But he is careful to understand this to mean no more than that God is the primary cause of our graced actions just as he is of all our actions. The will is the secondary cause of its graced actions. It is not, for example, an *instrument* of the Holy Spirit.[61] In effect, Scotus denies the need for an account of actual grace (in this technical sense, as opposed to habitual grace) at all.[62]

Central to Scotus's account of predestination, merit, and grace is God's sovereign freedom. God's decisions about predestination are made independently of any external influence (e.g., the foreseen good acts of certain creatures). And, likewise, his decision with regard to which acts to accept as meritorious is made irrespective of the natural moral values of those actions. God's decision to save people by means of a habit of grace is likewise contingent. God could have chosen to accept people without such a habit. Again, it is difficult not to be struck by the *contingency* of all this. God's freedom from any external constraint—his being wholly unconditioned—is the basic presupposition behind Scotus's account.

JESUS: GOD AND MAN

According to Christian orthodoxy, Jesus Christ is a person—the second person of the Trinity—who has both divine and human natures. As the Council of Chalcedon (451) puts it, the two natures are united in "a single person."[1] This union is usually referred to as the 'hypostatic' union (from 'hypostasis,' = 'person'). The point of the definition offered by Chalcedon is that the subject of divine and human attributes is the *person* of the Word. 'Person' here is not to be understood as referring to any sort of *psychological* concept. The crucial thing about a person, on the Chalcedonian view, is that it is a subject of characteristics. This was made a bit clearer at the third council of Constantinople in 680–81, where it was taught that Christ has two wills and two sorts of activity—divine and human.[2] So having human will and activity is not sufficient for being a person.[3]

Unsurprisingly, the medievals uniformly attempt to provide an account of the Incarnation that conforms to this Chalcedonian model. Oddly, however, they rarely refer explicitly to the Council's decree, and Scotus is no exception here. But they were well acquainted with the orthodox teaching through Boethius and John of Damascus, and by the late thirteenth century doubtless knew the Chalcedonian definition too.[4] Successfully defending the Chalcedonian position caused the medievals some difficulty. We can see this if we look at the issue that perhaps troubled the medievals most of all: how to characterize the *relation* that must exist between Christ's human nature and the second person of the Trinity.

1. The relation between Christ's human nature and the Word

Clearly, if the second person of the Trinity is to be the subject of the human nature, then the human nature must be related to it somehow. As the medievals saw, it must be related to the second person of the Trinity in a way analogous to the way in which a property is related to its subject. If it were not, then it would not be possible to speak of the second person of the Trinity as the subject of the human nature. Now, there is no property that is not either a necessary property or a contingent (accidental) property of its subject. So Christ's human nature must be either a necessary or a contingent property of the second person of the Trinity. But neither option looks very appealing. If Christ's human nature is a necessary property of the second person of the Trinity, then humanity is part of God's nature. This looks like a version of the monophysite heresy, according to which there is just one nature in Christ. But if Christ's human nature is an accidental property of the second person of the Trinity, then it will look as though that person has a passive potentiality that is actualized at some time. And the medievals were quite clear that God has no passive potentialities—that he is wholly unconditioned.[5]

Thomas Aquinas proposed a highly innovative solution to this problem—a solution with which almost everyone disagreed. Aquinas spells out his solution by appealing to his account of existence (*esse*),[6] drawing on an analogy afforded by created substance, that of a substance and its concrete parts. Aquinas's examples of such parts are (individual) hands, feet, eyes, heads, bodies, and souls. He argues that the concrete parts of a substance do not in any sense contribute existence to a substance. Aquinas sometimes claims that the concrete parts of a substance "share" in this substance's substantial existence.[7] In the passage on which I am basing my account here, he claims that the concrete parts of a substance constitute the substance. The relation of the human nature to the divine person is like this. The human nature *shares in the existence* of the divine person; and it does this by having the same sort of relation to the divine person as a concrete part has to its substance.

This account was certainly generally rejected by all medievals other than card-carrying Thomists. It is not difficult to see why. Concrete parts are themselves either essential or accidental. If the former—heads, bodies, and souls, for example—then it is of course reasonable enough to claim that they share in the substantial existence of a substance. But in this case the analogy of concrete part and substance cannot be a good one for the hypostatic union, because it would entail that the human nature is an essential property of the divine person, which would be a version of the monophysite heresy. Accidental concrete parts, however—hands, feet, and eyes, for example—must (like all accidents, according to Aquinas) contribute accidental existence to a substance. So characterizing the relation between the human nature and the second person of the Trinity as union in the existence of this person—at least as understood by Aquinas—cannot be right.[8]

Scotus explicitly targets Aquinas's account as a way of trying to characterize the hypostatic union.[9] He explains that the existence of a concrete part shares in the existence of its substance *just because* it is a part of its substance (or is, as Scotus puts it, perfected by the form of the substance):

> A part coming to a whole does not give existence to the whole, but rather receives [it], since it is perfected by the form of the whole. . . . But the human nature united to the Word is not informed by the Word.[10]

On this account, Aquinas's union in existence fails to be an accurate characterization of the union between the human nature and the second person of the Trinity. Scotus's reason for this is that the human nature is not (in the relevant sense) a part of the second person of the Trinity. And this seems quite right.

Aquinas's was not the only mid-thirteenth-century attempt to give some sort of account of the relation between the human nature and the Word. A different tradition was much happier than Aquinas to see the relation between an accident and a substance as the basic model for the hypostatic union. We find the view for example in William of Auxerre, writing between 1215 and 1225,[11] and there are clear antecedents to it.[12] Most important for Scotus was the acceptance of this model by William of Ware in the 1290s.[13] This sort of view, although heavily criticized by Aquinas, was common throughout the thirteenth century.[14] This tradition did not need to accept Aquinas's union in existence, and generally rejected Aquinas's claim that there is not more than one existence in the person of the Word.[15] Scotus accepts this tradition, and provides an extremely sophisticated defense of the basic claim.

Central to the sort of view accepted by Scotus is the claim that Christ's human nature is in some sense like an accident. Scotus tries to spell out exactly the ways in which Christ's human nature is like an accident, and those in which it is not. Scotus distinguishes two aspects of the relation between an accident and its substance: 'actualization' and 'dependence'. An accident is a property that its substance can lack. A substance has a passive potentiality for the property. This passive potentiality is *actualized* when the accident belongs to the substance. But there is a more basic relation than this too. If an accident is to actualize my passive potentiality, for example, there must be a sense in which the accident is *mine*, rather than yours. The accident *depends* on me in a way in which it does not depend on you. Scotus is fairly agnostic about this dependence element of the relation between an accident and a substance. All he says about it is this:

> An accident has a two-fold relation to its substance or subject: viz., of informing to informed (and this necessarily involves imperfection in the informed subject, namely in that [the subject] has potentiality with respect to a certain sort of act, i.e., accidental); and it has another, as of what is naturally posterior to the prior [thing] on which it depends. [This is] not like [dependence] on a cause.[16]

I called this dependence element of the accident-substance relation "more basic" than the actualization element, because Scotus clearly supposes that the dependence element can exist without the actualization element. What should we say about the supposition that something depends without actualizing any potentiality? Scotus is quite clear that such a dependent thing would be *like* an accident.[17] More importantly, it would clearly in some sense *belong to* the thing on which it depends. So the dependent thing would belong to its subject without actualizing any passive potentiality in its subject. Scotus uses this to interpret the claim that Christ's human nature is united to the Word in a way analogous to the way in which an accident depends on its substance. Just like an accident, Christ's human nature depends on its subject (the Word); unlike an accident, however, Christ's human nature actualizes no potentialities in its subject. As we saw in chapter 4, Scotus would argue that nothing outside God can bring about any effect internal to God; God has no passive potentialities. And Scotus argues that, because there is no logical impossibility in something's depending without actualizing any passive potentiality, there seems to be no logical impossibility in the human nature's depending on the Word without actualizing any passive potentiality in the Word.[18] In fact, as we saw in chapter 4, Scotus does not believe that there are any real relations in God to his creatures. The dependence relation is, putting it crudely, a one-way thing.[19] So the idea is that something can depend on its subject without any feature of that subject being altered—for example, without any of its potentiality being actualized. Thus Scotus is quite clear that sufficient for the divine person's being human is the actualization of *the human nature's* potentiality for dependence:

> It is not necessary for a mutation to have existed in anything said to have been made such, but only in that on account of whose passive change [*passio*] something is said to be made such; and here that was only the human nature.[20]

This seems to me a curious view to accept. We might think that this sort of account is consistent with what Scotus says elsewhere about ascribing extrinsic relational predicates to God. God is creator, for example, in virtue of real relations not in him but in his creatures. But the present case is very different from this. Scotus supposes that the incarnate divine person fails to be really related to one of its *properties* (i.e., the human nature). It is not clear how anything can have a property without being really related to this property. If Scotus's defense of the hypostatic union is correct, however, we will have to accept by stipulation that a substance *x* can have a property *F* merely in virtue of *F*'s relation to *x*.

2. Christ's human nature

Scotus's account of the relation between the human nature and the divine person seems to me to provide a way for him to avoid the charge of monophysitism that could perhaps be laid at Aquinas's Christology. But Scotus's account of the human nature has led some to suspect him of the opposite error—Nestorianism: the view that there are two persons, divine and human, in Christ. The theologians of the thirteenth century were generally quite clear that Christ's human nature is an *individual* thing, and that it is individuated by a principle *intrinsic* to it. Thus it is not, for example, a merely abstract property; neither is it individuated by its subject (i.e., the second person of the Trinity). Scotus agrees with this, citing the authority of John of Damascus: "The Word assumed a nature in particular (*in atomo*)."[21] Oddly, Scotus does not provide an argument for this claim. It was however a strong part of the tradition within which he was working.

The problem with seeing Christ's human nature as an individual is that the position begins to look a bit like a version of the Nestorian heresy. An individual human nature—including matter and form—seems to satisfy all the prima facie conditions that might be set for personhood. It is, for example, a concrete item, an agent, and rational. This would seem to imply that it satisfies Boethius's famous definition of 'person' as "an individual substance of rational nature."[22] If the human nature is a person, then we have some version of the Nestorian heresy, according to which Christ is the conjunction of two persons, divine and human.

Given the unacceptability of Nestorianism, the thirteenth-century schoolmen tried to find a way of allowing that Christ's individual human nature does not itself count as a human person. They tried two different approaches. One was to claim that some further non-privative or positive feature needs to be added to an individual nature in order to get a person; the second was to claim that the distinction between individual nature and person can be completely captured in terms of privative or negative properties, such that a person is simply an individual nature with one or more privative properties.

Scotus strongly rejects the first approach, and defends the second. He has both theological and philosophical reasons for this. Theologically, the first view seems to entail that Christ's human nature lacks something that all other human natures have (i.e., created personhood). But personhood seems to be the most important and characteristically human feature of all; so it would indeed be odd if Christ lacked it. Scotus cites John of Damascus to pick out a further theologically undesirable consequence of the first view. A positive feature of human existence would be beyond redemption. Created personhood is (on the first view) a positive feature of human existence that cannot be assumed by the second person of the Trinity; but "what cannot be assumed cannot be healed."[23] According to Scotus, there are philosophical difficulties too. The relation between the human nature and the Word is some sort of property of the human nature.

But Scotus is quite clear that it cannot be an essential property of that nature, since then there would have to be something about Christ's human nature that was essentially unlike any other human nature. According to Scotus, however, there is no such feature.[24] So the relation between the human nature and the Word is an accidental feature of the human nature. If it is accidental, it can be lost, such that God can bring it about that the human nature that is now Christ's *ceases* to belong to the second person of the Trinity, beginning to exist independently of this person. (Scotus is proposing this as a counterfactual possibility only; he [of course] does not believe that this will ever happen.) Now, suppose that the Word did cease to be incarnate, and that his human nature continued in existence:

> If human nature formally became a person by reason of some positive entity, the Word could not put off the nature he had assumed without either letting it remain depersonalized (which seems incongruous) or else giving it some new entity by which it would have created personhood. But this too is impossible. This could be no accidental entity, since an accident is not the formal reason why a substance is a person. Neither could this entity be substantial, be it matter, form, or a composite substance; for then it would no longer have the nature it had before, but it would have another matter, form, or composite substance.[25]

So the first view—according to which personhood is a positive feature of a nature—is false.

Given this, Scotus accepts instead the second view, that personhood is a merely privative or negative property of a nature.[26] Scotus considers two different forms of this theory. On the first, the negation of actual dependence is necessary and sufficient for the personhood of a human nature. On the second, the negation of actual dependence is necessary but not sufficient for personhood. On the second view, a further negative property is also required, a property that Scotus calls the negation of dispositional dependence. For an object to have dispositional dependence, it must be the case that the object depends on a subject unless prevented. Dependence on a subject must be a natural state for it. Accidents and substantial forms fit this description. A human soul, for example, is part of a human composite unless prevented. This is just as true of a disembodied human soul as it is of an embodied one. So a disembodied human soul is actually independent (it has the negation of actual dependence), but it is dispositionally dependent. If actual independence were sufficient for a human substance to have personhood, then a disembodied human soul would count as a person. Scotus believes however, citing Richard of St. Victor,[27] that a disembodied soul is not a person. So he concludes that actual independence is not sufficient for personhood. He opts instead for the second version of the negation theory: the negation of both actual and dispositional dependence is necessary and sufficient for personhood.[28] Scotus holds that independence and personhood are natural states for a human nature. But this inference seems open to an objection that he does not notice. The negation of dispositional dependence is satisfied as much by a nature in *neutral* potentiality for dependence as by one with dispositional independence. Ockham later accepts that the human nature is in neutral potentiality for dependence.[29]

Either version of the negation theory is sufficient to avoid Nestorianism. When considering the possibility of a divine person assuming a human person, Scotus claims that it is impossible that a created person is assumed, since then "two persons would be one person."[30] Scotus's negation doctrine in fact precludes Nestorianism. Necessary for being a person is *failing* to be assumed by the Word. Any nature assumed by the Word is *eo ipso* not a person.

As we have seen, Scotus holds that the dependence of the Word's human nature is an accidental property of that nature. Consistent with this, he holds that actual independence—a merely negative property necessary for personhood—is an accidental property of a human nature. Scotus holds that it is possible for *any* human nature to depend on the Word. According to Scotus, the negation doctrine by itself is sufficient to show this. Since all human natures are the same in all of their positive essential features, and since at least one can be assumed by the second person of the Trinity, it must follow that any can be.[31] (It does not of course follow that more than one *will* be.) There are thus no intrinsic barriers to dependence in any human nature.[32] Of course, if a person were (as is logically possible) to be assumed, then he or she would thereby cease to be a person—not by losing any positive feature, but by *gaining* one (viz., dependence on the Word).

On this account, it is clear that there will be some sort of distinction between a human nature and a human person. Scotus claims that there is in fact a *formal* distinction between a nature and a person. He argues that if there were not such a distinction, then a nature "could not exist

without its personhood."[33] The distinction Scotus means to make is between an individual nature and its personhood, where personhood is a
merely privative accidental property. Scotus (rightly) does not want this
property to count as any sort of thing.[34] Scotus does not go into any great
detail about this.[35] At one point, he offers a fairly agnostic account. Whatever the distinction between nature and person, it must be sufficient to
allow the following two statements both to be true:

(1) It is not possible that a created person is dependent;
(2) It is possible that a created nature is dependent.[36]

Note that (1) is consistent with the statement

(3) A created person is possibly dependent

(viz., something that is now a person could begin to be dependent [and
thus cease to be a person]). In *Quodlibet* 19, Scotus is quite clear that his
negation doctrine is necessary for the truth of (3); the existence of a positive entity guaranteeing independence would prevent dependence.[37]
(Recall that Scotus elsewhere reasons that such an entity would have to
be essential to the nature, as we saw above.)

One consequence of all this is that the word 'person' is not univocal.
Divine persons are such that they are necessarily independent. Because,
as we have just seen, persons whose personhood is constituted by a negation are possibly dependent, it follows that the personhood of a divine
person is constituted by some real, non-privative, property. Divine persons are, to this extent, unlike human persons.[38]

Scotus's account of the assumed human nature seems to me to have
much to offer. He stresses that this human nature lacks none of the positive features required for being human. It fails to be a person not in
virtue of anything that it lacks, but in virtue of an additional relational
property that it uniquely has. Christ is thus, on this account, fully human.
Equally, not even this relational property is essential to it. Christ's
human nature is essentially just the same as ours. In the next section, I
will look at Scotus's treatment of certain properties—grace, knowledge,
impeccability—which were held to distinguish Christ from other human
beings.

3. Grace, knowledge, and will

Scotus argues that Christ's human nature is essentially the same as all other human natures in a very strong sense. He holds that apart from its relation to the Word, the hypostatic union does not necessitate any further properties in Christ's human nature. (If it did, we would have to say that, necessarily, any incarnate nature has some properties—over and above that of dependence—that no other nature has. And this might serve to make any incarnate nature radically unlike any non-incarnate nature, a situation that Scotus wishes to avoid.) The relation of hypostatic dependence does not entail that Christ's human nature has grace:

> No new absolute is posited in this nature through the union, because for it to be united to the Word implies only its special dependence on the Word; and just as the nature remains [the same] with regard to its absolute [property], so [it remains] having the same capacity.[39]

Similarly, with regard to knowledge,

> From the power of the union, only the Word is present to the assumed soul, and this [is] according to personal existence. If therefore, from the power of the union [the Word] is present as an object moving [the assumed created intellect], this would mean just that the Word—and not the whole Trinity—moved the created intellect. But this is false, since the external actions of the Trinity are undivided.[40]

Equally, the hypostatic union does not entail that Christ is impeccable. Christ's impeccability follows rather from his human nature's enjoying the beatific vision.[41] Christ's human soul could lack the beatific vision. So Christ could sin:

> The human nature which he assumed was in itself able to sin, since it was not blessed as a result of the power of the union, and had free choice, and [was] thus able to choose either [action, viz., good or bad].[42]

It might be thought that Christ's human will was no more than an instrument of the second person of the Trinity, and thus impeccable for this reason. According to Aquinas, for example, Christ's human will operates in the manner appropriate to the human will of a divine person, such that "the [human will] always moves according to the nod of the divine will."[43] Scotus strongly rejects this position. He has two reasons. First, it is untrue that a will must act in a manner appropriate to its *per-*

son; it acts in a manner appropriate to its *nature*. And in the hypostatic union, the human will is of human nature.[44] Secondly, no external efficient causation can be attributed to one of the divine persons alone. So the Word cannot have any causal role in Christ's human actions that the other divine persons do not have. And this makes it look as though the causal influence of God on Christ's will is the same sort of influence as he has on any other will. The point is made clearly in the *Reportatio*:

> How is [the Word] said to be willing? I say that just as the Son of God is called "colored" because the body of Christ is colored, so he is called "willing" because the soul is thus willing; and because the nature subsists in the Word, he is for this reason thus denominated.[45]

None of this entails that Christ did not *in fact* have grace, the beatific vision, complete knowledge, and impeccability. Scotus holds that, as a matter of fact, Christ's human nature did have all of these properties. Christ's human nature has the highest possible grace any creature could have.[46] It enjoys the beatific vision,[47] and as a result of this knows everything that the Word knows—past, present, future, and possible—by "seeing" it in the Word.[48] This is, of course, a special kind of knowledge, beyond the unaided natural capacity of the human mind to achieve. But Christ has the sort of knowledge that can be gained by natural processes too. One sort of cognitive perfection achievable by the human mind is the abstractive knowledge of universals. God can infuse such universal "species" into the mind, and they can be known in this way. Scotus cites Augustine to the effect that these intelligible species are distinct from the things Christ's human mind sees in the Word.[49]

Scotus holds that the human mind can have intellectual knowledge of things specifically in their concrete presence too. It does this by means of what Scotus calls "intuitive" knowledge. Christ has this sort of knowledge.[50] This sort of knowledge can only be perfectly had in the presence of its object. So Christ's human mind can have perfect intuitive knowledge only of those things that are present to it.[51] Likewise, Christ can recollect—as past experiences—only those things he has actually experienced.[52] Since the store of Christ's memory of events actually experienced increases, Christ's knowledge is said to increase—as the Gospel of Luke testifies.[53] This seems a sensible way of trying to make sense of the Gospel testimony. Knowledge of an event experienced is different from knowledge that an event occurs. So the overall picture is that Christ knows all things by some sort of intuitive intellectual vision of the Word; that he knows those facts that could be known abstractively additionally by the infusion of intelligible species; and that he knows intuitively the individual things he experiences.

Equally, Scotus is clear that Christ is in fact impeccable.[54] He is sensitive to the worry that no human will can be both free and impeccable. But he argues that everyone who enjoys the beatific vision is impeccable.[55] So in principle there is no difficulty in Christ's being impeccable.

It might be thought that Christ's human nature—in Scotus's rather extravagant account—exhibits properties that no other human nature *could* exhibit; and thus that Christ fails to be really human at all. But Scotus denies this. There is no essential or accidental feature of Christ's human nature in virtue of which he is capable of any higher gifts or achievements than anyone else. We have already seen this in the case of impeccability. Scotus claims with regard to Christ's grace: "God in his absolute power can confer such grace on another nature [than Christ's], whether assumed or perhaps not assumed."[56] And there seems to me to be no reason why Scotus would not make this claim for Christ's knowledge too.[57] So Christ's human nature does not in fact receive gifts that another human nature could not; neither do the gifts it receives follow as a necessary consequence from the hypostatic union. Scotus thus has no difficulty in asserting Christ's complete humanity, "one who in every respect has been tempted as we are, yet without sinning."[58]

4. The incarnate divine person

As we saw in chapter 5, Scotus is quite clear that all external actions of the Trinity are undivided. This seems to raise a problem for the doctrine of the Incarnation: how can the Son become incarnate without the Father and Spirit also becoming incarnate? Scotus's answer is simple. For a person to be the end term of a dependence relation is not an action; but *causing* this relation is an action. So "the whole Trinity equally brought about the Incarnation";[59] but being the end term of the dependence relation of a human nature—"sustaining" that nature, as Scotus sometimes labels it[60]—can belong to one person alone, without belonging to the others.[61] Thus the Son can be incarnate without the Father and Spirit also being incarnate. Scotus considers some sophisticated alternative accounts. On the most interesting, the divine persons act externally *in concert*, such that each acts in the way proper to it. In the Incarnation, the proper action of the Son—but not of the Father or Spirit—is to be incarnate.[62] Scotus agrees that in every external action, the three persons act in concert; but he argues that these actions are different only if they have some direct connection with the Trinitarian origins of the three persons: "The Father acts from himself; the Son not from himself."[63] And Scotus evidently holds that this distinction is not sufficient to explain how only the Son is incarnate.

5. The communication of properties

Scotus, as we would expect, is clear that the second person of the Trinity is the subject of all predicates—divine and human[64]—with the exception of those that we use to describe the hypostatic union itself.[65] This exception is important: we need to be able to talk about—say—the dependence of the human nature on the Word without being forced to claim that the Word is dependent on itself. The situation is exactly the same in all cases of accidental dependence; I am the subject of my whiteness, but I am not the subject of its dependence on me. Scotus's discussion of individual cases is interesting, but in all cases conforms to the general rules just outlined.[66]

But the question of the communication of properties raises acutely a problem which—of all Christological problems—most exercises modern philosophical writing on the subject: the problem of coherence. If, for example, God is essentially uncreated, and human beings essentially created, how could anything be both God and human? (The problem arises, of course, for all sorts of seemingly contradictory pairs of attributes.)[67] Scotus was aware of this sort of difficulty, though a full discussion of his treatment would require dealing with each case separately. Perhaps an example, however, would be instructive. Is there any sense in which it is true to claim that Christ is a creature? Scotus thinks not. He reasons that we only use the word 'creature' of those substances that come into existence (after not existing). The incarnate divine person does not satisfy this description; so he is not a creature.[68] So Scotus must believe that being a creature is not essential for being human.[69]

Scotus's account of the hypostatic union is perhaps the most sophisticated to emerge from the middle ages, and is among the most philosophically astute defenses of orthodox Christology there is. Anyone who wants to take the complete humanity of the incarnate Word seriously, and who agrees with the medieval belief that this nature must—like any other human nature—be individuated independently of any union with the Word, will want to look at Scotus's subtle account of such a union very closely. Scotus's careful account of what it is to have a property is in any case just the sort of account that would need to be given of what it would be for the divine person to have a human nature.

JESUS: PREDESTINATION AND MERIT

I. The motive for the incarnation

One of the most interesting hard cases for the communication of properties discussed by Scotus is the following: "Christ was predestined to
be the Son of God."[1] Scotus claims that this statement is true, on the
basis that Christ's human nature was predestined to be united to the
second person of the Trinity. Much of the question is taken up with a
discussion of the motive for this predestination. Was Christ's human
nature predestined to be united to the Son of God because of the Fall
of Adam and the consequent need for redemption? Or was it predestined irrespective of the Fall? Aquinas holds that the incarnation was
a result of the Fall, and that speculation as to what might have happened
had Adam not fallen is pointless, since "we can only know about those
things which result merely from God's will (beyond anything owed to
a creature) if they are treated in scripture, through which the divine
will makes them known."[2]

But there was a clear if minority tradition, originating from Rupert
of Deutz (c. 1075–1129 or 1130), in favor of the view that Christ would
have become incarnate irrespective of the Fall. The motivation for this
sort of view—that Christ's humanity is the climax of creation—is at least
in part scriptural;[3] later, in the *Summa* once attributed to Alexander of

Hales, it is Dionysian: good is self-diffusive, and the incarnation represents the highest form of the self-diffusion of good.[4]

Scotus agrees with this minority tradition, though for strikingly different reasons (reasons that directly [though silently] attack Aquinas's account of our epistemic access to God's will). Scotus argues that natural reason will allow us to gain some insight into what God's decision-making process must look like, and he concludes that Christ would have become incarnate irrespective of the Fall of Adam. As far as I can tell, Scotus employs two different but related principles in establishing his conclusion:

(a) In any well-ordered action, the end is willed before the means;[5]

(b) In any well-ordered action, a greater good is willed before a lesser one.[6]

Using these two principles, Scotus establishes the following order in God's actions:

(1) God predestines Christ's soul to glory (i.e., to the beatific vision);

(2) God predestines Christ's human nature to depend on the Word;

(3) God predestines some other creatures to glory;

(4) God foresees the Fall of Adam;

(5) God predestines Christ to redeem fallen humanity.

The whole argument has to be gleaned from several passages. God must have decided to predestine Christ's human nature before any other nature, since the glory of Christ's human nature is a greater good than the glory of any other nature, and hence by (b) is willed first.[7] Equally, the predestination of Christ's soul to glory is prior to the predestination of Christ's human nature to hypostatic dependence, since hypostatic dependence is the means God has chosen to achieve his goal of the glorification of Christ's soul; and by (a) ends are willed before means.[8] But hypostatic dependence is a greater good than the glory of other creatures; so by (b) God's predestination of Christ's human nature to hypostatic dependence is prior to his willing glory for others.[9] (There is no suggestion that the hypostatic union would have been *necessary* for the glory of others.) Neither the predestination of Christ's human nature nor the predestination of any other nature can be dependent upon the Fall of Adam, since this would violate (b).[10] (Note that Scotus needs *only* this stage of his argument to establish his claim that Christ would have become incarnate irrespective of the Fall of Adam.) Equally, God's decision to redeem sinful humanity is subsequent to his decision to predestine creatures to glory, since the redemption is—given the Fall—God's chosen means to glory, and hence by (a) is willed after the end.[11]

Scotus's position here is a striking way of spelling out what he takes to be the significance of the Incarnation. It ties in neatly with his relatively lowly view of unfallen humanity. Adam did not have the vision of God, and (as we saw in chapter 7) had a passable body. Christ would have come with an impassible glorified body,[12] "The first-born among many brethren."[13]

2. Redemption

Christians hold that Christ's life, death, and resurrection have some sort of redemptive value, bringing about the remission of sins, justification, and the vision of God in everlasting life. The medievals located the redemptive value of Christ's work primarily in his passion and crucifixion, seeing Christ's death as making *satisfaction* for our sins, and as *meriting* our justification and everlasting life. The concepts of satisfaction and merit were used by Anselm of Canterbury in his *Cur Deus Homo* (*Why God Became Man*). Satisfaction is the voluntary repayment of a debt;[14] merit the earning of a reward.[15] According to Anselm, our sin places us in debt to God. This debt is paid by Christ—who thus makes satisfaction for our sin.[16] Since Christ was himself sinless, his satisfying for our sin earned him a reward—so Christ merits our salvation.[17] According to Anselm it is necessary for God to save us in this way, otherwise his plan is frustrated.[18]

Scotus makes use of Anselm's schema, though with certain modifications. Most importantly, he disagrees with Anselm that God has to redeem us by Christ's death. As Scotus presents Anselm's argument, it has four stages. (i) Humanity needs to be redeemed, otherwise God's plan would be frustrated; (ii) redemption can only be achieved through satisfaction for sin; (iii) satisfaction for human sin can only be made by a man who is God (i.e., by Christ); and (iv) satisfaction is best achieved by the death of a human being.[19] The crucial step is (iii). This step is entailed by two different sub-arguments: (iiia) the offense of human sin against God creates an infinite debt, since any wrong done to the all-good God is infinitely bad; but an infinite debt can be paid only by God;[20] and (iiib) a mere human being—even a sinless one—is obliged by God to every good deed he does, and hence cannot make satisfaction.[21]

Scotus disagrees with the crucial (iii) and its underlying claims.[22] Scotus claims against (iiia) that the offense caused by Adam's sin—and indeed all subsequent sin—is finite. But all that is required for satisfaction is equality; so a finite agent can make satisfaction simply by eliciting a finite act of love.[23] Neither will Anselm's (iiib) work. It is not true that we are obliged by God to every charitable act that we elicit. Some of our acts are *supererogatory*; and these can make satisfaction.[24]

Scotus argues, however, that God has decided to effect redemption through the passion of Christ. Like Anselm, though with very different results, he sees two significant actions in Christ's redemptive work: 'satisfaction' and 'merit'. Satisfaction is the voluntary return of equivalent for equivalent;[25] merit—as we saw in chapter 8—is the assignation of a reward to an act.[26] It is difficult to piece together Scotus's account of satisfaction, and more so without a clear grasp of his account of Christ's merit. So I will look at merit first, and then at satisfaction.

Scotus applies his account of merit—outlined in chapter 8—straightforwardly to Christ's meritorious work. On Scotus's account, an act is meritorious if and only if God assigns a reward for it. God assigned a reward to us because of Christ's affection for justice elicited in his willing submission to God's will in the passion.[27] This affection is an act of Christ's human will, and is therefore finite in value.[28] Although God could have assigned an infinite reward to it, he decided not to.[29] Nevertheless, the reward assigned to us is equal in value to Christ's merit.[30] In fact, given that an act merits if and only if God assigns a reward to it, it follows that Christ's work was meritorious only for those for whom God assigned a reward (i.e., the elect).[31] The idea is that Christ can only be said to have died for a person x if x receives the reward. And the reward is three-fold: the remission of sins,[32] the free gift of first grace (i.e., justification) given in baptism,[33] and the opening of the gates of heaven.[34]

Some commentators believe that Scotus's account of the redemption is sufficiently described in terms of merit, and thus that there is no satisfaction component in it at all.[35] Scotus usually applies the concept of satisfaction to our actions: *we* can make satisfaction for our sins in virtue of the merits of Christ.[36] And he likewise usually speaks not of Christ's death making satisfaction for sins, but (as we have just seen) of Christ's *meritorious* offering for the remission of sins.[37]

It is certainly true that Scotus clearly prioritizes the notion of Christ's merit over that of his satisfaction. On the other hand, there are clearly satisfaction elements in his theory. At one point Scotus expressly states, "When Christ . . . offered himself on the cross he made adequate satisfaction for an infinity of sins."[38] And Scotus does not elsewhere state explicitly that an Anselmian account of satisfaction is false. The burden of the discussion in *Ordinatio* 3.20.un. is that if Anselm's theory is true, it is only contingently so. In fact, in the *Reportatio* Scotus seems to claim that Anselm's position is a reasonably accurate account of the way God has decided to redeem humanity (*de potentia ordinata*).[39] Furthermore, Scotus is always happy to talk of Christ *placating* or *pleasing* the Trinity for original sin;[40] and talk of placation is very close to talk of satisfaction. Finally, at one point Scotus suggestively states that *if* Christ's death makes satisfaction, then it does so as a meritorious cause.[41] Presumably on this reading we would want to claim that Christ's death makes satisfaction for (i.e., merits the remission of) original sin and actual pre-baptismal sin, and that our cooperating makes satisfaction for (i.e., merits the remission of) actual post-baptismal sin.[42] This reading seems more plausible to me than that which denies a satisfaction component in Scotus's theory. The link, on my reading, between satisfaction and merit can be explained by the fact that, according to Scotus, satisfaction consists in receiving something from God (in this case, the remission of sins). So Christ's satisfaction can be spoken of as a sort of merit; it is that in virtue of which we receive a benefit from God.[43]

So it seems to me that Scotus does have a theory of satisfaction. I get the decided impression, however, that he is much happier with the concept of merit. We should also note that Scotus differs from Anselm in wanting to see Christ's work as an offering by the human nature to the Trinity, and not as an offering by the Son (the second person of the Trinity) to the Father.[44] Underlying this move is his account of the hypostatic union, according to which it is simply not possible for the Son alone, without the Father and Holy Spirit, to have any causal action over human nature—a principle Scotus reminds us of when explaining that it is not the case that, as Aquinas held, the value of Christ's work is infinite in virtue of the divine person.[45] Aquinas, of course, need do no more than appeal to the communication of properties to explain his position; Scotus seems to suppose that for an action *a* to have infinite intrinsic worth, it must be the case that *a* is *caused by*—not just predicated of—a divine person.[46]

3. Mary

One of Scotus's theological epithets is "Doctor marianus"—the Marian doctor. He owes this to his enthusiastic support for a doctrine that at the time was not very popular: the immaculate conception. According to the doctrine of the immaculate conception, Mary did not inherit original sin.[47] This doctrine is open to some formidable objections, put clearly by Aquinas. First, Mary was conceived in the natural way—and anyone so conceived inherits original sin.[48] Secondly, Christ's redemptive work saves us from sin; and it looks as though someone who lacked original sin would not need redeeming.[49]

Scotus does not believe these objections to be cogent. Scotus holds—as we saw in chapter 7—that original sin is not transmitted by the natural processes of procreation.[50] So Aquinas's first objection to the doctrine fails.

Mary is saved, according to Scotus, by Christ's meriting that she be preserved from original sin. Scotus is clear that Mary is prevented from having original sin in virtue of her having sanctifying grace.[51] On this account Mary's redemption is consistent with her never having contracted original sin.[52] This seems to be correct. Clearly, Christ's action on this view is sufficient for Mary's redemption. But the situation is a bit more complex than this. Mary's redemption on this account occurs *before* Christ's passion and death. This is just a particular instance of a general problem: how can those who lived before Christ be saved? In answer to this, Scotus generally holds that merit can be retroactive: God can assign a past reward to me on the basis of his knowledge of my present or future actions.[53] Again, this seems unobjectionable.[54] So the second objection presents no challenge to the doctrine of Mary's immaculate conception.

Scotus tries—rather implausibly—to demonstrate that the way in which he believes Mary to have been redeemed is in fact the most perfect form of redemption. First, the most perfect form of satisfaction is to prevent the offense. Second, the most perfect form of satisfaction removes the greatest available offense. But original sin is a greater offense to God than the deprivation of the beatific vision. Third, we are most perfectly under obligation to Christ only if he removes the greatest available offense.[55] Scotus uses these claims to try to show that the immaculate conception involves a more perfect form of redemption than any other available account of Mary's preservation from sin. So, he argues, "If it is not in conflict with the authority of the Church or the authority of Scripture, it seems probable that the more excellent should be attributed to Mary."[56]

How sympathetic we feel to the *argument* (setting aside the doctrine itself) will I suspect largely depend on how persuaded we feel by Scotus's attempts to show that the immaculate conception involves the most perfect form of redemption. Scotus's arguments for the doctrine seem to me to need more work. For example, if the most perfect form of redemption is to prevent the offense, we might be forgiven for inferring that we should *all* have been immaculately conceived. Variety in modes of redemption does not prima facie increase the perfection of the redemption. Equally, it is not clear whether there is any principled way of claiming that, on Scotus's account of the immaculate conception, Mary is genuinely redeemed. According to Scotus, Mary is redeemed in virtue of Jesus' preventing her from contracting the original sin which she would have contracted had Jesus not prevented her. Jesus pays the debt that Mary would have incurred had Jesus not paid it. Jesus, as it were, pays Mary's *potential* debt. Whether or not we are happy to classify this potential-debt payment as a case of genuine debt-payment—and hence, on the analogy, as a genuine form of redemption— seems to me an arbitrary matter. On the other hand, it is easy to be sympathetic to Scotus's claim that if there is a clearly graded order of perfection in modes of redemption, with an intrinsic maximum, then we should *ceteris paribus* ascribe the best one to God.

One odd result of Scotus's adherence to the doctrine of the immaculate conception is a lessening of the significance of Jesus' virgin birth. Clearly, on Scotus's view, virgin birth cannot be *necessary* to avoid original sin, since Mary was conceived in the natural way. This should not surprise us. Scotus's doctrine of original sin makes a strong disjunction between the natural process of conception and original sin. Furthermore, setting aside any factual questions, Scotus would deny that the virgin birth is *necessary* for the Incarnation. As we saw in the previous chapter, he is quite clear that God could if he wanted assume to hypostatic dependence a naturally generated human nature.

SACRAMENTS

According to Scotus, humanity has always needed signs of God's activity.[1] In the time of the New Covenant, sealed in Jesus' blood,[2] wayfaring humanity is in its closest state to beatitude. In this state, it consequently requires the most perfect signs of God's salvific activity.[3] The sacraments are such signs. They signify most appropriately the grace God confers through them. And the seven sacraments—baptism, Eucharist, confirmation, confession, unction, marriage, and ordination—correspond supernaturally to the seven requirements of natural life, individual and social: birth, nutrition, physical exercise, healing after illness, preparation for death, procreation, and the creation of spiritual leaders.[4] According to Scotus, citing the standard scriptural texts, these seven sacraments were instituted by Christ himself.[5]

In this chapter, I want to look at three features of Scotus's sacramental teaching in more detail. First, his account of the way in which the sacraments have a role in the causation of grace; second, his account of sacramental grace, and the indelible character given by three of the sacraments (baptism, confirmation, and ordination); third, his account of the Eucharist.

1. Sacramental causality

Scotus's definition of 'sacrament' weaves together several patristic themes:

> A sacrament is a sensible sign, ordered to the salvation of the wayfaring human being, efficaciously signifying—by divine institution—the grace of God, or a gratuitous effect of God.[6]

There is nothing much original about this. But the term 'efficaciously' requires comment. In what sense are the sacraments "efficacious"—in what sense do they *cause* grace? One powerful tradition, represented in the thirteenth century most typically by Bonaventure,[7] argues that the reception of a sacrament is no more than an *occasion* for a merely divine action. On this view, the reception of a sacrament has no *causal* role in the divine gift of grace. There is another view in the thirteenth century too, best represented by Aquinas. On this view, God uses the sacraments in the process of imparting grace. The sacraments have some sort of causal role; they are *instrumental causes* of grace. Aquinas argues that, if Bonaventure's view is correct, the sacraments are no more than signs of grace; they do not in any sense convey grace.[8]

As we have seen, the medievals often analyze cause-effect relationships in terms of causal powers. An agent has certain active powers in virtue of which it can produce an effect; and the corresponding patient has certain passive powers in virtue of which it can be affected or effected. Aquinas believes that every member of a casual chain has active causal powers. Consistent with this, he believes that, if the sacraments are instrumental causes of grace, then they must have certain active causal powers in virtue of which they can have a role in the process of conferring sacrament grace. He holds that such "instrumental" powers are caused by the motion of the principal agent, and presumably that they exist for only as long as the principal agent acts.[9] In the case of the sacraments, Aquinas is quite happy to claim that a supernatural power—the sort of power that could bring about a supernatural effect such as grace—could be given to a creature (in this case, to the sacrament).[10]

Scotus believes that Aquinas's view of sacramental causality is open to insuperable objections, and he much prefers the sort of occasionalist account defended by Bonaventure. Scotus agrees with Aquinas that agents have casual powers. He also agrees with Aquinas that instrumental causes do not have intrinsic causal powers. Just like Aquinas, he believes that the causal powers in virtue of which an instrumental cause has a role in the production of an effect are caused in it by the motion of the principal agent.[11] But, against Aquinas, Scotus believes that it would be logically contradictory that a material object have a *supernatural* causal power. So not even God could give such an object a supernatural power. The reason is that a supernatural form cannot be extended to exist throughout a material agent; and any causal power of a material object must be so extended.[12] Worse still, a sacrament is an aggregate of words, substances, and actions, and so in any case is not the sort of thing that could be an agent, or in which any sort of casual power could inhere.[13]

On Scotus's account, no natural agent could have a supernatural causal power. Could a sacrament, however, be an instrumental cause of grace without its having any supernatural powers? (For example, could it be an instrumental cause of grace in virtue of its own natural powers?) Scotus thinks not, claiming that it is impossible for a sacrament to be an instrumental cause of grace. First, no creature can be an instrumental cause of a supernatural effect.[14] Secondly, a sacrament is a temporally extended aggregate—it takes time to say all the required words. The infusion of grace by God is instantaneous. And no temporally extended aggregate can be in any sense the cause of an instantaneous action.[15]

Scotus's arguments against Aquinas rely on philosophical premises. In effect, Scotus is claiming that we can demonstrate that Aquinas's view is false. So the occasionalist option—the only other alternative—must be correct. Scotus thus argues that a sacrament is a non-causal "necessitating condition."[16] It does not *cause* God's action—after all, it has no causal powers, intrinsic or instrumental, in virtue of which it could bring about a divine action. God has decided, however, that *whenever* a sacrament is received, he will give the appropriate supernatural gift.[17] Indeed, this divine decision has been formalized in a covenant (*pactio*) made by God with the Church.[18] This does not commit Scotus to denying the reliability of sacramental grace. God's covenant guarantees sacramental reliability.[19]

Scotus argues similarly with regard to the consecration of the elements in the Eucharist. The priest's celebration of the Mass is an occasion for the conversion of the bread and wine into Christ's body and blood. But this conversion is not caused by the priest's words and actions in the mass. The priest's words and actions are a non-causal necessitating condition of a divine action. And all of this is the result of "the ordering of God making a covenant with the Church."[20]

One advantage of the Thomist account rejected by Scotus is that it allows a clear distinction between the sacraments of the New Covenant and the ceremonies of the Old. According to Aquinas, the sacraments have instrumentally causal powers; the Old Testament ceremonies are just *occasions* for divine grace. This way of distinguishing the sacraments from the Old Testament ceremonies is not open to Scotus's occasionalist account of sacramental causality. He therefore distinguishes the sacraments from the Old Testament ceremonies rather differently. He holds that Christ's life and death is the meritorious cause of God's salvific action exhibited in both the New Testament sacraments and the Old Testament ceremonies.[21] Whereas the Old Testament ceremonies owe their efficacy to Christ's *foreseen* merits, the New Testament sacraments owe their efficacy to the *actual* merits of Christ. But in things that owe their efficacy to merits in this way, greater efficacy is received in virtue of actual merits than of foreseen merits. So the New Testament sacraments are more effective in the conferring of grace than their Old Testament precursors.[22]

2. Grace and character

Scotus is clear that the effect of the sacraments—which as we have seen is brought about the merits of Christ—is the gift of grace.[23] Scotus distinguishes those sacraments that confer first grace (that grace in virtue of which we are saved)—baptism and confession—from those that confer second grace (i.e., an increase in grace).[24] Furthermore, one and the same grace, existing in the soul, has various different effects; and the sacraments are distinguished from each other in virtue of their relations to these different effects.[25] Thus, for example, God by means of baptism causes the remission of original sin[26] and actual sin,[27] without the need for penance,[28] remitting both the guilt of sin and the punishment due for it;[29] he gives spiritual birth,[30] adoption as sons of God,[31] and Church membership.[32] Confession brings about the remission of sins and the restoration of grace after its loss.[33] The Eucharist increases the force of the Christian's incorporation into Christ.[34]

Some sacraments—baptism, confirmation, and ordination—also confer some sort of indelible "mark" on their recipient. This mark is known technically as 'character'. Scotus provides a detailed description of the nature and effects of character. It is "an unrepeatable . . . spiritual form impressed by God."[35] It in some way makes those who possess it conform to Christ,[36] and it places those who have it under some sort of obligation to Christ.[37] It also places us in communion—here, a sort of family relationship—with others who have this character.[38]

According to Aquinas, this character is a quality—a non-relational perfection.[39] This quality inheres in the intellect, configuring the threefold structure of the mind to its Trinitarian model.[40] Furthermore, Aquinas sees character as an instrumental cause in the process of receiving sacramental grace.[41] Scotus disagrees with these claims of Aquinas. He argues that character is a relational property, that it inheres in the will, and that it functions merely as an occasion for God's giving us grace—it has no causal role, instrumental or otherwise.

According to Scotus, the very way in which character is defined involves relations to other items: conformity to Christ, and communion with other Christians. So character must in essence be a relation, not an absolute property.[42] Equally, character inheres in the will, not the intellect. Scotus's reason is that character places us under an obligation to God; and being obliged belongs to us not in virtue of our intellect but of our will.[43] Grace inheres in the will; and character, which is the occasion for the reception of grace, thus appropriately inheres in the will, too.[44]

Scotus distinguishes the different characters of baptism, confirmation, and ordination in terms of their effects. Baptismal character incorporates us into the family of Christ; confirmation gives us a role in the defense of the Church militant; the character of ordination allows us to lead others as parent and shepherd.[45]

3. Eucharist: Transubstantiation and sacrifice

According to Lateran IV (1215), in the Eucharist the bread and wine are transubstantiated into the body and blood of Christ.[46] The schoolmen understood this to entail that the *substance* of the consecrated bread and wine no longer exists, while the *accidents* of the bread and wine remain. Accidents are non-essential properties, paradigmatically analyzed by Aristotle as quantity, quality, relation, place, time, position, state, action, and passion.[47]

This doctrine raises three distinct problems. What sort of change is transubstantiation? How could the accidents of anything exist without their substance? How could Christ's body and blood be really present on the altar? I will look at these problems in turn, trying to see how effective are Scotus's proposed solutions. Scotus's major opponent here is Aquinas. So I will look briefly at Aquinas's view too.[48]

*What sort of change
is transubstantiation?*

Aquinas and Scotus agree that the Eucharistic change—transubstantiation—is best defined as "the conversion of one whole substance into another."[49] Both men understand this to entail that the matter and form of the bread is converted into the matter and form of Christ's body. Aquinas believes that this sort of change is the only way to explain how Christ's body can be really present in the Eucharist. He argues that there are only two ways in which a body can begin to be present at a place: by local motion from place to place and by transubstantiation. (In the first of these, the body undergoes a change; in the second, something else changes into the body.) The first of these changes, according to Aquinas, cannot explain Christ's real presence. For a body to move from place a to place b, it must cease being at a; it must travel through all the places between a and b; and if it is in place b it cannot be in any other place c. Christ's body in the Eucharist can satisfy none of these conditions: it remains in heaven while present on the altar; it does not travel from heaven to earth; and it can be present on more than one altar at the same time. So the only way to explain presence must be transubstantiation: the complete change of the bread into Christ's body.[50]

It is in fact difficult to see how Christ's body can begin to be present without it undergoing some sort of change, and Scotus attacks Aquinas's account for just this sort of reason. He argues that transubstantiation, as understood by Aquinas, is in fact no help in explaining how Christ's body begins to be present in the Eucharist. Transubstantiation is a doctrine about *substances*, not about the *places* they occupy; and to explain the presence of a material substance, we need to be able to talk about the place it occupies. As Scotus understands Aquinas's theory, it entails that the bread is transubstantiated into Christ's body; but it also entails that Christ's body remains in heaven—and so is not really present at all.[51] In order to explain how Christ's body begins to be present in the Eucharist, we need to appeal to something like local motion. Christ's body begins to be present in the Eucharist because it has in some sense *moved*.[52]

Aquinas's objections (just outlined) to this sort of account look formidable. Scotus answers them by appealing to an Aristotelian account of place that both he and Aquinas share. According to Aristotle, being in a place is a relation; a body is in a place if and only if it is contained by its immediate surroundings.[53] On this account, moving from place to place involves gaining and losing successive relations to different surroundings. In answering Aquinas's objections, Scotus appeals to various features that he believes all categorical relations share. One such feature is that, in general, a substance can have more than one relation of the same sort. Suppose I am the same height as my two friends. "Being the same height as" is a relation; and according to Scotus, I have two such relations, one to each of my two friends. Furthermore, I can gain and lose such relations; perhaps one of my friends grows a little hunched as he gets older, or I gain another friend of the same height. Scotus argues that place relations are like this. God could give me, simultaneously, the relation of being in place *a* and being in place *b*. If this were to happen, there would not, despite appearances, be two substances: just one substance in two places.[54]

On this account of place, it is easy to see how God could bring it about both that Christ's body is present in the Eucharist without his leaving heaven, and that his body is present on other altars at the same time.[55] And presumably, since Christ's body does not lose its first place—in heaven—there is no reason to suppose that it has to *travel* from heaven to earth, as Aquinas supposes would have to happen on this sort of scenario.

On Scotus's account, it is this change to Christ's body—and *not* transubstantiation—that properly explains the presence of Christ's body in the Eucharist. Scotus consequently thinks—unlike Aquinas—that there is no pressing theological reason for wanting to accept transubstantiation. He believes that consubstantiation—the doctrine that Christ's body comes to exist in the same place as the substance of the bread—is in principle preferable. It is simpler,[56] it is easier to understand (because it does not involve the claim that, despite appearances, the substance of the bread has changed),[57] and it is more scriptural.[58] Despite its intrinsic undesirability, however, Scotus believes that the doctrine of transubstantiation is true. His reason for this is just that it was taught "by the Roman Church" at Lateran IV.[59]

The separated accidents

The most telling objection to the doctrine of transubstantiation is that the existence of accidents without their substance is just impossible—the sort of absurdity satirized by Lewis Carroll in the Cheshire cat's grin. Clearly, if it is impossible for accidents to exist without their substance, then transubstantiation is false. But, as I have tried to show elsewhere, Scotus argues on straightforwardly *philosophical* grounds, without invoking any theological principle, that accidents can exist without their substances.

Scotus argues that for substance and accident to form an accidental whole *w*, it is necessary that none of the parts of *w* are essentially parts of *w*. On this account of the nature of an accidental whole, it is possible that accidents can "migrate" from substance to substance. Scotus believes (mistakenly) that this is a principle espoused by Aristotle.[60] Scotus (again mistakenly) argues that on his account of accidental unity, it follows that an accident can exist apart from any substance at all.[61] And this allows for the possibility of the separated accidents required for transubstantiation.

Presupposed to this argument is the claim, explicitly defended by Scotus, that accidents are individuated independently of their substances. (If they were not, it would be difficult to see how they could possibly exist without their substances.) Scotus argues that the individuation of something belonging to one of Aristotle's categories (e.g., an accident) cannot be explained by something existing in another of the categories (e.g., a substance).[62] Aquinas tries to give an account of transubstantiation that will be consistent with the claim that accidents are individuated by their substances. He claims—without making any attempt to justify his position—that an item can exist at a time t_n without its individuating feature if it was united to its individuating feature at t.[63] Scotus's attempt to find a stronger philosophical underpinning for the doctrine makes his account far more intellectually satisfying than Aquinas's more agnostic one.

Not all of the separated accidents in the Eucharist lack a subject. In fact, Scotus believes—adopting the standard thirteenth-century opinion—that it is most likely that only the quantity of the bread lacks a subject; the remaining accidents inhere in this quantity. His basic reason is Aristotelian:

quality is extended by being received into quantity.[64] On this account, the subject of—say—the color, or taste, of the consecrated host is its extension. What we see on the altar is in essence the *size* of the bread and wine.

The real presence

The claim that Christ's body is *present* in the Eucharist is itself problematic. Christ's body, after all, includes flesh, organs, bones, and so on; and it is much bigger than the consecrated bread on the altar. Furthermore, does talk of Christ's body being present entail that his *blood* is, or his *soul*, or—perhaps more importantly still—his *divinity*?

Aquinas develops a doctrine to answer all of these questions: the doctrine of 'concomitance'. Aquinas argues that Christ's body and all of its natural parts are really present; but that its quantity is present only concomitantly, "after the manner of substance," and not as it would be naturally. Aquinas understands this to mean that the various parts of Christ's body are not *distant* from each other.[65] We could think of Aquinas as holding that there is breakdown in the spatial relations between the various parts of Christ's body.[66]

Being present "concomitantly" seems to have another, more basic, meaning, too, for Aquinas. The Eucharistic change in itself is just from bread/wine to body/blood. So, in itself, only the body and blood come to be present properly in virtue of the change. But those things that are joined to the body come to be present concomitantly (i.e., as a natural result of the change to Christ's body/blood). As well as quantity, this includes Christ's soul and his divinity.[67] Equally, Christ's blood is concomitantly included in his body, and his body concomitantly in his blood.[68]

Scotus believes that Christ's body cannot be present in the way Aquinas describes. Scotus holds that it is a necessary feature of a body that it is physically extended. Specifically, he holds that the parts of a human body must be distant from each other if that body is to be the sort of body that could be the subject of an intellectual soul.[69] Equally, Scotus does not see how the fact of Christ's body coming to be present could in itself entail that Christ's body lacks any of its intrinsic natural properties—such as its spatial extension.[70]

Scotus argues instead that the body of Christ present on the altar includes its proper extension, and has organs that are spatially distant from each other. But Scotus argues that there is a breakdown in the relation between the different parts of Christ's body and the parts of the place that contains this body. Each part of Christ's Eucharistic body is spatially distant from all other parts of this body, and the whole of this body is spatially related to the whole of the place that contains it; but there are no spatial relations between the *parts* of Christ's body and the *parts* of the place that contains it. Rather, the whole body is present to each part of its place.[71]

One obvious objection to any doctrine of real presence is that Christ's body seems to be present in the same place as the bread, or at least the same place as the accidents of the bread. Scotus, as we might expect, does not believe that this dual presence offers any real difficulties. Being the place of a body—containing this body—is an extrinsic relational property, and such relations can be multiplied, allowing one place to contain two bodies.[72]

Scotus believes, then, that the quantity of Christ's body is present naturally, not merely concomitantly. But he agrees with Aquinas's claim that Christ's soul and blood are present with the body only concomitantly. Even though Christ's soul and blood are not the proper end term of the conversion from bread to body, nevertheless they are automatically present wherever Christ's living body is. Their presence is thus concomitant upon the presence of the body.[73]

The Eucharistic sacrifice

The Reformers were greatly exercised by the medieval doctrine of the Eucharistic sacrifice, believing that it derogated from the sufficiency of Christ's "one oblation of himself once offered" on Calvary. The Council of Trent, however, usefully clarified the Catholic view. In the Eucharist, Christ offers himself by means of the ministry of his priests, making the sacrifice of Calvary present again.[74] Central to both Tridentine and Reformed views is the notion of *anamnesis*: the Eucharist *recalls* Christ's offering on Calvary, either—on the Catholic view—by making that sacrifice somehow present, or—on the Protestant view—by reminding the assembled congregation of Christ's salvific work.

Scotus accepts the Catholic view that the Eucharistic offering makes Christ's offering on Calvary present—it "represents" it.[75] The merits of the Eucharist are given "through the passion."[76] And Scotus claims that Christ somehow offers himself in the Eucharist.[77] Scotus does not spell out this last claim. But there are clear indications that he would want to reject the obvious possible sense: that Christ offers himself in the Eucharist using the priest as his instrument. Scotus is quite clear that the priest— or at any rate the Church—does not have any sort of *instrumental* role in sacrifice of Christ's body in the mass; the Church is rather the *principal agent* offering the Eucharistic sacrifice.[78] And elsewhere Scotus puzzlingly argues on scriptural grounds that there is no obvious sense in which Christ sacrifices himself in the Eucharist.[79]

In fact, Scotus is clear that there is a real sacrifice in the Mass that is *distinct* from the sacrifice of Calvary. So his view seems dangerously close to the view of the Eucharistic sacrifice later rejected by both Protestants and Catholics alike. He argues that, in the Eucharist, the Church offers Christ's body and blood to God.[80] By making this offering, the Church gains merit for its members.[81] On Scotus's, view, then, not only is the Eucharistic sacrifice distinct from Christ's sacrifice on Calvary, it is offered not by Christ but by the Church. Presumably, the sorts of causal powers involved in offering Christ's body and blood to God are not supernatural, because, as we have seen, none of the causal powers of a creature can be supernatural. Scotus must be assuming that the Church has some sort of natural active causal power in virtue of which its priests can offer Christ's body and blood, and that this power can be delegated to the priest. (Scotus claims that the priest is the 'organ' of the Church.)[82] Doubtless, Scotus would want to see that power as related in some way to the priest's power for being an occasion of divine sacramental activity, but he does not discuss this and I do not know what further speculation to offer about it.

APPENDIX

As we saw in chapters 2 and 3 above, Scotus's account of God's existence and nature makes a great deal of use of his theory of the transcendentals. This theory, at least as manifested in Scotus's account of God's simplicity, is itself bound up with his famous formal distinction, a distinction that Scotus uses frequently in his accounts of both God and humanity. In this appendix, I want to look very briefly at these two distinctive Scotist doctrines, along with a third that is central in Scotus's account of human freedom: Scotus's compatibilist insight that the possession of a free causal power is sufficient for freedom, even in the absence of any opportunity to exercise this causal power. Scotus discusses this insight when discussing how it is that Jesus and the saints, enjoying the beatific vision, are both free and impeccable.

1. Metaphysics and the transcendental attributes

Scotus holds that there are a number of facts about God that we can know without revelation. The specific philosophical discipline that Scotus holds to be responsible for proving these facts about God is *metaphysics*. Metaphysics, for Scotus, is the study of what he labels the 'transcendentals':[1]

those of a thing's attributes that transcend the classification of predicates proposed by Aristotle in the opening chapters of the *Categories*.[2] In *Categories*, Aristotle argues that all predicates are either substantial (i.e., essential: telling us about the *kind* of thing the subject is) or accidental (telling us about the non-essential attributes of the subject). Aristotle came to realize that this classification cannot be quite right. In his *Metaphysics*, Aristotle notes that 'being' and 'unity' are features of things that defy classification in the way outlined in the *Categories*.[3] The medievals were quick to pick up on this observation, and during the thirteenth century began tentatively to outline a theory of the 'transcendentals'.[4] Scotus extended the account of the transcendentals to include more than just those attributes that cannot fit into Aristotle's proposed taxonomy. For Scotus, the list of transcendentals includes not only the sorts of attributes just mentioned, but also those attributes that can be instantiated by that being (viz., God) that cannot itself be the subject of categorical attributes.[5] Metaphysics, according to Scotus, is the academic discipline whose subject is the transcendental attributes, specifically, 'being', of which the other transcendentals are in a sense properties.[6]

Being is the most basic transcendental attribute; there is a sense in which substances, accidents, and God all *exist*. Following standard medieval accounts, Scotus argues that there are certain other transcendental attributes that are *coextensive* with being: unity, truth, and goodness (i.e., desirability).[7] Possibly following a hint in Bonaventure,[8] Scotus notes that there are some non-categorical *disjunctive* attributes, again coextensive with being: necessary-or-contingent, actual-or-potential, infinite-or-finite, cause-or-caused, prior-or-posterior, independent-or-dependent, absolute-or-relative, a-goal–or–goal-directed, simple-or-composite, one-or-many, exceeding-or-exceeded, substance-or-accident, same-or-diverse, equal-or-unequal.[9] A final group of transcendental attributes are those 'pure perfections' that can be predicated of God—whether common to God and creatures or proper to God alone—and that have not been included in any of the first three groups. Common to God and creatures we would include, for example, knowledge, will, power; proper to God we would include, for example, omniscience and omnipotence.[10] As Scotus understands metaphysics, a correct elucidation of the transcendental attributes will allow us to infer God's existence. Proving the existence of God, then, is the *goal* of metaphysics,[11] and metaphysics for Scotus is fundamentally natural theology.[12]

2. The formal distinction

Scotus holds that there is a distinction mid-way between a real distinction and a merely rational or conceptual distinction. He calls it the 'formal distinction'. Roughly two realities—two aspects of one thing—are formally distinct if and only if they are both really identical and susceptible of definition independently of each other.[13] Scotus's criterion for real identity is real inseparability. In fact, real inseparability (such that the real separation of two or more realities is *logically impossible*) is *necessary and sufficient* for real identity.[14] Conversely, real separability is necessary and sufficient for real distinction. More precisely, two objects x and y are inseparable if and only if, both, it is not possible for x to exist without y, and it is not possible for y to exist without x; conversely, two objects x and y are separable if and only if at least one of x and y can exist without the other. On this showing two really identical but formally distinct realities will be something like distinct essential (i.e., inseparable) properties of a thing.

Scotus makes use of his formal distinction in his account of individuation. He argues that any individual created item (including a composite substance) can be analyzed into two really identical but formally distinct aspects: essence and individuating feature (or 'haecceity').[15] What this amounts to, roughly, is that any individual created item has two different essential properties: its nature or kind, and its individuating, non-repeatable, haecceity.

3. The beatific vision

After death, the saints whom God has predestined enjoy the vision of God in heaven. The medievals discerned both a cognitive and an appetitive aspect to this. The vision of the Trinity of persons is a cognitive act.[16] The enjoyment of these persons is appetitive.[17] Scotus spends some time debating—inconclusively—whether this enjoyment is an *act*—an act of love—or merely *passive*—the delight caused in us by something we like.[18]

According to Catholic doctrine, the saints in heaven enjoy the beatific vision for ever, such that they cannot lose this vision.[19] One way in which—if it were possible—the beatific vision would be lost would be if such a saint were to sin. So the saints in heaven must be impeccable. There is, however, an obvious objection to this. If the saints are impeccable, it looks as if they cannot be free. And freedom is a feature of human existence that we would probably be loath to lose. The schoolmen proposed a variety of solutions to this problem. Aquinas is happy to concede that we will not be free in heaven. It is central to Aquinas's action theory that our will responds automatically to whatever we perceive will make us happy. Sometimes, of course, we fail to see that God, who truly makes us happy, is the ultimate goal of our existence. So we sometimes fail to will true happiness for ourselves. But this is the result of an intellectual mistake. In the beatific vision, however, God shows himself directly to the will. So the problem of intellectual error is precluded, and we cling to God necessarily.[20] Our lack of freedom in heaven coincides exactly with the general contours of Aquinas's action theory.

Scotus believes Aquinas's account to be profoundly mistaken. The basis for this belief is Scotus's radically different account of the human will. According to Scotus, the will always has the power to will other than it does. This is just the sort of thing the will is.[21] A change in the external circumstances of the will (e.g., the presence of God) cannot alter the way the will acts.[22] Scotus claims instead that the will, in eliciting an act of love for God in the beatific vision, retains its power for refraining from eliciting this act.[23] God, however, removes the opportunity for the will to exercise this power. So while the will retains its power for sinning (by failing to love God), it cannot use this power because it lacks the opportunity to do so:

> A secondary cause, bringing about one opposite, can never, if prevented by a higher cause, by proximate power go to the other opposite.[24]

The will clings to God with firmness or steadfastness.[25]

Scotus does not believe that we *usually* lack the opportunity for exercising our freedom. But we do lack this opportunity in the beatific vision. Scotus's basic account of freedom is thus compatibilist: freedom and determinism—in the sense of 'determinism' just outlined—are compatible. This does not entail that all of our actions are determined. But it does mean that, even when they are determined, Scotus is happy to see them as free. Retaining the *power* for opposites—even without the opportunity for exercising this power—is sufficient for freedom.

Scotus's view of the beatific vision is open to a strong objection that he himself raises. How can we retain a power for refraining from loving

God if we cannot exercise this power? Is it really a power in this case at all? Douglas Langston summarizes Scotus's answer well:

> Scotus . . . claims that determination of an agent by an agent that is metaphysically superior does not infringe on the freedom of the lower agent. Only determination of an agent that is metaphysically inferior to the agent in question is contrary to the freedom of this agent.[26]

So Scotus claims that freedom is compatible with determinism only if the determining agent is "metaphysically superior." Langston notes:

> According to Scotus, part of what is meant by a metaphysically superior agent is that it is powerful enough to prevent the actions of an agent inferior to it. Thus, a metaphysically superior agent can determine the activity of an inferior agent by controlling the actions of an inferior agent. But on the other hand, a metaphysically inferior agent can determine a metaphysically superior agent only indirectly, by affecting the nature of the superior agent.[27]

So a metaphysically superior agent can affect the actions of an inferior agent without interfering with the inferior agent's nature—and thus without interfering with its causal powers. And this, according to Scotus, is how we explain the impeccability of the saints enjoying the beatific vision in heaven.

Scotus elsewhere claims that this sort of firmness or steadfastness in the will is a perfection.[28] We need to be careful about the claim that steadfastness is a perfection—a component of a perfect free act. Steadfastness is a perfection of a free act; but it is not an essential part of every free act.[29]

It is worth keeping in mind finally that what Scotus claims about the beatific vision is not (despite prima facie appearances to the contrary) inconsistent with his claim that the will cannot be coerced. As Scotus understands coercion, it entails that the cause of such an action is wholly outside the agent being coerced. Scotus notes, citing Aristotle, that in such cases "the person . . . contributes nothing."[30] Thus, the coerced action does not spring from the causal powers of the coerced agent. In the case of the beatific vision, however, the action does indeed spring from the causal powers of the agent; one whose opportunity to act otherwise is removed.

NOTES

1. See F. Bąk, "Scoti schola numerosior est omnibus aliis simul sumptis," *Franciscan Studies*, 16 (1956): 144–65.

2. In the discussion that follows I rely on C. K. Brampton, "Duns Scotus at Oxford, 1288–1301," *Franciscan Studies*, 24 (1964), 5–20; Allan B. Wolter, "Reflections on the Life and Works of Scotus," *American Catholic Philosophical Quarterly*, 67 (1993): 1–36; Wolter, "Duns Scotus at Oxford," in Leonardo Sileo (ed.), *Via Scoti: Methodologica ad mentem Joannis Duns Scoti*, Atti del Congresso Scotistico Internazionale, Roma, 9–11 Marzo 1993, 2 vols. (Rome: Antonianum, 1995), 1:183–91; and Wolter, "Reflections about Scotus's Early Works," in Ludger Honnefelder, Rega Wood, and Mechthild Dreyer (eds.), *John Duns Scotus: Metaphysics and Ethics*, STGM, 53 (Leiden, New York, and Cologne: E. J. Brill, 1996), 37–57. For a useful summary, see also C. Balić, "Life and Works of Duns Scotus," in John K. Ryan and Bernardine Bonansea (eds.), *John Duns Scotus, 1265–1965*, Studies in Philosophy and the History of Philosophy, 3 (Washington, D. C.: Catholic University of America Press, 1965), 1–27. A different version of events can be found in William J. Courtenay, "Scotus at Paris," in Sileo (ed.), *Via Scoti*, 1:149–64.

3. John Major, *Historia Maioris Britanniae tam Angliae tam Scotiae* 4.16 (Paris, 1521), p. 74ʳ.

4. Duns Scotus, *Ord.* 1.4.1.un., n. 1 (*Opera Omnia*, ed. C Balić and others [Vatican City: Typis Polyglottis Vaticanis, 1950–], 4:1) [= Vatican].

5. Among these we should include (in addition to Henry) Giles of Rome (c. 1243/7–1316), Godfrey of Fontaines (1250–1306/9), and William of Ware (fl. 1290).

6. Literature on Scotus's theology is fairly sparse. In the chapters that follow, I indicate specialized monographs that should be consulted by those who want more detailed discussion of the theological issues treated here. But there are at least four general discussions that focus on Scotus's theology. Still useful on Scotus's theology is Reinhold Seeberg's groundbreaking study, *Die Theologie des Johannes Duns Scotus: Eine dogmengeschichtliche Untersuchung*, Studien zur Geschichte der Theologie und der Kirche, 5 (Leipzig: Dieterich'sche Verlags-Buchhandlung, 1900). Very basic introductions to Scotus's theology can be found in Léon Veuthey, *Jean Duns Scot: pensée théologique* (Paris: Éditions Franciscaines, 1967), and Mary Elizabeth Ingham, "John Duns Scotus: An Integrated Vision," in Kenan B. Osborne (ed.), *The History of Franciscan Theology* (St. Bonaventure, N. Y.: The Franciscan Institute, 1994), 185–230.

Most important is the recent work by Antonie Vos Jaczn., *Johannes Duns Scotus*, Kerkhistorische Monografieën (Leiden: J. J. Groen en Zoon, 1994). Vos argues that the driving force behind Scotus's theology is an attempt to spell out the implications of what Vos takes to be Scotus's central insight: the notion of synchronic contingency. (On this issue, see chapter 4, section 3, below.) My own presentation of Scotus's thought is more conventional. Part of my reason for this is that I judge Scotus's basic insights on the relation between philosophy and theology to be similar to those of Aquinas. (It thus makes good sense to begin with metaphysics and conclude with theology.) I argue for this claim in the later sections of this chapter. But there is a clear precedent for my approach in Scotus's own writings. As he makes clear, his metaphysical proof for God's existence found classically in his treatise *De Primo Principio* was intended by him to be the first part of a bipartite work, the second part of which was to be on theology: "In this first treatise I have tried to show how the metaphysical attributes affirmed of you can be inferred in some way by natural reason. In the treatise which follows, those shall be set forth that are the subject of belief, wherein reason is held captive—yet to Catholics, the latter are more certain since they rest firmly on your most solid truth and not upon our intellect which is blind and weak in many things" (Duns Scotus, *DPP* 4.86 [ed. and trans. Allan B. Wolter (Chicago: Franciscan Herald Press, 1982), p. 146]; on the bipartite nature of these two works, see Wolter's introduction to his edition, pp. xiii–xiv). Secondly, it seems to me far from clear that Vos has made his case. Synchronic contingency is an important Scotist insight, but it is one of many that drive Scotus's theology. It seems to me that a strong case could be made, for example, for seeing Scotus's theological project as in part an attempt to spell out the implications of God's being wholly unconditioned, that is, such that nothing in him can be caused by anything external. God's unconditioned nature is, of course, a commonplace of scholastic debates. But even the notion of synchronic contingency merely spells out claims that must be held implicitly by anyone who believes a timeless God can act freely. Scotus invented the terminology of logical possibility and its cognates; but he can scarcely be held to have invented the notion. (For some of the literature on this, see chapter 4, below, for the notion of logical possibility see, e.g., Aquinas, *ST* 1.25.3 [ed. Petrus Caramello, 3 vols. (Turin and Rome: Marietti, 1952–56), 1(1):140^b]: "Something is called possible or impossible absolutely, from the relation of the terms: possible, because the predicate is not incompatible with the subject, as for Socrates to sit; impossible absolutely, because the predicate is incompatible with the subject, as for a human being to be an ass.")

7. Duns Scotus, *Lect.*, Vatican, vols. 16–19.

8. See *Ord.* prol.2.un., n. 112 (Vatican, 1:77), where Scotus mentions this date as present. Book 1 and book 2 distinctions 1–3 are in Vatican, vols. 1–7; the rest of book 2 and books 3–4 are in Scotus, *Opera Omnia*, ed. Luke Wadding, 12 vols. (Lyons: Durand, 1639), vols. 6–10 [= Wadding]. Where convenient I check the Wadding text against MS Assisi, Biblioteca Communale, MS 137 [= MS A], the base text used by the Vatican editors for books 1, 3, and 4. An *Ordinatio* is a version of a work edited and finalized for publication by the author.

9. Books 2–4 of the *Reportatio* can be found in Wadding, vol. 11; for book 1 (which has never been printed) I use MS Vienna, Österreichische Nationalbibliothek, MS 1453 [= MS V].

10. This is published as book 1 of the *Reportatio* in Wadding, vol. 11.

11. An uncritical Latin text can be found in Wadding, vol. 12.

12. See Wolter's edition of *DPP*, pp. ix–xiii.

13. Duns Scotus, *In Metaph.*, Wadding, vol. 4. The new critical edition of Scotus's *Metaphysics* questions, recently published by the Franciscan Institute at St. Bonaventure University, appeared too late for me to be able to use it here.

14. See Wadding, vol. 1, for Scotus's questions on Aristotle's *Cat.*, *Int.*, (= Scotus, *Super Praed.*), and *Soph. el.*; see Wadding, vol. 2, for his questions on *De an.*

15. See Stephen D. Dumont, "The Question on Individuation in Scotus's 'Quaestiones super Metaphysicam,'" in Sileo (ed.), *Via Scoti*, 1:193–227; also Timothy B. Noone, "Scotus's Critique of the Thomistic Theory of Individuation and the Dating of the 'Quaestiones in Libros Metaphysicorum,' VII q. 13," in Sileo (ed.), *Via Scoti*, 1:394–96. Allan B. Wolter notes, on the

basis of the work done by Dumont and Noone, that book 7 of the *Metaphysics* questions dates between book 2 of the *Ordinatio* and book 2 of the *Reportatio*; see his "Reflections about Scotus's Early Works," 52. I have argued elsewhere that book 5 of the *Metaphysics* questions should be dated before the *Lectura*, and thus that at least books 1 to 5 of *Metaphysics* should be given an early date (see my *The Physics of Duns Scotus: The Scientific Context of a Theological Vision* [Oxford: Clarendon Press, 1998], chapter 13).

16. The object of *theologia in se* is principally the divine essence (*Ord.* prol.3.1–3, n. 154 [Vatican, 1:102–103]). But since the divine essence in some sense includes all of God's knowledge, God's theology extends to everything that he knows (*Ord.* prol.3.1–3, nn. 200–201 [Vatican, 1:135–36]).

17. *Ord.* prol.3.1–3, n. 141 (1:95–96).

18. *Ord.* prol.3.1–3, nn. 151, 167–68, 170–71 (Vatican, 1:102, 109–114).

19. *Ord.* 1.3.1.1–2, nn. 56–57 (Vatican, 3:38–39 = *PW*, pp. 25–26).

20. Note that these attempts will appeal only to someone who accepts Christian revelation; they will not be sufficient to prove the need for theology to someone who does not accept revelation. I examine Scotus's discussion of the possibility of a proof for our need of theology in section 4 of this chapter.

21. Duns Scotus, *Quod.* 14, n. 9 (Wadding, 12:356 = AW, p. 323 [n. 14.34]). In *Quod.* 8, Scotus attempts to prove by natural reason that the three persons of the Trinity must always act as *one* causal principle; see *Quod.* 8, nn. 6, 21 (Wadding, 12:205–206, 216 = AW, p. 201 [n. 8.10], pp. 212–13 [nn. 8.41–43]). Interestingly, Scotus elsewhere is happier with the thought that there might be some convincing considerations in favor of God's Trinitarian nature, arguing in *Lect.* 1.2.2.1–4, n. 165 (Vatican, 16:167) that these considerations are "perhaps more demonstrative than many demonstrations posited in metaphysics are." Later, Scotus is for theological reasons more reluctant to allow any demonstrative force to the arguments (see *Ord.* 1.2.2.1–4, nn. 242, 252 [Vatican, 2:274, 277], also, puzzlingly, *Lect.* 1.2.2.1–4, n. 185 [Vatican, 16:175]). In *Ord.* 1.42.un., n. 16 (Vatican, 6:246–47), Scotus notes that his arguments in favor of the Trinity fail because their premises are not known by us to be true. For the arguments themselves, see, for example, *Ord.* 1.2.2.1–4, nn. 221–22, 226, 238–39, 301–302 (Vatican, 259–60, 263, 270–72, 305–308); also *Quod.* 2, n. 25 (Wadding, 12:59–60 = AW, p. 54 [n. 2.78]).

22. *Quod.* 14, n. 16 (Wadding, 12:377 = AW, p. 332 [n. 14.63]). I discuss some related claims in chapter 4, below.

23. For the medieval debate on the Bible as the source for revealed doctrine, see Paul de Vooght, *Les sources da la doctrine chrétienne d'après les théologiens du XIVᵉ siècle et du début du XVᵉ avec le texte intégrale des XII premières questions de la Summa inédite de Gérard de Bologne († 1317)* (Paris: Desclée de Brouwer, 1954).

24. *Ord.* prol.2.un., n. 123 (Vatican, 1:87); *Ord.* prol.3.1–3, nn. 204, 207 (Vatican, 1:137–38, 140).

25. *Ord.* 1.11.1, n. 20 (Vatican, 5:7–8).

26. See *Ord.* 4.6.9, n. 14 (Wadding, 8:344) for character; *Ord.* 4.11.3, n. 13 (Wadding, 8:616–17) for transubstantiation. (On these, see chapter 11, below.) For a discussion of Scotus's "two-source" theory of revelation, see Josef Finkenzeller, *Offenbarung und Theologie nach der Lehre des Johannes Duns Scotus: eine historische und systematische Untersuchung*, BGPTM, 38(5) (Münster: Aschendorff, 1961), parts 2 and 3.

27. *Ord.* prol.3.1–3, n. 205 (Vatican, 1:138); *Ord.* 3.24.un., n. 7 (Wadding, 7:480); *Ord.* 4.9.6, n. 13 (Wadding, 8:343); see also, for example, *Sum. Fr. Alex.* 1.2.3 c (4 vols. [Quaracchi: Collegium Sancti Bonaventurae, 1924–48], 1:33^b); Aquinas, *ST* 2-2.1.4 c (2:6^b), *ST* 2-2.1.5 c (2:7^b); Henry of Ghent, *SQ* 6.1 (2 vols. [Paris, 1520], 1:42^{v}B).

28. *Ord.* prol.4.1–2, n. 214 (Vatican, 1:146–47). This text is specifically about *theologia in se*; but I take it that a fortiori its claim is true of *theologia nostra* too. We do, of course, use claims from other sciences in forming and understanding theological conclusions; see, for example, *Ord.* 3.24.un., n. 16 (Wadding, 7:484). For theology as the science of things believed (*credita*), see *Ord.* 3.24.un., n. 4 (Wadding, 7:478–79).

29. Aquinas makes much the same point when he speaks of the things that we can know about God by natural reason as "preambles to the articles [of faith]": *ST* 1.2.2 ad 1 (1[1]:11^b). On the methodological priority of metaphysics over theology in Scotus, see note 6 to this chapter.

30. Metaphysics studies the so-called transcendentals, and by means of this study allows us to infer God's existence. I discuss the subject and object of metaphysics in the Appendix, section 1.

31. On these claims, see chapter 6, below.

32. Scotus is happy to assert that *theologia in se* is a science, as is the theology of the blessed in heaven. *Ord.* prol.4.1–2, nn. 208–212 (Vatican, 1:141–46). For an implicit assertion that *theologia nostra* is a science, see *Ord.* prol.5.1–2, nn. 314, 332 (Vatican, 1:207–208, 217). Elsewhere, for a reason that I make clear in the next note, Scotus claims that the only scientific human theology is that of the prophets and apostles, the direct recipients of revelation (*Ord.* 3.24.un., n. 17 [Wadding, 7:485]; see also *Quod.* 7, n. 10 (Wadding, 12:174 = AW, p. 169, [n. 7.27]). For a discussion of this issue, referring to the prologues to *Reportatio* and *Additiones Magnae*, see Stephen Dumont, "Theology as a Practical Science and Duns Scotus's Distinction between Intuitive and Abstractive Cognition," *Speculum*, 64 (1989): 579–99. Basically, the idea is that God gives to the recipient of revelation some sort of abstractive knowledge of his (i.e., God's) essence. (Someone enjoying the

beatific vision has an intuitive understanding of the divine essence. On the distinction between intuitive and abstractive knowledge, see chapter 4, section 2, below.) Claiming that God's theology—*theologia in se*—is a science makes a stronger claim for the scientific nature of theology than can be found in any other medieval thinker. Scotus believes that theological truths are *intrinsically* ordered as a set of scientific propositions. This order does not extend merely to the way we discover theological truths. Certain theological claims are genuinely explanatory of others, even in God's understanding of things. On the scientific nature of theology for Scotus, see, in addition to Dumont, "Theology as a Practical Science," Finkenzeller, *Offenbarung und Theologie*, part 6; Aegidius Magrini, *Ioannis Duns Scoti doctrina de scientifica theologiae natura*, Studia Antoniana, 5 (Rome: Antonianum, 1952); Stephen F. Brown, "Scotus's Method in Theology," in Sileo (ed.), *Via Scoti*, 1:229–43. For Aquinas's claim that theology is a science, see John I. Jenkins, *Knowledge and Faith in Thomas Aquinas* (Cambridge: Cambridge University Press, 1997).

33. *Ord.* prol.4.1–2, n. 208 (Vatican, 1:141–42), referring to Aristotle, *An. post.* 1.2 (71ᵇ9–12). See also *Ord.* 3.24.un., n. 13 (Wadding, 7:482–83), where Scotus lists, in addition to the requirement that a science be deductive, three Aristotelian criteria that must be satisfied by the axioms of a science: (i) certainty, (ii) necessity, (iii) (self-)evidence. He notes that even the "scientific" theology of the prophets and apostles (which does satisfy [i] and [ii]), fails to satisfy the last of these (*Ord.* 3.24.un., n. 17 [Wadding, 7:485]), and that this scientific theology cannot include contingent theological facts on the grounds that the necessity of its claims is a necessary feature of a science (*Quod.* 7, n. 10 [Wadding, 12:174 = AW, p. 169 (n. 7.27)]).

34. For the distinction, see Aristotle, *Eth. Nic.* 6.1 (1139ᵃ11–15).

35. *ST* 1.1.4 c (1[1]:4ᵇ). Scotus discusses a series of views similar to Aquinas's in *Ord.* prol.5.1–2, nn. 270–302 (Vatican, 1:183–99). These views defend the claim that theology is purely theoretical. Aquinas's view, that it is theoretical with practical elements, is mentioned by Scotus in *Ord.* prol.5.1–2, n. 313 (Vatican, 1:206).

36. The claim that theology is an affective science is associated with the Dominican Albert the Great, the Franciscans Gonsalvus of Spain and Bonaventure, and the Augustinian Giles of Rome (see Scotus, *Ord.* prol.5.1–2, n. 303 [1:200]); the claim that it is contemplative is associated with the Franciscan William of Ware (see Scotus, *Ord.* prol.5.1–2, n. 304 [1:200–201]).

37. *Lect.* prol.4.1–2, n. 164 (Vatican, 16:54 = *WM*, p. 137); *Ord.* prol.5.1–2, n. 227 (Vatican, 1:154).

38. *Lect.* prol.4.1–2, n. 133 (Vatican, 16:47 = *WM*, p. 127); *Ord.* prol.5.1–2, n. 228 (Vatican, 1:155).

39. *Lect*. prol.4.1–2, n. 164 (Vatican, 16:54 = *WM*, p. 137); *Ord*. prol.5.1–2, nn. 314, 332 (Vatican, 1:207–208, 217).

40. *Lect*. prol.4.1–2, n. 163 (Vatican, 16:54 = *WM*, p. 137); *Ord*. prol.5.1–2, n. 310 (Vatican, 1:204–205).

41. *Lect*. prol.4.1–2, n. 164 (Vatican, 16:54 = *WM*, p. 137); *Ord*. prol.5.1–2, nn. 236–37 (Vatican, 1:161–62).

42. This claim might make it look as though every science is practical on Scotus's account. "The heavens declare the glory of God" (Ps. 19.1), so we might think that the religiously minded astronomer could be led by his or her studies to a greater love for God. But I do not think that this would be quite the right reading of Scotus here. Presumably, what distinguishes theology from, say, astronomy, is that the subject of theology is God; and, as we shall see in chapter 7, below, the only necessary ethical precepts are those that oblige us to act in certain ways towards God (e.g., to love him). On metaphysics as a theoretical (and not a practical) science: see *Ord*. prol.5.1–2, n. 352 (1:228). For a challenging attempt to fit Scotus's insight about theology into the history of ideas, see Nicholas Lobkowicz, *Theory and Practice: The History of a Concept from Aristotle to Marx* (Notre Dame: University of Notre Dame Press, 1967), 71–74. Lobkowicz argues that Scotus's insight "anticipates . . . the notion that man's ultimate achievement is practice, not theory" (p. 74). But I think that we should keep in mind that 'praxis', for Scotus, does not refer to *atheoretical* practice in the same sort of sense we might find in Marx. Just as for Aquinas, so for Scotus, properly human action cannot take place without intellectual knowledge of practical truths.

43. See, for example, William of Ockham, *Quod. Sept.* 2.3 ad 3 (*OT*, 9:119–20 = FK, 1:103), where Ockham argues that the doctrine of the Trinity appears philosophically incoherent. For Aquinas's opposite claim, that theology can never be philosophically incoherent, see *ST* 1.1.8 c (1[1]:7ᵇ).

44. *Ord*. prol.1.un., n. 5 (Vatican, 1:4 = *WFS*, p. 242).

45. Aquinas is perhaps the clearest adherent of this view; see *ST* 1.1.1 c (1[1]:2ᵇ).

46. *Ord*. prol.1.un., n. 5 (Vatican, 1:5 = *WFS*, p. 242).

47. *Ord*. prol.1.un., nn. 54–55 (Vatican, 1:32–34 = *WFS*, pp. 257–59); see also *Ord*. prol.2.un., n. 120 (Vatican, 1:85). Bonaventure is a good example of someone who also prima facie accepts this claim; see Bonaventure, *Comm. Sent.* 3.25.1.2 arg. 6 and ad 6 (*Opera Omnia*, 10 vols. [Quaracchi: Collegium Sancti Bonaventurae, 1882–1902], 3:540ᵃ, 541ᵇ).

48. *Ord*. prol.1.un., n. 12 (Vatican, 1:9 = *WFS*, p. 244).

49. William E. Mann, "Duns Scotus, Demonstration, and Doctrine," *Faith and Philosophy*, 9 (1992): 437. Mann argues that this position, which

appears in a marginal note in MS A, is most likely to represent Scotus's own opinion on the matter.

50. *Ord*. prol.1.un., n. 71 (Vatican, 1:43 = *WFS*, p. 264). Mann argues against this reading that the prima facie sense of the first of the arguments that Scotus gives against the philosophers—according to which we can *show* that natural reason is not sufficient to reveal whether our ultimate goal can be attained naturally (*Ord*. prol.1.un., nn. 13–16 [Vatican, 1:9–11])—is misleading, and that when read correctly it is consistent with the agnostic marginal annotation (Mann, "Duns Scotus, Demonstration, and Doctrine," 451–62). Mann might be right, of course, in suggesting that Scotus never successfully demonstrates the claim that I am labeling his "second answer."

51. *Ord*. prol.2.un., nn. 101–119 (Vatican, 1:61–85). Scotus derives his knowledge of the Sibylline Oracle from Augustine, *De Civ. Dei* 18.23 (CCSL, 48:613–15).

52. *Ord*. prol.2.un., n. 110 (Vatican, 1:61).

53. See my *The Physics of Duns Scotus*, especially chapter 1, where I argue this point in the case of Scotus's natural philosophy. But it seems to me to be unequivocally true of all of Scotus's philosophical endeavors.

CHAPTER 2

1. I discuss the nature and goal of metaphysics in the Appendix, section 1.

2. Although Aquinas allows himself to claim "And this all call God" (or something like this claim) at the conclusion of each of his five proofs for God's existence in the *Summa Theologiae*, it is clear that this claim is wholly inessential to the overall structure of his argument, which is first to prove the existence of something prior to everything else in certain respects, and then to argue that the relevant kinds of priority entail certain (divine) attributes. See *ST* 1.2.3 (1[1]:12[a]–13[b]) for the proofs, and questions 3–26 (1[1]:14[a]–146[b]) for the attributes.

3. See *Lect*. 1.2.1, nn. 38–135 (Vatican, 16:124–57); *Ord*. 1.2.1, nn. 39–190 (Vatican, 2:148–243 = *PW*, pp. 35–95); *Rep*. 1.2.1 (WA, pp. 253–321 = FW, pp. 41–73); *DPP* (pp. 2–150). In the following discussion, I do not discuss Scotus's early *Lectura* account. The differences between the various versions, though interesting, are not really all that important. Later versions merely offer refinements to an argument whose basic contours remain unchanged. For useful introductory discussions of Scotus's argument, see Rega Wood, "Scotus's Argument for the Existence of God," *Franciscan Studies*, 47 (1987): 257–77; William Lane Craig, *The Cosmological Argument from Plato to Leibniz*, Library of Philosophy and Religion (London and Basingstoke:

Macmillan, 1980), chapter 5; and Allan B. Wolter, "Duns Scotus on the Existence and Nature of God," *Proceedings of the American Catholic Philosophical Association*, 28 (1954): 94–121, reprinted in Wolter, *The Philosophical Theology of John Duns Scotus*, ed. Marilyn McCord Adams (Ithaca, N.Y., and London: Cornell University Press, 1990), 254–77.

4. In so describing efficient causation, I do not intend Scotus to be committed to the claim that causal chains might not be complex, each effect being brought about immediately by a number of different jointly sufficient causes. Equally, it is important to bear in mind that Scotus understands *every* cause to have causal powers, and to be (in this sense) an agent. Agency, for Scotus, applies to many more substances than we might be inclined to assume.

5. For both examples, see Aquinas, *ST* 1.46.2 ad 7 (1[1]:238$^{a–b}$); see also Scotus, *Ord.* 1.3.3.2, n. 496 (Vatican, 3:293–94).

6. *DPP* 3.11 (p. 46); see also *Ord.* 1.2.1.1–2, nn. 48–51 (Vatican, 2:154–55 = *PW*, pp. 40–41); *Rep.* 1.2.1.1–2, nn. 17–20 (WA, pp. 261–63 = FW, pp. 45–47).

7. For a more detailed account of an E-series, see Patterson Brown, "Infinite Causal Regression," *Philosophical Review*, 75 (1966): 510–25, reprinted in Anthony Kenny (ed.), *Aquinas: A Collection of Critical Essays*, Modern Studies in Philosophy (London and Melbourne: Macmillan, 1969), 214–36. On this account, x's causal action is not *causally* sufficient for z's being G. For z to be G, after all, there is required the causal action of y (even if this causal action is just the result of x's action). (I discuss the nature of such essentially ordered causes in chapter 4, below. Roughly, an item is a member of such a series only if it uses its own causal powers in bringing about an effect.) But z's being G is *logically* entailed by x's bringing about its effect. For a useful account of E-series in Scotus, see William A. Frank, "Duns Scotus on Autonomous Freedom and Divine Co-Causality," *Medieval Philosophy and Theology*, 2 (1992): 153–56; see also the literature cited therein on page 153.

8. On this account, x's action is neither causally nor logically sufficient (in the sense just given) for z.

9. *Rep.* 1.2.1.1–2, n. 12 (WA, p. 259 = FW, p. 43); *DPP* 3.6 (p. 42); see *Ord.* 1.2.1.1–2, n. 43 (Vatican, 2:151 = *PW*, p. 39).

10. *Ord.* 1.2.1.1–2, n. 43 (Vatican, 2:151–52 = *PW*, p. 39); see also *Rep.* 1.2.1.1–2, n. 12 (WA, 259 = FW, p. 43); *DPP* 3.8 (p. 44).

11. *Rep.* 1.2.1.1–2, n. 21 (WA, p. 263 = FW, p. 47); see *Ord.* 1.2.1.1–2, n. 53 (Vatican, 2:157 = *PW*, p. 41).

12. We might be inclined to argue that, if there were no first cause to an E-series, we could not find the *real* cause of any effect. (For the argument, see Brown, "Infinite Causal Regression," 522 [232 in the reprint].) Richard

Swinburne notes that this argument falls victim to what he labels the 'completist fallacy': if y causes z, then it really does explain the existence of z, even if y itself requires explanation. For the fallacy, see his *The Existence of God*, 2nd ed. (Oxford: Clarendon Press, 1991), 73; for its application to E-series, see Swinburne, *The Existence of God*, 89. Scotus's argument is made more complicated by his claim that even if *per impossibile* there were an infinite series of causes, each one would have to depend on some first cause that was *outside* the series; *Ord.* 1.2.1.1–2, n. 53 (Vatican, 2:157 = *PW*, pp. 41–42); *Rep.* 1.2.1.1–2, n. 21 (WA, p. 263 = FW, p. 47); *DPP* 3.13 (p. 46). But this just blurs the distinction between an E-series and an A-series. On Scotus's initial definitions, an E-series will be self-sufficient; it will not depend on any cause outside itself.

13. *Rep.* 1.2.1.1–2, n. 27 (WA, pp. 265–67 = FW, p. 49); see *Ord.* 1.2.1.1–2, n. 54 (Vatican, 2:159–60 = *PW*, p. 43); *DPP* 3.14 (p. 48). Since an A-series (unlike an E-series) can be temporally extended (by the third property of an E-series), Scotus like Aquinas would prima facie have no difficulty allowing for the logical possibility of an everlasting universe with no beginning in time. His opinion here will thus be diametrically opposed to that of his great Franciscan predecessor Bonaventure. (For Bonaventure's opinion, see *Comm. Sent.* 2.1.1.1.2 [*Opera Omnia*, 2:20b–22a]; for that of Aquinas, see *ST* 1.46.2 [1(1):237a–38b].) In fact, however, Scotus is not quite as sanguine as Aquinas with regard to the possibility of a backwardly everlasting universe. When giving his *ex professo* treatment of the topic, Scotus gives the two opposing views—those of Bonaventure and Aquinas—and notes three reasons why Aquinas's is a stronger view; see *Ord.* 2.1.3, n. 154 (Vatican, 7:77). Furthermore, Scotus is quite clear that there is no distinction between creation and conservation. So he ought to be able to offer unequivocal support for Aquinas against Bonaventure. Basically, he argues—like Aquinas—that creation and conservation are best understood *relationally;* every creature "equally and always depends essentially on God"; 'creation' refers to God's causal activity in the first temporal instant of a creature's existence, and 'conservation' refers to the same causal activity at any later instant in the creature's existence. (See *Ord.* 2.2.1.1, n. 63 [Vatican, 7:184], referred to in *Ord.* 2.1.3, n. 156 [Vatican, 7:78].)

14. *Rep.* 1.2.1.1–2, n. 28 (WA, p. 267 = FW, pp. 49–51); see *Ord.* 1.2.1.1–2, n. 56 (Vatican, 2:161 = *PW*, p. 44).

15. *An. post.* 1.5 (74b5–39).

16. It is difficult to see why Scotus should be worried about satisfying the strict account of demonstration, since even his revised formulation fails to satisfy another of Aristotle's criteria for a strict demonstration: namely, that the premises should be a sufficient *causal* explanation of the conclusion.

For the criterion, see *An. post.* 1.13 (78^a22–$^b23$). The idea here is that the existence of effects does not in any way explain God's existence.

17. *Ord.* 1.2.1.1–2, n. 56 (Vatican, 2:161–62 = *PW*, p. 44);*Rep.* 1.2.1.1–2, n. 28 (WA, p. 267 = FW, p. 51); *DPP* 3.5 (p. 42).

18. *Ord.* 1.2.1.1–2, n. 56 (Vatican, 2:162 = *PW*, p. 44); *Rep.* 1.2.1.1–2, n. 28 (WA, p. 267 = FW, p. 51); *DPP* 3.5 (p. 42).

19. *Ord.* 1.2.1.1–2, n. 56 (Vatican, 2:162 = *PW*, p. 45); *DPP* 3.7 (p. 44). Logically, the impossibility of an infinite E-series, although sufficient for (3), is certainly not necessary for it. Below, I describe a further Scotist argument that does not invoke this impossibility. Scotus mistakenly expresses the argument from (1) to (3) using *de re* modalities. Thus, his premise is "Something can be caused," and his conclusion is "Something can be a first agent." But he clearly intends the *de dicto* way of putting the argument, as I have expressed it here. Unlike (1), "Something can be caused" is not a logically necessary truth—and Scotus's professed aim in formulating the modal version of his argument is to satisfy the Aristotelian necessity criterion. In fact, Scotus expressly notes that "Something can be a first agent" claims no more than possible existence for a first agent—that is, that the modality is *de dicto*, equivalent to my (3). As we shall see in a moment, he provides an argument to get from (3) to the stronger, factual, *de re* claim. Equally, the *de re* way of expressing the argument is clearly invalid.

20. For the premise, see *Ord.* 1.2.1.1–2, n. 58 (Vatican, 2:164 = *PW*, p. 46);*Rep.* 1.2.1.1–2, n. 29 (WA, p. 269 = FW, p. 51);*DPP* 3.19 (p. 52). Scotus again phrases (4) misleadingly in terms of *de re* modality: thus, "Anything to whose nature it is repugnant to receive existence from something else, can exist of itself if it can exist at all." Understanding "exist of itself" to entail necessary existence, and expressing the modalities as *de dicto*, this yields "If it is possible that something is an essentially uncaused being, then it is possibly necessary that something is an uncaused being"; but given that the relevant sort of necessity is logical necessity, "possibly necessary" is equivalent to "necessary." And this yields (4). I owe the observation that Scotus's argument does not presuppose standard versions of the principle of sufficient reason to Timothy O'Connor's excellent article, "Scotus's Argument for the Existence of a First Efficient Cause," *International Journal for Philosophy of Religion*, 33 (1993): 18–19. Scotus is committed to stronger versions of the principle of sufficient reason; crucially, however, his argument does not presuppose them.

21. For the argument, see *Ord.* 1.2.1.1–2, n. 59 (Vatican, 2:165 = *PW*, p. 47); *Rep.* 1.2.1.1–2, n. 29 (WA, p. 269 = FW, p. 51); *DPP* 3.20 (p. 52).

22. On metaphysics, transcendental attributes (such as causation, necessity, and contingency), and the proof for God's existence, see the Appendix, section 1.

23. For the argument, see *DPP* 3.13 (p. 48); *Ord.* 1.2.1.1–2, n. 53 (Vatican, 2:158–59 = *PW* p. 43); *Rep.* 1.2.1.1–2, n. 29 (WA, p. 269 = FW, p. 51). (In the *Reportatio* account, Scotus brands the argument as merely "persuasive.") For O'Connor's helpful discussion of the argument, see "Scotus on the Existence of a First Cause," 27–28.

24. *Ord.* 1.2.1.1–2, n. 60 (Vatican, 2:165–66 = *PW*, p. 47); *DPP* 3.29 (p. 58).

25. See, for example, *Eth. Nic.* 1.1 (1094ᵃ3–5).

26. Anselm, *Pros.* 3 (*Opera Omnia*, ed. Franciscus Salesius Schmitt, 6 vols. [Edinburgh: Thomas Nelson and Sons, 1946–61], 1:102–103.

27. *Rep.* 1.2.1.1–2, n. 30 (WA, p. 269 = FW, p. 51); see *Ord.* 1.2.1.1–2, n. 64 (Vatican, 2:167 = *PW*, p. 48); see also *DPP* 3.35–37 (p. 60).

28. *Rep.* 1.2.1.3, n. 73 (WA, p. 301 = FW, pp. 65–67); see *Ord.* 1.2.1.1–2, n. 138 (Vatican, 2:210 = *PW*, pp. 73–74); *DPP* 4.65 (pp. 122–24).

29. Interestingly, Scotus denies that "God exists" is known per se; roughly, he denies that it is a priori. The reason for this is that without detailed reflection we only have a rough idea of the meaning of the term 'God', in itself insufficient to allow us to *realize* that the proposition "God exists" is analytic (i.e., necessarily true). See especially *Ord.* 1.2.1.1–2, nn. 15–19, 28, 35–36 (Vatican, 2:131–34, 140, 145–46).

30. *Ord.* 1.2.1.1–2, n. 61 (Vatican, 2:166 = *PW*, pp. 47–48); *Rep.* 1.2.1.1–2, n. 31 (WA, pp. 269–71 = FW, p. 53); *DPP* 3.31–32 (pp. 58–60).

31. *Ord.* 1.2.1.1–2, n. 50 (Vatican, 2:154–55 = *PW*, p. 49). For Scotus's discussions of the coextensiveness of the three properties, see *Ord.* 1.2.1.1–2, nn. 61, 65, 68–69 (Vatican, 2:166, 167–69 = *PW*, 47–49).

32. For the argument, which I omit here, see *Ord.* 1.2.1.1–2, nn. 70–73 (Vatican, 2:169–73 = *PW*, pp. 49–52); *Rep.* 1.2.1.1–2, nn. 36–40 (WA, pp. 275–79 = FW, pp. 55–59); *DPP* 3.24–26, 43–62 (pp. 54–58, 62–70). The sense Scotus has in mind is that the three properties fail to define the class "God" and that they are still non-exemplifiable by anything else.

33. See Aquinas, *ST* 1.3 (1[1]:14ᵃ–20ᵇ) for simplicity, *ST* 1.7.1–2 (1[1]: 32ᵇ–33ᵇ) for the inference from simplicity to infinity, and *ST* 1.11.3 c (1[1]:49ᵇ) for the inference from simplicity to unicity.

34. *Ord.* 1.2.1.1–2, nn. 140–41 (Vatican, 2:211 = *PW*, p. 74). For a helpful discussion of Scotus's attempt to infer the sorts of attributes a being exhibiting the threefold primacy must have, see Timothy O'Connor, "From First Efficient Cause to God: Scotus on the Identification Stage of the Cosmological Argument," in Honnefelder, Wood, and Dreyer (eds.), *John Duns Scotus: Metaphysics and Ethics*, 435–54.

35. *Ord.* 1.2.1.1–2, nn. 125–29 (Vatican, 2:201–205 = *PW*, pp. 68–69); *DPP* 4.48 (pp. 102–104); *Rep.* 1.2.1.3, nn. 69–70 (WA, pp. 297–99 = FW, p. 63).

36. *Ord.* 1.2.1.1–2, nn. 111–24 (Vatican, 2:189–201 = *PW*, pp. 64–68); *Rep.* 1.2.1.3, nn. 64–88 (WA, pp. 293–97 = FW, pp. 59–63); *DPP* 4.67–72 (pp. 124–32).

37. *Ord.* 1.2.1.1–2, n. 130 (Vatican, 2:205–206 = *PW*, 70–71); *Rep.* 1.2.1.3, n. 75 (WA, pp. 301–303 = FW, p. 67); *DPP* 4.66 (p. 124).

38. *Ord.* 1.2.1.1–2, n. 131 (Vatican, 2:206 = *PW*, p. 71); *Rep.* 1.2.1.3, n. 71 (WA, 301 = FW, p. 65); *DPP* 4.63 (p. 120).

39. *Ord.* 1.2.1.1–2, n. 132 (Vatican, 2:206–207 = *PW*, p. 71); *Rep.* 1.2.1.3, n. 73 (WA, p. 301 = FW, p. 65); *DPP* 4.64 (p. 120).

40. *Ord.* 1.3.1.1–2, n. 59 (Vatican, 3:41 = *PW*, p. 27).

41. *DPP* 4.88 (p. 148).

42. Arguments closely related to this can be found in recent discussions of the issue. See William J. Wainwright, "Monotheism," in Robert Audi and William J. Wainwright (eds.), *Rationality, Religious Belief, and Moral Commitment: New Essays in the Philosophy of Religion* (Ithaca, N.Y., and London: Cornell University Press, 1986), 296–97; and T. W. Bartel, "Could there be More than One Lord?" *Faith and Philosophy*, 11 (1994): 358–61.

43. *Ord.* 1.42.un., nn. 8–9 (Vatican, 6:342–44); *Quod.* 7, nn. 4, 32 (Wadding, 12:169, 185 = AW, pp. 162 [n. 7.8], 184–85 [nn. 7.89–90]).

44. I discuss this distinction in detail in chapter 4, below.

45. *Ord.* 1.2.1.3, nn. 172–73 (Vatican, 2:230–31 = *PW*, p. 87); *DPP* 4.91 (p. 150).

46. This assertion is not inconsistent with Scotus's description of an E-series. In an E-series, there is an important sense in which earlier causes are not *causally* sufficient, even though the causal activity of an earlier cause is *logically* sufficient for any later effect in the series.

47. For a sophisticated presentation of much the same argument as Scotus's, see Wainwright, "Monotheism," 301–305; also Richard Swinburne, *The Christian God* (Oxford: Clarendon Press, 1994), 171.

48. *Ord.* 1.2.1.3, n. 180 (Vatican, 2:235 = *PW*, p. 90); see *Rep.* 1.2.2.un., nn. 100–101 (WA, pp. 315–17 = FW, p. 71).

49. *Ord.* 1.2.1.3, n. 181 (Vatican, 2:235 = *PW*, p. 90); *Rep.* 1.2.2.un., n. 102 (WA, p. 317 = FW, p. 71).

50. *Rep.* 1.2.2.un., n. 102 (AW, p. 317 = FW, p. 73); the first appears also in *Ord.* 1.2.1.3, n. 181 (Vatican, 2:236 = *PW*, pp. 90–91).

51. *DPP* 4.75 (p. 134).

52. *Ord.* 1.8.1.1, n. 16 (Vatican, 4:160); *DPP* 4.4 (p. 74).

53. On matter and form, see chapter 6, below.

54. For Aquinas on these various sorts of simplicity, see *ST* 1.3.1–3, 5–7 ($1[1]:14^a$–16^b, 18^b–20^a) for (i), (iii), (iv), and (v); *ST* 1.10.2 ($1[1]:43^{a-b}$) for (ii); and *ST* 1.13.4 c ($1[1]:66^b$) for (vi). Aquinas also believes that God lacks any

sort of composition between his essence and his existence: see *ST* 1.3.4 (1[1]:16ᵃ–17ᵇ). Scotus never addresses this Thomist claim directly. At one point, however, he clearly denies that there is a distinction between any substance's existence and its essence: "I do not know that fiction according to which existence is something that supervenes on an essence" (*Ord.* 4.11.3, n. 46 [Wadding, 8:649]). What he wants to deny is that there is any *part* of a substance that is not part of that substance's individual essence. As should be clear already, Scotus is happy to claim that God is a necessary existent— and thus, roughly, that existence is a defining property of his. And, as we shall see, he is clear that all creatures are contingent—and thus, roughly, that existence is not a defining property of any creature. For an illuminating discussion of Aquinas, see Christopher Hughes, *On a Complex Theory of a Simple God: An Investigation in Aquinas's Philosophical Theology*, Cornell Studies in the Philosophy of Religion (Ithaca, N.Y., and London: Cornell University Press, 1989).

55. *Ord.* 1.8.1.1, nn. 17, 19 (Vatican, 4:160–61); *DPP* 4.76 (p. 134).

56. *DPP* 4.80 (p. 138); for a different argument, see *Ord.* 1.8.1.1, n. 15 (Vatican, 4:159).

57. It is certainly false in mathematics, as the work of Cantor and his successors has shown. For a useful summary of some of the mathematical issues, see A. W. Moore, *The Infinite*, Problems of Philosophy: Their Past and their Present (London and New York: Routledge, 1990), 118–22, 147–58. The point is that if something infinite actually exists, it will probably be false to claim that it (logically) cannot be a part of some greater whole.

58. *Ord.* 1.8.1.1, n. 7 (Vatican, 4:154–55).

CHAPTER 3

1. Scotus assumes this in the argument discussed in chapter 2, section 3, above.

2. See Thomas V. Morris, *Anselmian Explorations: Essays in Philosophical Theology* (Notre Dame: University of Notre Dame Press, 1987), 2. For a sophisticated modern presentation of a perfect-being theology, see Morris, "The God of Abraham, Isaac, and Anselm," *Faith and Philosophy*, 1 (1984): 177–87, reprinted in Morris (ed.), *Anselmian Explorations*, 10–25.

3. See Anselm, *Monol.* 15 (*Opera Omnia*, 1:28–29).

4. *Ord.* 1.3.1.1–2, n. 38 (Vatican, 3:25–26 = *PW*, p. 24). See also *Ord.* 1.2.2.1–4, nn. 382–84 (Vatican, 2:346–47); *Ord.* 1.8.1.1, n. 22 (Vatican, 4:162); *Ord.* 1.8.1.4, n. 167 (Vatican, 4:239–40); *Quod.* 1, n. 8 (Wadding, 12:10 = AW, p. 12 [n. 1.22]); *Quod.* 5, n. 13 (Wadding, 12:128 = AW, p. 119 [n. 5.31]).

5. *Quod.* 1, n. 8 (Wadding, 12:10 = AW, p. 12 [n. 1.22]), quoting Anselm, *Monol.* 15 (1:28–29). On wisdom, see chapter 4, below.

6. *Quod.* 6, n. 14 (Wadding, 12:150 = AW, p. 142 [n. 6.34]). For a discussion of eternity in Scotus, see my "Duns Scotus on Eternity and Timelessness," *Faith and Philosophy*, 14 (1997): 3–25.

7. *Ord.* 1.3.1.1–2, n. 39 (Vatican, 3:26 = *PW*, p. 25). As we shall see in chapter 4, below, Scotus is not always so sure that intellect and will count as pure perfections, and he offers a different set of arguments for God's possession of these powers.

8. *Ord.* 1.8.1.4, n. 167 (Vatican, 4:240), quoting Augustine, *De Trin.* 15.8 (CCSL, 50:470).

9. See *Ord.* 1.3.1.3, n. 135 (Vatican, 3:84). I discuss the coextensive transcendentals in the Appendix, section 1.

10. *Ord.* 1.8.1.4, n. 167 (Vatican, 4:240); *Quod.* 5, n. 13 (Wadding, 12:128 = AW, p. 119 [n. 5.31]).

11. Scotus's Anselmian methodology is far removed from the sorts of method used by Aquinas. For Aquinas, we come to know things about God by our natural reason in two ways: by the *via remotionis*, eliminating imperfections from God, and by the relational method, seeing how created things relate to God. On these, see Norman Kretzmann, *The Metaphysics of Theism: Aquinas's Natural Theology in "Summa Contra Gentiles" I* (Oxford: Clarendon Press, 1997), 91–92, 140. Scotus certainly uses the eliminative method—fox example, in his attempt to establish God's simplicity and immutability (for simplicity, see chapter 2, above; for immutability, see chapter 4, below). But he emphasizes that the result of an application of the eliminative is not any sort of apophatic view of God: "Negations are not the object of our highest love" (*Ord.* 1.3.1.1–2, n. 10 [Vatican, 3:5 = *PW*, p. 14]). Scotus argues that negative propositions can only be formulated about something if we can formulate affirmative propositions about that thing as well. On Scotus's views of negative theology, see Rolf Schönberger, "*Negationes non summe amamus*: Duns Scotus's Auseinandersetzung mit der negativen Theologie," in Honnefelder, Wood, and Dreyer (eds.), *John Duns Scotus: Metaphysics and Ethics*, 475–96.

12. Henry of Ghent, *SQ* 21.2 c. (2 vols. [Paris, 1520], 1:124^{r}F–5^{r}S); see Scotus, *Ord.* 1.3.1.1–2, n. 20 (Vatican, 3:12 = *PW*, p. 18).

13. *SQ* 21.2 ad 3 (1:124^{v}O–125^{r}S).

14. *SQ* 21.2 (1:124^{r}G).

15. *SQ* 21.2 ad 3 (1:125^{r}S).

16. FW, pp. 142–43.

17. *ST* 1.13.5 c (1[1]:67^b–68^a).

18. Scotus sometimes obscures this point by distinguishing too sharply between univocal *concepts* and univocal *terms*. For example, Wolter notes that Scotus consistently claims that the concept of being, though *not* the term 'being', is univocal. What Scotus is drawing our attention to is that we (rather misleadingly) use just one term, 'being', to pick out a number of different complex concepts, where each concept is related to the other concepts by analogy, related in virtue of the univocal common concept of being. (See Allan B. Wolter, *The Transcendentals and their Function in the Metaphysics of Duns Scotus*, Franciscan Institute Publications, Philosophy Series, 3 [St. Bonaventure, N.Y.: The Franciscan Institute, 1946], p. 47, n. 35.) On the univocity of being in Scotus, see, for example, Douglas C. Langston, "Scotus and Ockham on the Univocal Concept of Being," *Franciscan Studies*, 39 (1979): 105–129; and Stephen Dumont, "The Univocal Concept of Being in the Fourteenth Century: I. John Duns Scotus and William of Alnwick," *Mediaeval Studies*, 49 (1987): 1–75.

19. I do not want to discuss Aquinas's theory in detail, since its interpretation is a controversial matter (see usefully Gerard J. Hughes, *The Philosophical Assessment of Theology: Essays in Honor of Frederick C. Copleston* [Tunbridge Wells: Search Press; Washington, D.C.: Georgetown University Press, 1987], 37–39), and since Scotus in any case targets Henry's theory.

20. *Ord.* 1.3.1.1–2, n. 26 (Vatican, 3:18 = *PW*, p. 19).

21. *Ord.* 1.3.1.1–2, *textus interpolatus* (Vatican, 3:29).

22. William Alston, "Aquinas on Theological Predication," in Eleonore Stump (ed.), *Reasoned Faith: Essays in Philosophical Theology in Honor of Norman Kretzmann* (Ithaca, N.Y., and London: Cornell University Press, 1993), 167–68.

23. See *Ord.* 1.3.1.1–2, nn. 27–28 (Vatican, 4:18 = *PW*, p. 20). In fact, both Aquinas and Henry provide alternative, causal, accounts of how we might assign truth values to theological statements. For Aquinas's awareness of this problem, see *ST* 1.13.5 c (1[1]:68ª), where Aquinas argues that analogy is sufficiently guaranteed by the similarity that obtains between effect and cause. (For Henry, see above.) I have already indicated why Scotus would find this account of similarity without univocity puzzling.

24. *Ord.* 1.3.1.1–2, n. 40 (Vatican, 3:27 = PW, p. 25); see also *Ord.* 1.8.1.3, n. 67 (Vatican, 4:183).

25. *Lect.* 1.3.1.1–2, n. 113 (Vatican, 16:266–67).

26. *Ord.* 1.3.1.1–2, n. 35 (Vatican, 3:21–22 = *PW*, p. 22).

27. *Ord.* 1.3.1.1–2, n. 26 (Vatican, 3:18 = *PW*, p. 20 = FW, p. 109).

28. In a recent discussion, Janice Thomas notes that analogous and equivocal terms can easily be made to satisfy Scotus's descriptions (Janice Thomas, "Univocity and Understanding God's Nature," in Hughes (ed.),

The Philosophical Assessment of Theology, 90–93). But Scotus does not claim that satisfying the two descriptions is sufficient for univocity; merely that it is necessary. So I do not see that his position is significantly threatened by Thomas's criticism.

29. This theory clearly entails that there is some kind of commonality between creaturely and divine attributes. I discuss exactly how Scotus spells out this commonality below.

30. *Ord.* 1.8.1.3, n. 113 (Vatican, 4:206). On the transcendental attributes, see the Appendix, section 1.

31. *Ord.* 1.3.1.1–2, n. 39 (Vatican, 3:26–27 = *PW*, p. 25).

32. Scotus never makes this point explicitly. But Wolter has argued for it convincingly in *The Transcendentals*, 40–48. The argument has several steps. The first is that Scotus is quite clear that complex concepts proper to God "do not apply to creatures" (*Ord.* 1.3.1.1–2, n. 58 [Vatican, 3:40 = *PW*, p. 27]). The next step is that Scotus clearly allows for analogical senses for terms referring to crucial transcendental attributes such as being; see, for example, his *In Metaph.* 4.1, n. 12 (Wadding, 4:578ᵃ); and *Super Praed.* 4, n. 7 (Wadding, 1:130ᵇ). Finally, Scotus is quite clear that his arguments in favor of the univocity theory show no more than that *some* concepts must be univocal when applied to God and creatures: "Secondly, I say that God is conceived not only in a concept analogous to the concept of a creature"; *Ord.* 1.3.1.1–2, n. 26 (Vatican, 3:18 = *PW*, p. 19).

33. *Ord.* 1.8.1.3, n. 82 (Vatican, 4:190). I will explain in section 4 of this chapter why Scotus makes this move.

34. *Ord.* 1.8.1.3, n. 139 (Vatican, 4:223).

35. *Ord.* 1.8.1.3, n. 153 (Vatican, 4:228). Scotus appeals (perhaps surprisingly) to Aristotle for support. According to Aristotle's standard account, as Scotus notes, predicates applied to things *quidditatively* (i.e., telling us about the *kind* of thing we are talking about) are classifiable only as genus or definition (*Ord.* 1.8.1.3, n. 120 [Vatican, 4:212], referring to Aristotle, *Top.* 1.4 [101ᵇ15–28]). But Scotus notices that Aristotle himself sometimes allows for another kind of common attribute, and that Aristotle therefore "implicitly teaches that some transcendental predicate which is neither genus nor definition is said quidditatively"; *Ord.* 1.8.1.3, n. 127 (Vatican, 4:216).

36. "In quadam descriptione"; *Ord.* 1.3.1.1–2, n. 58 (Vatican, 3:40 = *PW*, p. 27).

37. On infinity in Scotus, see FW, pp. 151–55; and Francis J. Catania, "John Duns Scotus on *Ens Infinitum*," *American Catholic Philosophical Quarterly*, 67 (1993): 37–54, and the literature cited therein.

38. *ST* 1.7.1 c (1[1]:32ᵇ).

39. See *In Metaph.* 2.6, n. 2 (Wadding, 4:563ᵃ): "The infinite negates

finitude with the positing of a contrary, such as: an extended finite thing without boundaries."

40. *Ord.* 1.2.1.1–2, n. 143 (Vatican, 2:212 = *PW*, p. 75).

41. *Ord.* 1.2.1.1–2, n. 142 (Vatican, 2:212 = *PW*, p. 75). The earliest account of infinity as an intrinsic mode in Scotus is *Lect.* 1.8.1.3, nn. 103–104 (Vatican, 17:35–36). For earlier accounts of the infinite, upon which Scotus may be drawing, see Meldon C. Wass, *The Infinite God and the Summa Fratris Alexandri* (Chicago: Franciscan Herald Press, 1964), 47–70.

42. For an account of the process, see FW, pp. 151–55; and Catania, "John Duns Scotus on *Ens Infinitum*," 42–43. Also see AW, pp. 110–111, n. 4.

43. *Quod.* 5, n. 2 (Wadding, 12:118 = AW, pp. 108–109 [n. 5.5]): see Aristotle, *Ph.* 3.6 (207^{a}7–9).

44. *Quod.* 5, n. 2 (Wadding, 12:118 = AW, p. 109 [n. 5.6]). Scotus's description of this process is strikingly similar to descriptions of the actual infinite found in post-Cantor mathematics. David Hilbert, for example, describes the actual infinite as follows: "We meet the true infinite when we regard the totality of numbers 1, 2, 3, 4,. . . itself as a completed unity, or when we regard the points of an interval as a totality of things which exists all at once. This kind of infinity is known as *actual infinity*" (Hilbert, "On the Infinite," in Paul Benacerraf and Hilary Putnam (eds.), *Philosophy of Mathematics* [Englewood Cliffs, N. J.: Prentice-Hall, 1964], 139, quoted in William Lane Craig, *The Kalām Cosmological Argument*, Library of Philosophy and Religion [London and Basingstoke: Macmillan, 1979], 149–50.

45. *Quod.* 5, n. 3 (Wadding, 12:118 = AW, pp. 109–110 [n. 5.7]).

46. FW, pp. 153–54.

47. *Quod.* 5, n. 3 (Wadding, 12:118 = AW, p. 110 [n. 5.7]).

48. I discuss in more detail Scotus's claim that an infinite being (in Scotus's sense) could not be composed of parts at the end of chapter 2, above.

49. *Ord.* 1.3.1.1–2, n. 58 (Vatican, 3:40 = *PW*, p. 27).

50. *Quod.* 5, n. 4 (Wadding, 12:119 = AW, pp. 111–12 [n. 5.10]).

51. On Scotus's formal distinction, see the Appendix, section 2.

52. For Scotus's discussion of the distinction between an attribute and its intrinsic mode, see *Ord.* 1.8.1.3, nn. 138–40 (Vatican, 4:222–23); also *Ord.* 1.3.1.1–2, n. 58 (Vatican, 3:40 = *PW*, p. 27). The distinction between an attribute and its intrinsic mode is not quite a formal distinction, since an intrinsic mode is not at all a quidditative reality: it just tells us "how much" of the attribute is present. But the two are not in every respect identical. For a thorough discussion of the issue in this context, see Wolter, *The Transcendentals*, 24–27; and recently, in considerable detail and including a translation of *Ord.* 1.8.1.3, nn. 138–40, Peter King, "Duns Scotus on the Com-

mon Nature and Individual Differentia," *Philosophical Topics*, 20 (1992): 60–64, 70–1. Scotus' doctrine of intrinsic modes is worked out in great detail in his discussion of the degrees of a quality. On this, see my *The Physics of Duns Scotus*, chapter 9 (in particular, pp. 179–79, 186–87).

53. We should perhaps also keep in mind that, according to Scotus, a simple attribute (unlike a genus) is not in any sense *potential* to its intrinsic mode; so the sort of complexity Scotus proposes here does not compromise God's pure actuality (*Ord.* 1.8.1.3, n. 148 [Vatican, 4:226]). I examine Scotus's account of God's pure actuality (i.e., God's being wholly unconditioned) in chapter 4, below. Scotus uses his account of divine infinity to show how God cannot belong to a genus, or be composite in the sense of being definable in terms of genus and difference. Infinity is an intrinsic mode of a thing; and an intrinsic mode—an *amount* of something—cannot be a specific difference: it cannot help tell us about the *sort* of thing we are dealing with. See *Ord.* 1.8.1.3, n. 108 (Vatican, 4:202–203); on the contrast between a species and a complex transcendental mode, see *Ord.* 1.8.1.4, nn. 219–20 (Vatican, 4:274–75). Equally, any general concept that applies to God is "indifferent to [being] finite or infinite." But no concept that is indifferent to being finite or infinite is precise enough to be a concept of a genus; see *Ord.* 1.8.1.3, n. 101 (Vatican, 4:199–200). Scotus's approach here is quite different from that of Aquinas. Aquinas argues that God cannot be defined because he is *pure actuality*, and a genus is necessarily *potential* to a specific difference; see *ST* 1.3.5 c (1[1]:18ᵃ).

54. *Ord.* 1.8.1.4, n. 192 (Vatican, 6:192).

55. *Ord.* 1.8.1.4, n. 193 (Vatican, 4:261–62).

56. One important modern account of divine simplicity has argued that the coextensiveness of the divine attributes is sufficient for their all being classified as exactly the same attribute; see William E. Mann, "Divine Simplicity," *Religious Studies*, 18 (1982): 451–71. Scotus would regard this sort of account, I think, as inimical to the whole task of doing metaphysics. And his doctrine of the commonality between divine and human attributes is probably sufficient—if it is true—to refute Mann's approach.

57. *Ord.* 1.8.1.4, n. 192 (Vatican, 4:261).

58. *Ord.* 1.8.1.4, n. 209 (Vatican, 4:209); see also *Ord.* 1.8.1.3, n. 95 (Vatican, 4:198).

59. *Ord.* 1.2.2.1–4, n. 400 (Vatican, 2:355).

60. *Ord.* 1.8.1.4, n. 202 (Vatican, 6:266). Scotus is clear that God's simplicity entails that everything in God is identical with him (*Ord.* 1.30.1–2, n. 50 [Vatican, 6:192]), presumably in the sense that there are no real distinctions between different parts in God.

61. *Ord.* 1.8.1.4, n. 210 (Vatican, 4:270).

62. For various reasons, partly philosophical, partly historical, Scotus is not too happy labeling God's essence a 'substance'. Philosophically, Scotus argues that 'substance' is a generic term, capable of further determination; *Ord*. 1.8.1.3, nn. 122, 134 (Vatican, 4:212–13, 220). Historically, Augustine was reluctant to label God a substance because 'substance' implies being the subject of accidents; see *Ord*. 1.8.1.3, n. 97 (Vatican, 4:198–99), referring to *De Trin*. 7.10 (CCSL, 50:260–61). On the other hand, if 'substance' is used merely to pick out the fact of *subsistence* (independent existence), then Scotus has no difficulty in calling God a substance; see *Ord*. 1.8.1.3, n. 134 (Vatican, 4:220). Equally, Scotus is happy repeating John of Damascus's "infinite sea of substance"; see *De Fide Orth*. 1.9 (PG, 94:835B) = 9 (ed. Eligius Buytaert, Franciscan Institute Publications: Text Series, 8 [St. Bonaventure, N.Y.: The Franciscan Institute; Louvain: E. Nauwelaerts; Paderborn: F. Schöningh, 1955], p. 49), cited in *Ord*. 1.8.1.4, n. 198 (Vatican, 4:264).

63. For Scotus's separability condition for real distinction, see the Appendix, section 2.

64. *Ord*. 1.8.1.4, n. 214 (Vatican, 4:271–72).

65. *Ord*. 1.8.1.4, n. 200 (Vatican, 4:265–66).

66. *ST* 1.13.4 c (1[1]:66a). Aquinas claims that the words we use to refer to these attributes fail to be synonymous *despite* the fact that the attributes are "one thing." The reason is that our intellect forms different conceptions of God, such that the words we use of him have diverse meanings "in virtue of diverse negated properties, or in virtue of the diverse effects connoted [by the words used]."

67. William Alston argues that a strong account of divine simplicity need not entail rejecting what I have labeled the univocity theory of religious language; see "Aquinas on Theological Predication," 176–78. Aquinas and Scotus, I believe, both disagree with this claim.

68. *ST* 1.3, introductory passage (1[1]:13a).

CHAPTER 4

1. Scotus argues that a pure perfection—the sort of perfection we argue for using Anselm's perfect-being theology—is only such if we can be sure that it is better for a maximally excellent nature to have it than not. But it is not clear that intellect and will are like this; see *DPP* 4.22 (pp. 86–90). Scotus's reason is that it is not always better to have intellect than not to have it. It is not, for example, better for a dog to have it than not to have it, since intellect is inconsistent with canine nature. This argument is puzzling, since it looks prima facie to be fatal for any putative pure perfection, and thus for a whole aspect of Scotus's metaphysical methodology. But Scotus clarifies: "The situa-

tion is different with the properties of being in general [i.e., the transcen-
dentals], for they are characteristic of every being either commonly or in
disjunction" (*DPP* 4.22 [p. 88]). Intellect is not like this. (On the transcendentals, see the Appendix, section 1.)

2. *Ord.* 1.2.1.1–2, n. 79 (Vatican, 2:176 = *PW*, pp. 53–54); *DPP* 4.15
(p. 82).

3. *Ord.* 1.2.1.1–2, n. 80 (Vatican, 2:176–77 = *PW*, p. 54); *DPP* 4.15
(p. 82). See also *Ord.* 1.8.2.un., nn. 281–82 (Vatican, 4:313–14).

4. *DPP* 4.26 (p. 92).

5. *Ord.* 1.2.1.1–2, n. 81 (Vatican, 2:177 = *PW*, p. 54); *DPP* 4.15 (p. 82).

6. *Ord.* 1.2.1.1–2, n. 78 (Vatican, 2:176 = *PW*, p. 53); *DPP* 4.14 (p. 82).

7. *Ord.* 1.30.1–2, n. 50 (Vatican, 6:192). On God's immutability, see
Ord. 1.8.2.un., n. 229 (Vatican, 4:229), where Scotus argues that God's simplicity prevents him from receiving any new substantial or accidental form,
and that God's necessity entails that he cannot be annihilated. The relevant
sort of identity in the claim that everything in God is identical with him is
of course consistent with formal distinction. On this, see chapter 3, note 60,
above.

8. *Ord.* 1.30.1–2, n. 51 (Vatican, 6:192).

9. *Ord.* 1.8.2.un., nn. 275–77 (Vatican, 4:310–11).

10. *Ord.* 1.30.1–2, n. 51 (Vatican, 6:192). In *Quod.* 1, n. 8 (Wadding, 12:10
= AW, pp. 11–12 [nn. 1.20–22]), Scotus offers a different argument: "Relation to a creature cannot be a pure perfection, because it involves a term that
is potential," and every essential divine attribute is a pure perfection. On
God's pure perfections, see chapter 3, section 1, above.

11. *Ord.* 1.3.3.1, nn. 352, 354, 360, 370 (Vatican, 3:211–14, 218, 225);
Ord. 1.36.un., nn. 45–46 (Vatican, 6:288–89). Note that this "calling to mind"
is a distinct activity from *recalling* a past thing or fact; on recall and remembering in Scotus, see John Marenbon, *Later Medieval Philosophy (1150–1350):
An Introduction* (London and New York: Routledge, 1987), 164–68, referring to *Ord.* 4.45.3. For a further discussion, including text from MS A and
a translation, see Allan B. Wolter and Marilyn McCord Adams, "Memory
and Intuition: A Focal Debate in Fourteenth Century Cognitive Psychology," *Franciscan Studies*, 53 (1993): 175–230.

12. *Ord.* 1.3.1.4, n. 277 (Vatican, 3:170). Scotus posits an elaborate
mechanism for the abstraction of these intelligible objects from extra-mental objects. We do not need to know about this in order to understand what
Scotus has to say about God's knowledge. Note that we can in principle have
intelligible objects corresponding to both universals and particulars. For
universals, see, for example, *Ord.* 1.3.3.1, nn. 349, 352, 370 (Vatican, 3:210–
212, 225); for particulars, see, for example, *Ord.* 3.14.3, n. 5 (Wadding,

7:303–304). Also see Allan B. Wolter, "Duns Scotus on Intuition, Memory, and Our Knowledge of Individuals," in his *The Philosophical Theology of John Duns Scotus*, 115.

13. *Ord.* 1.3.3.1, n. 367 (Vatican, 3:223–24). On this, see Dominik Perler, "What Am I Thinking About? John Duns Scotus and Peter Aureol on Intentional Objects," *Vivarium*, 32 (1994): 73–81.

14. See Aristotle, *Int.* 1 (16ᵃ3–9). For a discussion of the scholastics, see Marenbon, *Later Medieval Philosophy*, 110–115, 125–27); and Claude Panaccio, "From Mental Word to Mental Language," *Philosophical Topics*, 20 (1992): 125–47. For Aquinas, see Robert Pasnau, *Theories of Cognition in the Later Middle Ages* (Cambridge: Cambridge University Press, 1997), 256–71; and Bernard J. Lonergan, *Verbum: Word and Idea in Aquinas*, ed. David B. Burrell (London: Darton, Longman and Todd, 1968), especially chapters 1, 2, and 4.

15. *Ord.* 1.27.1–3, nn. 20, 78 (Vatican, 6:72, 94); *Ord.* 1.2.2.1–4, n. 310 (Vatican, 2:313–14); *Ord.* 1.3.3.1, nn. 394–97 (Vatican, 3:340–342); *Ord.* 1.3.3.2, nn. 487–89, 494 (Vatican, 3:289, 292–93); *Ord.* 1.32.1–2, n. 23 (Vatican, 230–231); *Quod.* 15, n. 7 (Wadding, 12:421 = AW, p. 350 [n. 15.19]); *Quod.* 15, n. 8 (Wadding, 12:422 = AW, p. 351 [n. 15.26]); *Quod.* 15, n. 9 (Wadding, 12:423 = AW, pp. 352–53 [n. 15.31]); *Quod.* 15, n. 20 (Wadding, 12:430 = AW, p. 362 [n. 15.60]). As noted above, Scotus identifies memory with Aristotle's possible intellect (or at least as part of Aristotle's possible intellect); *Quod.* 15, n. 24 (Wadding, 12:445 = AW, p. 368 [n. 15.87]). The idea is that the presence of an intelligible species (produced by the agent intellect), along with the causal powers of the possible intellect, causes the mental word identified as actual knowledge.

16. Memory and intelligence are two "sub-powers" of the intellect; see *Ord.* 1.27.1–3, n. 51 (Vatican, 6:85); see also *Ord.* 1.2.2.1–4, n. 323 (Vatican, 2:319–320). On the powers of the soul, see chapter 7, section 1, below.

17. Scotus contrasts this mental quality with the action that produces it. See *Ord.* 1.3.3.4, nn. 601–604 (Vatican, 3:354–57); see also *Ord.* 1.2.2.1–4, nn. 325–26 (Vatican, 2:321); *Ord.* 1.6.un., n. 14 (Vatican, 4:93–95); *Quod.* 13, nn. 3–4 (Wadding, 12:302 = AW, pp. 285–86 [n. 13.10]); *Quod.* 13, n. 5 (Wadding, 12:302–303 = AW, p. 287 [n. 13.16]); *Quod.* 15, n. 2 (Wadding, 12:411 = AW, pp. 345–46 [n. 15.6]).

18. *Ord.* 1.35.un, nn. 38–40 (Vatican, 6:260–261). Scotus is an essentialist, and thus believes that there are necessarily true propositions about the natures of things; see, for example, *Lect.* 1.43.un., n. 15 (Vatican, 17:533); *Ord.* 1.36.un., nn. 60–63 (Vatican, 6:296–97).

19. *Ord.* 1.38.un., n. 10 (Vatican, 6:307); *Ord.* 1.43.un., nn. 14, 16 (Vatican, 6:358–360); *Ord.* 1.3.1.4, n. 269 (Vatican, 3:164–65); *Lect.* 1.39.1–5, n. 62 (Vatican, 17: 500 = Vos, p. 142).

20. *Ord.* 1.2.1.1–2, n. 109 (Vatican, 2:188); *In Metaph.* 1.5, nn. 3–4 (Wadding, 4:538ᵃ⁻ᵇ); also *Ord.* 2.3.1.5–6, n. 191 (Vatican, 7:486); and Duns Scotus *Add. Mag.* 1.36.4, nn. 26–27 (Wadding, 11:213ᵃ).

21. The Augustinian *locus classicus* for the medievals is *De Div. Qu.* 46 (CCSL, 44A:70–73). See *ST* 1.15.1, 1[1]:90ᵃ⁻ᵇ); and *Ord.* 1.36.un., n. 1 (Vatican, 6:244).

22. See, for example, *Lect.* 1.39.1–5, nn. 20–21 (Vatican, 17:485 = Vos, pp. 74, 76). Scotus is sometimes reluctant to use the word 'idea': see *DPP* 4.85 (p. 146).

23. *Ord.* 1.2.2.1–4, n. 394 (Vatican, 2:352); *Ord.* 1.10.un., n. 62 (Vatican, 4:366); *Ord.* 1.35.un., nn. 14, 32, 49 (Vatican, 6:249–50, 258, 266).

24. For intuitive cognition see, for example, *Ord.* 1.3.3.2, n. 500 (Vatican, 3:296–97); *Quod.* 13, n. 10 (Wadding, 12:310 = AW, p. 292 [n. 13.33]; also *Quod.* 13, n. 8 (Wadding, 12:309 = AW, p. 291 [n. 13.29]); *Quod.* 14, n. 10 (Wadding, 12:369 = AW, pp. 324–25 [n. 14.36]). It is not clear whether the intuitive knowledge defended by Scotus in general should be regarded as a form of direct realism. For a useful discussion of this, see Wolter, "Duns Scotus on Intuition, Memory, and Our Knowledge of Individuals," 120–21.

25. *Ord.* 1.2.1.1–2, n. 95 (Vatican, 2:183 = *PW*, p. 58).

26. Bonaventure, *Comm. Sent.* 1.35.un.1 (*Opera Omnia*, 1:601ᵃ⁻ᵇ); *Comm. Sent.* 1.35.un.3 (1:608ᵃ–609ᵇ); *Comm. Sent.* 1.35.un.4 (1:610ᵃ⁻ᵇ). Scotus helpfully summarizes Bonaventure's view at *Ord.* 1.35.un., nn. 9–11 (Vatican, 6:247–48).

27. *Ord.* 1.36.un., nn. 2, 4–5 (Vatican, 6:272–74); see Henry of Ghent, *SQ* 21.4 (1:127ʳN–ᵛQ).

28. *Ord.* 1.35.un., n. 15 (Vatican, 6:250).

29. *Ord.* 1.36.un., n. 13 (Vatican, 6:276).

30. *Ord* 1.36.un., n. 14 (Vatican, 6:276). On this, see John F. Wippel, *Metaphysical Themes in Thomas Aquinas*, Studies in Philosophy and the History of Philosophy, 10 (Washington, D.C.: Catholic University of America Press, 1984), 173–84.

31. *Ord.* 1.35.un., n. 32 (Vatican, 6:258).

32. *Ord.* 1.3.1.4, n. 277 (Vatican, 3:169–70).

33. *Ord.* 1.3.1.4, n. 268 (Vatican, 3:168–69); see also *Ord.* 1.30.1–2, nn. 56–57 (Vatican, 6:194–95); *Ord.* 1.36.un., nn. 19, 39–40 (Vatican, 6:278, 286–87).

34. *Ord.* 2.3.2.3, n. 395 (Vatican, 7:594).

35. *Ord.* 1.2.2.1–4, n. 394 (Vatican, 2:352); *Ord.* 1.35.un., nn. 14, 32, 49 (Vatican, 6:249–50, 258, 266); *Quod.* 14, n. 14 (Wadding, 12:376 = AW, p. 330 [n. 14.55]).

36. Scotus's position here is rather complex. Simo Knuuttila has re-

cently argued—convincingly to my mind—that according to Scotus necessary truths and logical possibilities have their respective modal properties (i.e., being necessary/possible) irrespective of their actual *existence*. Necessary truths and logical possibilities have their existence caused by God; but their having such and such a modal property is not likewise caused by God. In fact they can have these properties without their needing to *exist* in any sense, whether as thought-objects or as extra-mental realities. See Simo Knuuttila, "Duns Scotus and the Foundations of Logical Modalities," in Honnefelder, Wood, and Dreyer (eds.), *John Duns Scotus: Metaphysics and Ethics*, 127–43.

37. *Ord.* 1.2.1.1–2, n. 98 (Vatican, 2:184 = *PW*, p. 58).

38. *Lect.* 1.39.1–5, nn. 43–44 (Vatican, 17:492–93 = Vos, pp. 104, 106); *Ord.* 1.38.un., nn. 5–6 (Vatican, 6:304–305). A lot of presuppositions about God's goodness and unconditioned nature appear in this argument. I will consider some of them in more detail in chapter 7, section 2, below.

39. *Lect.* 1.39.1–5, n. 62 (Vatican, 17:500 = Vos, p. 142); see also *Ord.* 2.37.2, n. 3 (Wadding, 6: 991). A revised text can be found in Allan B. Wolter, "Scotus's Paris Lectures on God's Knowledge of Future Events," in his *The Philosophical Theology of John Duns Scotus*, 324, n. 96; also *Rep.* 1.38, edited in Wolter, "Scotus's Paris Lectures," 288–89, n. 9. See also William A. Frank, "Duns Scotus on Autonomous Freedom and Divine Co-Causality," 146–47.

40. For these, see *Ord.* 1.2.1.1–2, nn. 98–104 (Vatican, 2:184–87).

41. See, for example, *Quod.* 2, n. 30 (Wadding, 12:64 = AW, p. 58 [n. 2.94]); "In the divine only that which is actual is possible."

42. *Lect.* 1.39.1–5, n. 64 (Vatican, 17:500–501 = Vos, p. 144), discussing Henry of Ghent, *Quodlib.* 8.2 (2 vols. [Paris, 1518], 2:301H–I); see also Scotus, *Rep.* 1.38, discussed in Wolter, "Scotus's Paris Lectures," 291.

43. *Lect.* 1.39.1–5, n. 65 (Vatican, 17:501 = Vos, p. 146); see Wolter, "Scotus' Paris Lectures," 291–93.

44. *Ord.* 2.37.2, n. 7 (Wadding, 6:994); a revised text is found in Wolter, "Scotus's Paris Lectures," 324–25, nn. 96–100.

45. Wolter, "Scotus's Paris Lectures," 333; Frank, "Duns Scotus on Autonomous Freedom and Divine Co-Causality," 163. In *Rep.* 1.38, Scotus makes it clear that it is a mistake to see God's causal activity as sufficient for a creaturely effect; see Wolter, "Scotus's Paris Lectures," 301 (for the text, see note 46 of Wolter's article).

46. Frank, "Duns Scotus on Autonomous Freedom and Divine Co-Causality," 154–55. The example makes it quite clear that both causes here are supposed to be *immediate* causes of the effect. Neither acts by means of a causal chain.

47. Frank, "Duns Scotus on Autonomous Freedom and Divine Co-Causality," 153.

48. See my "Duns Scotus on Eternity and Timelessness," 7, 11–13; see *Quod.* 6, n. 14 (Wadding, 12:150 = AW, p. 141 [n. 6.34]); *Ord.* 1.9.un., n. 11 (Vatican, 4:333); *Ord.* 1.13.un., n. 83 (Vatican, 5:110); *Ord.* 2.1.3, n. 155 (Vatican, 7:78).

49. See Norman Kretzmann's seminal article "Omniscience and Immutability," *Journal of Philosophy*, 63 (1966): 409–421; for the opposing view—with which Scotus would doubtless have been sympathetic—see H.-N. Castañeda, "Omniscience and Indexical Reference," *Journal of Philosophy*, 64 (1967): 203–210.

50. *Ord.* 1.30.1–2, n. 41 (Vatican, 6:187–88); see also *Lect.* 1.39.1–5, n. 73 (Vatican, 17:504 = Vos, p. 160). For a more detailed discussion of the whole issue, including Scotus's debate with Henry of Ghent on this matter, see my "Duns Scotus on Eternity and Timelessness," 13–15.

51. *Ord.* 1.30.1–2, n. 42 (Vatican, 6:188).

52. *Ord.* 4.1.1, nn. 26–27 (Wadding, 8:47ᵃ–49).

53. *Ord.* 4.13.1, n. 37 (Wadding, 8:807).

54. On instrumental activity, see chapter 11, below.

55. *Quod.* 7, n. 4 (Wadding, 12:169–70 = AW, pp. 161–62 [n. 7.8]); *Quod.* 7, n. 19 (Wadding, 12:179 = AW, p. 175 [n. 7.51]); *Ord.* 1.42.un., n. 9 (Vatican, 6:343–44).

56. *Quod.* 7, n. 19 (Wadding, 12:179 = AW, p. 175 [n. 7.52]).

57. *Quod.* 7, n. 19 (Wadding, 12:179 = AW, p. 175 [n. 7.53]).

58. *Quod.* 7, n. 19 (Wadding, 12:179 = AW, p. 175 [n. 7.54]).

59. *Quod.* 7, n. 20 (Wadding, 12:179 = AW, p. 175 [n. 7.55]); *Ord.* 1.42.un., n. 10 (Vatican, 6:344).

60. *Quod.* 7, n. 23 (Wadding, 12:180 = AW, p. 177 [n. 7.63]).

61. *Lect.* 1.39.1–5, n. 46 (Vatican, 17:493–94 = Vos, p. 110).

62. *Lect.* 1.39.1–5, n. 53 (Vatican, 17:496–97 = Vos, p. 124).

63. *Lect.* 1.39.1–5, nn. 53–54 (Vatican, 17:496–97 = Vos, pp. 124, 126).

64. *Lect.* 1.39.1–5, nn. 49–51 (Vatican, 17:496–97 = Vos, pp. 116, 118).

65. *Lect.* 1.39.1–5, n. 62 (Vatican, 17:500 = Vos, p. 143).

66. For earlier developments of the power distinction, see most recently Lawrence Moonan, *Divine Power: The Medieval Power Distinction up to Its Adoption by Albert, Bonaventure, and Aquinas* (Oxford: Clarendon Press, 1994), and the works cited in chapter 1 therein.

67. *Ord.* 1.44.un., n. 10 (Vatican, 6:367 = *WM*, p. 259).

68. Eugenio Randi contrasts Scotus's treatment of the two powers with Ockham's: "Scotus claims that God can do *de potentia absoluta* (i.e., de facto)

different things from those that he does *de potentia ordinata* (i.e., de iure). Nothing striking, but the fact that Ockham uses this parallelism the other way round: *de potentia absoluta* God can do things that *de potentia ordinata*, that is de facto, he never did, nor does, nor will do." Randi, "A Scotist Way of Distinguishing between God's Absolute and Ordained Powers," in Anne Hudson and Michael Wilks (eds.), *From Ockham to Wyclif*, Studies in Church History: Subsidia, 5 (Oxford: Basil Blackwell, 1987), 44–45. In fact, nothing about Scotus's exposition of his own position should lead us to infer that Scotus in any way understood God's absolute power as a special realm of action—perhaps the realm of the miraculous. Anything that Scotus's God can do is done lawfully—"ordainedly." Interestingly, and corresponding to my account, the idea of a pact between God and his creatures—a covenant in which God guarantees that he will act reliably and lawfully, cannot be found in Scotus. On this, see also M. A. Pernoud, "The Theory of the *Potentia Dei* according to Aquinas, Scotus and Ockham," *Antonianum*, 47 (1972): 69–95.

69. See Moonan, *Divine Power*, for a discussion of the difficulties. The problem is not that the thinkers of the thirteenth century lacked any sense of what we would label the 'logically possible' (see, e.g., my discussion in chapter 1, note 6, above), but that they did not have any clear theoretical way of talking about this sort of possibility.

70. Simo Knuuttila, "Modal Logic," in Norman Kretzmann, Anthony Kenny, and Jan Pinborg (eds.), *The Cambridge History of Later Medieval Philosophy* (Cambridge: Cambridge University Press, 1982), 355; see also his *Modalities in Medieval Philosophy*, Topics in Medieval Philosophy (London and New York: Routledge, 1993), 139–49. In addition to the passages from *Lect.* 1.39.1–5 discussed above, see also *Ord.* 1.2.2.1–4, n. 196 (Vatican, 2:249): "The possible is that which does not include a contradiction"; also *Ord.* 1.2.2.1–4, n. 262 (Vatican, 2:282); *Ord.* 1.7.1, n. 27 (Vatican, 4:118–19).

71. *Ord.* 1.8.2.un., n. 294 (Vatican, 4:322); see also *Ord.* 2.1.2, n. 86 (Vatican, 7:45).

72. *Ord.* 2.1.2, n. 85 (Vatican, 7:44–45). Scotus is also clear that a timeless God does not have to wait for his effect; *Ord.* 1.8.2.un., n. 297 (Vatican, 4:324).

CHAPTER 5

1. See, for example, Basil of Caesarea (probably to be attributed to Gregory of Nyssa), *Ep.* 38 (ed. Yves Courtonne, Collections des Universités de France, 3 vols. [Paris: Les Belles Lettres, 1957] 1:81–92).

2. For a detailed discussion of Scotus's Trinitarian thought, see Friedrich Wetter, *Die Trinitätslehre des Johannes Duns Scotus*, BGPTM, 41(5) (Münster: Aschendorff, 1967).

3. *Ord.* 1.9.un., n. 7 (Vatican, 4:331).

4. For the Trinitarian analogy of memory, understanding, and will, see Augustine, *De Trin.* 10.13–19 (CCSL, 50:326–32), discussed in *Ord.* 1.3.3.4, nn. 580, 583–86 (Vatican, 3:343–47), and *Ord.* 2.16.un., n. 20 (Wadding, 6:774); for mind, knowledge, and love, see *De Trin.* 9.8–16 (CCSL, 50:300–308), discussed in *Ord.* 1.3.3.4, n. 583 (Vatican, 3:334).

5. *Quod.* 14, n. 14 (Wadding, 12:376 = AW, p. 329 [n. 14.53]). Note that, as we saw in chapter 4, above, the divine essence is known directly by the divine mind; there is no "intelligible object" in God representing his essence. In this Trinitarian context, Scotus does not include creatures, or creaturely essences, in this object of knowledge. *Ord.* 1.27.1–2, n. 95 (Vatican, 6:102).

6. *Ord.* 1.2.2.1–4, nn. 292–94, 312 (Vatican, 2:299–301, 315); *Ord.* 1.27.1–3, nn. 78, 85–86 (Vatican, 94, 98–99); *Ord.* 1.32.1–2, nn. 24–25 (Vatican, 6:231–33). Scotus's account of the procession of the Son is immensely complex. I present only the barest outline here.

7. *Ord.* 1.2.2.1–4, nn. 291, 320 (Vatican, 2:299–300, 317–18); *Ord.* 1.27.1–3, n. 64 (Vatican, 6:88); *Ord.* 2.1.1, n. 40 (Vatican, 7:23–24).

8. *Quod.* 2, nn. 28–29 (Wadding, 12:62 = AW, pp. 56–57 [nn. 2.89, 2.91]).

9. See *Ord.* 1.2.2.1–4, nn. 311–12 (Vatican, 2:314–15); *Quod.* 1, nn. 19–20 (Wadding, 12:28 = AW, pp. 26–27 [nn. 1.67–71]); *Quod.* 1, n. 22 (Wadding, 12:29 = AW, p. 28 [n. 1.76]); *Quod.* 2, n. 8 (Wadding, 12:40 = AW, p. 38 [n. 2.26]); *Quod.* 14, n. 14 (Wadding, 12:276 = AW, p. 330 [n. 14.55]). Scotus also denies that the divine Word belongs to the divine intelligence; *Ord.* 1.2.2.1–4, n. 321 (Vatican, 2:318); *Ord.* 1.27.1–3, nn. 64, 71 (Vatican, 88, 91).

10. 'Notional' here picks out a divine feature belonging properly to one or more of the divine persons rather than to the divine essence; see, for example, *Quod.* 1, nn. 5–6 (Wadding, 12:7–8 = AW, pp. 9–10 [n. 1.14]).

11. *Ord.* 1.11.1, nn. 15–16 (Vatican, 5:5–6); *Ord.* 1.10.un., n. 62 (Vatican, 4:365).

12. *Ord.* 1.12.1, n. 19 (Vatican, 5:35).

13. *De Trin.* 15.27 (CCSL, 50:501).

14. *De Trin.* 6.7 (CCSL, 50:235); see *Ord.* 1.12.1, n. 1 (Vatican, 5:25).

15. *Quod.* 5, n. 7 (Wadding, 12:125 = AW, p. 114 [n. 5.16]); *Ord.* 1.13.un., n. 39 (Vatican, 5:85).

16. *Ord.* 1.12.1, n. 20 (Vatican, 5:20).

17. *Ord.* 1.12.1, n., 48 (Vatican, 5:53); see also *Ord.* 1.12.1, n. 37 (Vatican, 5:44–45).

18. See *De Trin.* 15.27 (CCSL, 50:501); for the *filioque*, see also *De Trin.* 5.15 (CCSL, 50:222–23).

19. *Ord.* 1.11.1, n. 9 (Vatican, 5:28).

20. *Ord.* 1.11.1, n. 10 (Vatican, 5:29–30).

21. *Ord.* 1.11.1, n. 11 (Vatican, 5:4).

22. *Ord.* 1.12.1, n. 36 (Vatican, 5:44).

23. *Ord.* 1.12.2, n. 60 (Vatican, 5:59).

24. Aquinas, *ST* 1.36.2 c (1[1]:183^b–4^b).

25. *Ord.* 1.11.2, n. 40 (Vatican, 5:16); see also *Ord.* 1.11.2, n. 49 (Vatican, 5:21).

26. *Ord.* 1.2.2.1–4, n. 239 (Vatican, 2:271–72).

27. *Ord.* 1.2.2.1–4, nn. 233, 235 (Vatican, 2:266–69); *Ord.* 1.10.un., n. 9 (Vatican, 4:342).

28. *Lect.* 1.2.2.1–4, n. 165 (Vatican, 16:168); see *Ord.* 1.2.2.1–4, n. 222 (Vatican, 260–61); *Ord.* 1.10.un., n. 9 (Vatican, 4:342).

29. *Ord.* 1.2.2.1–4, n. 222 (Vatican, 2:260–61); *Lect.* 1.2.2.1–4, n. 165 (Vatican, 16:167–68). See also *Ord.* 1.10.un., n. 9 (Vatican, 4:342).

30. *De Trin.* 5.4 (CCSL, 50:208–209).

31. *De Trin.* 5.6 (CCSL, 50:210).

32. *De Trin.* 5.6 (CCSL, 50:210–211). Scotus cites *De Trin.* 5.6 in *Quod.* 3, n. 18 (Wadding, 12:83 = AW, p. 76 [n. 3.51]), seemingly with approval. See also *Quod.* 4, n. 32 (Wadding, 12:115 = AW, pp. 106–107 [n. 4.68]).

33. On this, see the Appendix, section 2.

34. See *Lect.* 1.26.un., n. 66 (Vatican, 17:337), where Scotus claims that the theory is more probable. In *Ord.* 1.26.un., nn. 70–71 (Vatican, 6:28–29), Scotus tries to show that the theory is consistent with Church teaching, referring to Lateran IV and the Council of Lyons.

35. *Ord.* 1.26.un., n. 24 (Vatican, 6:6); *Lect.* 1.26.un., n. 17 (Vatican, 17:320).

36. *Ord.* 1.26, n. 26 (Vatican, 6:6).

37. *Ord.* 1.26.un., nn. 80, 82 (Vatican, 6:36–37); *Lect.* 1.26.un., n. 59 (Vatican, 17:334–35).

38. *Ord.* 1.26.un., n. 38 (Vatican, 6:13); *Lect.* 1.26.un., n. 29 (Vatican, 17:323).

39. *Ord.* 1.26.un., nn. 45, 47 (Vatican, 6:15–16); *Lect.* 1.26.un., n. 34 (Vatican, 17:324–25).

40. *Ord.* 1.26.un., n. 84 (Vatican, 6:39–44); *Lect.* 1.26.un., n. 68 (Vatican, 17:337–38).

41. *Ord.* 1.26.un., n. 93 (Vatican, 6:49); *Lect.* 1.26.un., n. 75 (Vatican, 17:75–76).

42. It is possible that Scotus's defense of the absolute-property theory got him into trouble; see Vatican, 6:23*. For some of the debates, see Michael Schmaus, *Die Liber Propugnatorius des Thomas Anglicus und die Lehrunterschiede zwischen Thomas von Aquin und Duns Scotus. II. Teil: Die Trinitarischen*

Lehrdifferenzen. Erste Band: Systematische Darstellung und historische Wür-digung, BGPTM, 29(1) (Münster: Aschendorff, 1930), 482–550.

43. *Ord.* 3.1.5 (MS A, fol. 142va).

44. *Ord.* 3.1.5 (MS A, fol. 142vb); see also the *textus interpolatus* to *Ord.* 1.26.un. (Vatican, 6:49, l. 18–50, l. 2), which here reproduces the text from *Ord.* 3.1.5 (on this, see the editorial comments in Vatican, 6:4*–8*); also *Quod.* 3, n. 6 (Wadding, 12:72 = AW, pp. 65–66 [n. 3.24]).

45. See also the very late *Quod.* 1, n. 7 (Wadding, 12:9 = AW, p. 10 [n. 1.16]): "Everything notional is something relative internally, and vice versa." Nevertheless, even at this late date, Scotus sees the issue as still basically undecided; see *Quod.* 4, n. 2 (Wadding, 12:88 = AW, pp. 80–81 [n. 4.3])

46. *Rep.* 1.26.2 (MS V, fol. 77^{ra-b}) cited in Wetter, *Die Trinitätslehre*, 334; see also *Quod.* 1, nn. 23–24 (Wadding, 12:33 = AW, pp. 29–30 [n. 1.78–80]) on the generic difference between absolute and relational items.

47. See *Ord.* 1.11.2, n. 45 (Vatican, 5:19); *Ord.* 1.26.un., n. 1 (Vatican, 6:1); *Ord.* 1.28.1–2, nn. 45–46 (Vatican, 6:131); *Ord.* 1.28.3, nn. 55, 93 (Vatican, 6:139–140, 155); and *Quod.* 4, n. 25 (Wadding, 12:109–110 = AW, pp. 100–101 [nn. 4.52, 4.57]) for the Father's property. See *Ord.* 1.11.2, nn. 40–41 (Vatican, 5:16–17); *Ord.* 1.26.un., n. 1 (Vatican, 6:1); and *Quod.* 2, n. 1 (Wadding, 12:35 = AW, pp. 31–32 [n. 2.3]) for the Son's property. See *Ord.* 1.26.un., n. 49 (Vatican, 6:16–17); and *Quod.* 2, n. 1 (Wadding, 12:35 = AW, pp. 31–32 [n. 2.3]) for the Spirit.

48. *Ord.* 1.26.un., n. 10 (Vatican, 6:3); *Ord.* 1.28.1–2, nn. 19–20, 27, 30, 45–46 (Vatican, 6:116–17, 120, 123–24, 131).

49. *Ord.* 1.28.3, n. 90 (Vatican, 6:153).

50. Scotus is here supposing that the property "not-F" is necessarily shareable by different things.

51. *Ord.* 1.28.1–2, n. 44 (Vatican, 130); *Quod.* 4, n. 7 (Wadding, 12:94–95 = AW, pp. 85–86 [nn. 4.18–19]).

52. Lateran IV, const. 2 (Tanner, 1:*231–*2).

53. *Ord.* 1.5.1.un., n. 10 (Vatican, 4:14); see also *Ord.* 1.23.un., n. 15 (Vatican, 355–57), where Scotus makes it clear that God is one substance (and hence that Boethius's definition of 'person' as "individual substance of rational nature" cannot apply in the case of God; see Boethius, *De Per.* 3 [*The Theological Tractates. The Consolation of Philosophy*, ed. H. F. Stewart, E. K. Rand, and S. J. Tester, Loeb Classical Library (Cambridge: Harvard University Press; London: Heinemann, 1978), p. 85]).

54. See, for example, *Ord.* 1.2.2.1–4, n. 437 (Vatican, 2:375–76).

55. *Ord.* 1.2.2.1–4, n. 381 (Vatican, 2:346).

56. *Ord.* 1.2.2.1–4, nn. 379–80 (Vatican, 2:345–46).

57. On the formal distinction, see the Appendix, section 2.

58. *Ord.* 1.2.2.1–4, n. 381 (Vatican, 2:346); see also *Quod.* 1, n. 24 (Wadding, 12:33 = AW, pp. 29–30 [n. 1.80]); and *Quod.* 3, n. 17 (Wadding, 12:82–83 = AW, pp. 74–75 [n. 3.49]). Wolter's translation of Augustine's 'incommutabilis' (*De Trin.* 7.10 [CCSL, 50:261], quoted in *Quod.* 1, n. 3 [Wadding, 12:3 = AW, p. 7 (n. 1.6)]), as 'incommunicable', obscures this important point.

59. *Ord.* 1.2.2.1–4, n. 381 (Vatican, 2:346). The point is made neatly at *Lect.* 2.1.1, n. 48 (Vatican, 18:17): "Deity is 'this' in itself, and thus God is this God in virtue of this deity, which is common to the three persons." On God's Trinitarian nature as "this God," see chapter 1, section 2, above.

60. Aquinas holds that God's essence is incommunicable; see *ST* 1.11.3 c (1[1]:49^b). This leaves no room for an account of the three persons as somehow having the same essence.

61. *Ord.* 1.2.2.1–4, n. 387 (Vatican, 2:349).

62. *Ord.* 1.2.2.1–4, nn. 386–87 (Vatican, 2:348–49); see *Ord.* 1.2.2.1–4, n. 412 (Vatican, 2:362); *Ord.* 1.5.2.un., n. 135 (Vatican, 4:76–77); *Ord.* 1.26.un., n. 64 (Vatican, 6:25–26).

63. *Ord.* 1.2.2.1–4, n. 385 (Vatican, 2:348); see also *Ord.* 1.2.2.1–4, n. 367 (Vatican, 2:339); *Ord.* 1.5.2.un., n. 117 (Vatican, 4:69); *Ord.* 1.26.un., n. 82 (Vatican, 6:37); *Ord.* 1.26.un., *textus interpolatus* (Vatican, 6:50, lines 28–37); and *Ord.* 2.3.1.7, n. 227 (Vatican, 7:500).

64. *Ord.* 1.2.2.1–4, n. 388 (Vatican, 2:349); *Quod.* 3, n. 10 (Wadding, 12:76–77 = AW, pp. 68–69 [n. 3.33]).

65. *Ord.* 1.2.2.1–4, nn. 389, 391, 393, 398, 403 (Vatican, 2:349–52, 354–57); for the formal distinction between essence and property, see *Ord.* 1.2.2.1–4, nn. 396–408 (Vatican, 2:353–58).

66. *Ord.* 1.2.2.1–4, nn. 415, 417 (Vatican, 2:363–64). For similar arguments, solved in similar ways, see *Quod.* 5, nn. 5–6 (Wadding, 12:120–21 = AW, pp. 112–13 [nn. 5.12–14]); *Quod.* 5, n. 17 (Wadding, 12:130 = AW, pp. 121–22 [n. 5.37]); and *Quod.* 5, n. 18 (Wadding, 12:131 = AW, pp. 122–23 [n. 5.41]).

67. *Ord.* 1.2.2.1–4, nn. 417–18 (Vatican, 2:364–65).

68. *Ord.* 1.2.2.1–4, n. 415 (Vatican, 2:363–64).

69. *Ord.* 1.2.2.1–4, n. 421 (Vatican, 2:366–67).

70. For Scotus's claim that the persons are numerically three, see *Ord.* 1.24.un., n. 7 (Vatican, 5:368); also *Ord.* 1.3.2.un., n. 301 (Vatican, 3:183–84).

71. One standard Patristic way of explaining the divine unity was to appeal to the doctrine of perichoresis: the mutual indwelling of the divine persons. See, for example, John of Damascus, *De Fide Orth.* 1.8 (PG, 94:829A); *De Fide Orth.* 1.14 (PG, 94:860B); and *De Fide Orth.* 4.18 (PG, 94:1181B). Some medievals reduced the doctrine of perichoresis to the numerical identity of the divine essence; the divine persons indwell each other in virtue of the fact

that their essence is numerically one. Henry of Ghent records this opinion, and attributes it to John of Damascus; see *SQ* 53.10, 2:73^{v}N). Scotus does not believe this account of perichoresis to be strong enough. He interprets perichoresis as the indwelling of the persons in each other, over and above the unity they exhibit in virtue of the divine essence (*Ord*. 1.19.2, nn. 42, 54, 67 (Vatican, 5:284, 290, 298). The doctrine is superfluous to requirements in Scotus's theology, since he does not need it to account for divine unity. But its inclusion is certainly a welcome component from the Eastern Trinitarian tradition.

72. See, for example, Augustine, *Contra Max*. 2.10.2 (PL, 42:765); *De Trin* 1.7 (CCSL 50:36); and *De Trin*. 2.3 (CCSL, 50:83). Scotus cites *De Trin*. 5.15 (CCSL, 50:223) in *Quod*. 8, n. 3 (Wadding, 12:205 = AW, p. 199 [n. 8.6]).

73. Henry of Ghent, *Quodlib*. 6.2 (*Opera Omnia*, ed. R. Macken and others, Ancient and Medieval Philosophy, De Wulf-Mansion Centre, Series 2 [Leuven: Leuven University Press; Leiden: E. J. Brill, 1979–], 10:36–40).

74. *Ord*. 2.1.1, n. 6 (Vatican, 7:3–4).

75. *Ord*. 2.1.1, n. 8 (Vatican, 7:5). On this matter, see chapter 7, section 1, below.

76. *Ord*. 2.1.1, n. 18 (Vatican, 7:10–11).

77. *Ord*. 2.1.1, n. 19 (Vatican, 7:11). In the *Quodlibetal Questions*, Scotus offers a series of different arguments. See *Quod*. 8, nn. 4–5 (Wadding, 12:205 = AW, pp. 200–201 [nn. 8.7–9]); *Quod*. 8, n. 7 (Wadding, 12:206 = AW, p. 203 [n. 8.14]); *Quod*, 8, n. 15 (Wadding, 12:210–211 = AW, p. 209 [n. 8.30]); *Quod*. 8, n. 20 (Wadding, 12:216 = AW, pp. 212–13 [nn. 8.41–43]); and *Quod*. 1, n. 9 (Wadding, 12:10 = AW, p. 13 [n. 1.24]).

CHAPTER 6

1. For Scotus's account of matter and form, see my *The Physics of Duns Scotus*, chapters 2 and 3.

2. For Aquinas's claim that forms are individuals, see, for example, *ST* 1.50.2 c (1[1]:253^b). For Scotus, see my *The Physics of Duns Scotus*, chapter 3, section 1.

3. See, for example, *ST* 1.76.3 c (1[1]:362^b), where Aquinas argues that the unity of a substance can only be explained if we posit just one substantial form; also see *ST* 1.76.4 c (1[1]:364^a), where Aquinas argues that, unless there were just one substantial form, there could be no principled way of distinguishing between substantial unities and merely accidental unities. For Scotus's attempts to refute these arguments, see *Ord*. 4.11.3, nn. 46, 50 (Wadding, 8:649, 651). I discuss the arguments in *The Physics of Duns Scotus*, chapter 4, section 3.

4. *ST* 1.76.1 c (1[1]:358ᵃ).

5. See, for example, Aquinas, *Script. Sent.* 4.44.1.1.2 ad 3 (*Opera Omnia*, ed. Roberto Busa, 7 vols. [Stuttgart and Bad Constatt: Fromann and Holzburg, 1980], 1:636ᵃ).

6. *Ord.* 4.11.3, n. 54 (Wadding, 8:653). I discuss the argument in *The Physics of Duns Scotus*, chapter 4, section 3.

7. For the condemnation, see proposition 13 "in naturalibus" condemned by Kilwardby at Oxford in 1277: "That a dead body is equivocally a body, and that a dead body [considered] as a dead body is a body in a derivative sense" (*Cartularium Universitatis Parisiensis*, ed. H. Denifle and E. Chatelain, 4 vols. [Paris: Delalain, 1889–97], 1:559). Aquinas defended the condemned proposition (before it was actually condemned, by which time Aquinas was dead) in *Quae. Quod.* 3.2.2 (ed. R. M. Spiazzi [Turin and Rome: Marietti, 1949], pp. 42ᵇ–43ᵃ) (Easter 1270), where he claims that Christ's dead body is only equivocally a body at all. But by Easter 1271 he rejected it; see *Quae. Quod.* 4.5.un. (p. 76ᵇ) where he claims that Christ's dead body is numerically the same as his living body on the grounds that bodily identity is determined by the identity of the *person* whose body it is. (On the dates of the two *Quodlibets*, see Jean-Pierre Torrell, *Saint Thomas Aquinas. Volume 1: The Person and His Work*, trans. Robert Royal [Washington, D. C.: Catholic University of America Press, 1996], 211.) Scotus discusses the heterodoxy of the one-form position in *Ord.* 4.11.3, nn. 28, 31 (Wadding, 8:630, 632).

8. I discuss this theory in *The Physics of Duns Scotus*, chapter 4, sections 3 and 4. For the background, see Roberto Zavalloni, *Richard de Mediavilla et la controverse sur la pluralité des formes*, Philosophes Médiévaux, 2 (Louvain: L'Institut Supérieur de Philosophie, 1951).

9. *Ord.* 4.11.3, n. 46 (Wadding, 8:649).

10. For this claim, see my *The Physics of Duns Scotus*, chapter 5. The classic Scotist discussion of these matters is *Ord.* 3.2.2, nn. 7–11 (Wadding, 7:76–81).

11. Most of the schoolmen believe that it is possible to *demonstrate* this claim. An exception is William of Ockham; see his *Quod. Sept.* 1.10 (*OT*, 9:63–64 = FK, 1:56–57).

12. *Ord.* 4.43.2, n. 10 (Wadding, 10:24 = *PW*, p. 141).

13. *Ord.* 4.43.2, n. 10 (Wadding, 10:24–25 = *PW*, p. 142).

14. In the *Ordinatio*, Scotus argues further that we have some knowledge whose *subject* cannot be a sense organ. Mere sense knowledge of a given sort is "limited to the sensibles of some determined kind," just as "every [sense] organ is determined to a certain sort of sensible"; *Ord.* 4.43.2, n. 7 (Wadding, 10:23 = *PW*, p. 139). But our knowledge is greater than this, since we can know "how one kind of sensible differs from another"; *Ord.* 4.43.2,

n. 7 (Wadding, 10:23 = *PW*, p. 140). And to do this, we need more than mere sense knowledge. In the *Quodlibetal Questions*, however, Scotus denies that the non-organic nature of our knowledge is sufficient to allow us to infer its immateriality: "Even a purely material form like fire is not said to act through an organ, provided it be uniformly in the whole and each part thereof" (*Quod.* 9, n. 10 [Wadding, 12:229 = AW, p. 225 (n. 9.26)]).

15. *Ord.* 4.43.2, n. 12 (Wadding, 10:26 = *PW*, pp. 143–44). In the *Quodlibetal Questions*, however, Scotus denies this inference: "To get the conclusion we want [viz., that the intellect is an immaterial power], one would have to show that this operation which has the universal as its object could not be communicated to matter in some way" (*Quod.* 9, n. 11 [Wadding, 12:230 = AW, p. 226 (n. 9.27)]). In this late text, Scotus suggests that we could infer the immateriality of the soul as follows: "What is proximately and properly the recipient subject of intellection is the form and not something material" (*Quod.* 9, n. 11 [Wadding, 12:230 = AW, p. 226 (n. 9.28)]). Scotus gives, however, no argument in favor of this claim. So I take it that he becomes increasingly pessimistic about the possibility of proving the soul's immateriality.

16. *Ord.* 4.43.2, n. 12 (Wadding, 10:26 = *PW*, p. 144–45). I discuss Scotus's account of human freedom in chapter 7, below.

17. *ST* 1.76.4 ad 2 (1[1]:364^b).

18. *Ord.* 4.43.2, n. 6 (Wadding, 10:23 = *PW*, p. 139). Elsewhere, Scotus claims that there is no reason why an angel cannot causally affect a human body in a way analogous to the way in which a soul can affect its body; see *Ord.* 2.8.un., n. 2 (Wadding, 6:585).

19. *Ord.* 4.43.2, n. 6 (Wadding, 10:23 = *PW*, p. 139).

20. *Quod.* 9, n. 11 (Wadding, 12: 230 = AW, pp. 226–28 [nn. 9.28–29]); *Ord.* 2.8.un., n. 4 (Wadding, 6:587); *Ord* 4.10.7, n. 3 (Wadding, 8:560); and *Ord.* 1.3.3.2, nn. 471, 504 (Vatican, 3:282–83, 299). See also *ST* 1.51.3 (1[1]: 259^{a–b}).

21. *Ord.* 2.8.un., nn. 4–5 (Wadding, 6:587).

22. *ST* 1.89.1 c (1[1]:436^b).

23. *Ord.* 4.45.2, n. 12 (Wadding, 10:182).

24. *Ord.* 4.1.1, n. 30 (Wadding, 8:52). Presumably the attribute of nobility will here include attributes such as complexity, set of causal powers, and so on. The argument will thus be that a more complex agent cannot be caused by a less complex one.

25. Scotus has a complex argument for this claim. I discuss it in *The Physics of Duns Scotus*, appendix. Whether or not the argument is successful, Scotus accepts as part of the Christian faith that creatures cannot themselves create; see *Ord.* 4.1.1, n. 27 (Wadding, 8:49). Creation, according to the faith, requires infinite power; no creature has infinite power.

26. See, for example, *ST* 1.75.6 c (1[1]:355[b]). I discuss Aquinas's arguments in "Is Aquinas's Attempt to Prove the Indestructibility of the Soul Successful?" *British Journal for the History of Philosophy*, 5 (1997): 1–20.

27. *ST* 1.76.1 ad 6 (1[1]:359[b]–60[a]). Aquinas denies that this entails that the soul is only accidentally the form of the body, but he is obviously wrong about this.

28. *Ord.* 4.43.2, n. 16 (Wadding, 10:28–29 = *PW*, pp. 148–49).

29. *De an.* 2.2 (413[b]29–31).

30. *Ord.* 4.43.2, n. 13 (Wadding, 10:27 = *PW*, p. 145).

31. *Ord.* 4.43.2, n. 17 (Wadding, 10:29 = *PW*, p. 149).

32. *Quod.* 9, n. 12 (Wadding, 12:230 = AW, p. 228 [n. 9.30]).

33. *Ord.* 4.43.2, n. 23 (Wadding, 10:30 = *PW*, pp. 154).

34. I discuss this in *The Physics of Duns Scotus*, chapter 3, section 1.

35. *Ord.* 4.43.1, n. 11 (Wadding, 10:18).

36. *Ord.* 4.43.3, nn. 9–13 (Wadding, 10:44–45, 54–55). I discuss Scotus's claims in "Identity, Origin, and Persistence in Duns Scotus's Physics," *History of Philosophy Quarterly*, 16(1999): 1–19. See also Marilyn McCord Adams, "The Resurrection of the Body According to Three Medieval Aristotelians: Thomas Aquinas, John Duns Scotus, William Ockham," *Philosophical Topics*, 20 (1992): 9–18.

37. *Ord.* 4.43.3, n. 20 (Wadding, 10:62).

38. *Ord.* 4.43.3, n. 11 (Wadding, 10:44).

39. *Ord.* 4.43.3, nn. 21–22 (Wadding, 10:64).

40. *Ord.* 4.43.3, n. 22 (Wadding, 10:64); and *Ord.* 4.43.4, n. 5 (Wadding, 10:68).

41. *Ord.* 4.43.2, n. 24 (Wadding, 10:33–34 = *PW*, p. 155).

42. *Ord.* 4.43.2, n. 24 (Wadding, 10:33 = *PW*, p. 154); see Aristotle, *Cael.* 2.3 (286[a]18).

43. *Ord.* 4.43.2, n. 24 (Wadding, 10:33–34 = *PW*, p. 155). Scotus thus correctly sees, against Aquinas, that there is no sense in which union with the body can be essential to the human soul.

44. See *Script. Sent.* 4.44.1.1.2 ad 3 (1:636[a]). For a recent discussion of this issue in Aquinas, with an analysis of some of its problems, see Christopher Hughes, "Aquinas on Continuity and Identity," *Medieval Philosophy and Theology*, 6 (1997): 93–108.

45. *Ord.* 4.43.1, n. 3 (Wadding, 10:5), referring to Augustine, *De Civ. Dei* 22.20 (CCSL, 48:840).

46. *Ord.* 4.43.1, n. 3 (Wadding, 10:5).

47. *Ord.* 4.43.1, n. 4 (Wadding, 10:5); see my "Identity, Origin, and Persistence," for some of the metaphysical presuppositions underlying this argument.

48. *Ord.* 4.44.1, nn. 16–17 (Wadding, 10:115).

49. I discuss this claim in "Identity, Origin, and Persistence."

50. *Ord.* 4.43.1, n. 4 (Wadding, 10:5); I discuss this argument in detail in "Identity, Origin, and Persistence."

51. 1 Cor. 15.37–38, 44.

52. *Ord.* 4.49.14, n. 4 (Wadding, 10:595).

53. *Ord.* 4.49.14, n. 11 (Wadding, 10:602–603).

54. *Ord.* 4.49.15, nn. 2–3 (Wadding, 10:606, 608).

55. *Ord.* 4.49.16, n. 17 (Wadding, 10:620–621). (Scotus is thinking of passages such as Jn. 20.19.) I discuss some related arguments in *The Physics of Duns Scotus*, chapter 11.

56. *Ord.* 4.49.16, n. 19 (Wadding, 10:621).

57. *Ord.* 4.49.13, n. 9 (Wadding, 10:587).

58. Dan. 3.25–27.

CHAPTER 7

1. *ST* 1.77.1, esp. ad 5 (1[1]:370^b).

2. *Ord.* 2.1.6, n. 316 (Vatican, 7:154); and *Ord.* 2.16.un., nn. 15–16, 18 (Wadding, 6:770–71, 773).

3. *Ord.* 2.16.un., n. 15 (Wadding, 6:770).

4. *Ord.* 2.16.un., n. 8 (Wadding, 6:767).

5. *Lect.* 2.25.un, nn. 55, 68 (Vatican, 19:247, 252); *Ord.* 4.49.9–10, n. 5 (Wadding, 10:513 = *WM*, p. 189).

6. *Ord.* 2.42.1–4, nn. 10–11 (Wadding, 6:1051–52 = *WM*, 173–75).

7. *ST* 1.82.1 c (1:399^a).

8. *ST* 1-2.77.2, esp. ad 4 (1[2]:356^a).

9. *ST* 1-2.2.8 (1[2]:15^{a-b}).

10. *ST* 2-2.47.1–2 (2:234^b–36^a).

11. *ST* 1.83.1 c (1[1]:403^b).

12. *In Metaph.* 9.15, n. 6 (Wadding, 4:798^a = *WM*, p. 155); see *Ord.* 2.6.2, n. 11 (Wadding, 6:541 = *WM*, p. 475); *Lect.* 2.25.un., n. 37 (Vatican, 19:240). Scotus also holds that the contingency of the intellect with regard to assent and dissent can only result in the intellect's sometimes being mistaken; so if freedom consists in the intellect's contingency, freedom would indeed be "a miserable thing." *Lect.* 2.25.un., n. 35 (Vatican, 19:239).

13. *Metaph.* 9.2 (1046^{b}1–4).

14. *In Metaph.* 9.15, n. 2 (Wadding, 4:797^a = *WM*, p. 147). Important for Scotus's account of the will's indeterminism is the notion of choice at an instant. Basically, Scotus holds that for genuine indeterminism, it must be the case that, at the very same time as a will is exercising its causal power in

bringing about an action *a*, it must retain its causal power to bring about not-*a*; *Lect.* 1.39.1–5, nn. 51–52 (Vatican, 17:495–96 = Vos, pp. 118, 122); see also *In Metaph.* 9.15, nn. 12–13 (Wadding, 4:800^b = *WM*, pp. 167–69). This does not seem quite right. Assume that an agent *x*'s possession of a causal power at time *t* to bring about an action *a* is necessary for *x*'s bringing about *a* at *t*. Suppose *x* brings about *a* at *t*, and that *x* has a causal power until *t*$_{-n}$— but not at *t*—to bring about not-*a*. On this scenario, *x* does not have a causal power to bring about not-*a* at *t*. But *x*'s bringing about *a* at *t* can still be free, because *x* could simply refrain from bringing about *a*; it need not exercise any causal power at *t* at all.

15. *In Metaph.* 9.15, n. 2 (Wadding, 4:796^a–97^b = *WM*, p. 147); for the contrast, see *In Metaph.* 9.15, n. 4 (Wadding, 4:797^b = *WM*, p. 151). For a full account of self-motion in Scotus's physics, see Peter King, "Duns Scotus on the Reality of Self-Change," in Mary Louise Gill and James G. Lennox (eds.), *Self-Motion from Aristotle to Newton* (Princeton, N.J.: Princeton University Press, 1994), 229–90. Scotus holds in fact that freedom thus described is compatible with determinism. The reason is that his account of freedom just outlined does not entail that we have the *opportunity* to exercise our causal powers. On this, see the Appendix, section 3 on the beatific vision and freedom. It is, however, important to keep in mind that Scotus does not believe that we usually, under normal circumstances, lack the opportunity for exercising our causal powers. So Scotus is a genuine indeterminist with regard to human freedom.

16. *Lect.* 1.39.1–5, n. 40 (Vatican, 17:491 = Vos, p. 100); also *In Metaph.* 9.15, n. 5 (Wadding, 4:798^a = *WM*, p. 153).

17. *Ord.* 1.1.2.2, n. 93 (Vatican, 2:67–68). On the nature of a natural power, see below.

18. *Ord.* 1.1.2.2, n. 92 (Vatican, 2:66–67).

19. *In Metaph.* 9.15, n. 4 (Wadding, 4:797^b = *WM*, p. 151). Note, of course, that Scotus does not believe anything to be genuinely random (see *Ord.* 1.36.un., n. 39 [Vatican, 6:287]); hence the disjunction he proposes is not between *free*, *determined*, and *random*, but rather just between *free* and *determined*.

20. *In Metaph.* 9.15, n. 5 (Wadding, 4:798^a = *WM*, pp. 153–55).

21. *Ord.* 3.26.un., nn. 17–18 (Wadding, 7:635 = *WM*, pp. 179–81; note that the Wadding text here is very defective); *Ord.* 2.6.2, n. 8 (Wadding, 6:539–40 = *WM*, pp. 469–73). For the Anselmian source, see *De Casu Diab.* 4 (*Opera Omnia*, 1:240–42).

22. See Thomas Williams, "How Scotus Separates Morality from Happiness," *American Catholic Philosophical Quarterly*, 69 (1995): 436–38. The crucial passage is *Ord.* 2.6.2, n. 11 (Wadding: 6:541 = *WM*, p. 477), where

Scotus argues that the will is capable of moderating its willing "in accordance with the rule of justice received from a higher will."

23. *Ord*. 4.49.9–10, nn. 2–3 (Wadding, 10:505–506 = *WM*, pp. 183–87); *Ord*. 2.6.2, n. 8 (Wadding, 6:539–40 = *WM*, pp. 469–71). (This last passage also makes it clear that the intellect presents several options to the will.)

24. *Ord*. 4.49.9–10, n. 5 (Wadding, 10:513 = *WM*, p. 189).

25. *Ord*. 4.49.9–10, nn. 2–3 (Wadding, 10:505–506 = *WM*, pp. 183–87).

26. *Ord*. 4.49.9–10, n. 3 (Wadding, 10:506 = *WM*, p. 185).

27. *Ord*. 3.26.un., n. 17 (Wadding, 7:635 = *WM*, p. 179); *Ord*. 2.6.2, n. 8 (Wadding, 6:540 = *WM*, p. 471). We could, of course, have an account of freedom as superabundant sufficiency without an account of the two inclinations of the will (see John Boler, "Transcending the Natural: Duns Scotus on the Two Affections of the Will," *American Catholic Philosophical Quarterly*, 67 [1993]: 115). But for reasons just outlined we could not do so on the assumption that one of the ways in which the will operates is as a natural power. Boler further argues that the two inclinations of the will are not sufficient for freedom. Again, I am not so sure that he is right. If one of the will's inclinations is natural, then the other cannot be (since one substance in an Aristotelian universe cannot have two natural goals); but possessing a non-natural inclination is sufficient for freedom. See also Sukjae Lee, "Scotus on the Will: The Rational Power and the Two Affections," *Vivarium*, 36 (1998): 40–54.

28. *Ord*. 2.6.2, n. 9 (Wadding, 6:540 = *WM* pp. 471–73). Note that among the natural goals of human existence is included the vision of God (see chapter 1, above); Scotus will argue, as we shall see, that we can desire this goal in the wrong way.

29. *Ord*. 4.49.9–10, n. 3 (Wadding, 10:506 = *WM*, pp. 185–87).

30. *Ord*. 2.6.2, n. 9 (Wadding, 6:540 = *WM*, p. 471). One of these defects, presumably, occurred when Satan fell.

31. Presumably, Scotus is supposing that these sorts of occasion are frequent; otherwise his argument to freedom from introspection would seem to prove that we are free on more occasions than we really are—assuming, at any rate, that it appears, for example, to me that I am free in most of my actions.

32. See *Ord*. 4.49.9–10, n. 6 (Wadding, 10:513 = *WM*, p. 191); *Ord*. 2.43.2, n. 2 (Wadding, 6:1073 = *WM*, p. 479).

33. Rom. 7.15: "I do not understand my own actions. For I do not do what I want, but I do the very thing I hate."

34. *Ord*. 2.43.2, n. 2 (Wadding, 6:1073 = *WM*, p. 479).

35. *Ord*. 4.49.9–10, nn. 8–9 (Wadding, 10:513–14 = *WM*, p. 193).

36. *Lect*. 2.25.un., nn. 69–70 (Vatican, 19:253).

37. *Lect*. 2.25.un., n. 28 (Vatican, 19:236).

38. *Lect*. 2.25.un, n. 55 (Vatican, 19:247).

39. Scotus did not, as has sometimes been thought, change his mind about this: see the editors' introduction in Vatican, 19:38*–41*. Presupposed to Scotus's view is the claim that the intellect is causally as well as logically necessary for the will's action: see *Lect*. 2.25.un., n. 58 (Vatican, 19:248). It is difficult to see why this should be so.

40. See, helpfully, Robert Merrihew Adams, "A Modified Divine Command Theory of Ethical Wrongness," in his *The Virtue of Faith and Other Essays in Philosophical Theology* (New York and Oxford: Oxford University Press, 1987), 97–122.

41. See, for example, Aquinas, *ST* 1=2.94.2 c (1[2]:426^b–7^a).

42. *Ord*. 4.17.un., nn. 4–5 (Wadding, 9:297 = *WM*, p. 265).

43. *Lect*. 2.21–2.1–2, n. 29 (Vatican, 19:206).

44. Anthony Quinton, "British Philosophy," in P. Edwards (ed.), *The Encyclopedia of Philosophy*, 8 vols. (London: Collier-Macmillan, 1965), 1:373); see Wolter, *WM*, p. 3.

45. *Ord*. 2.40.un., n. 3 (Wadding, 6:1028 = *WM*, p. 227).

46. *Quod*. 18, nn. 5–6 (Wadding, 12:476, 479 = *WM*, pp. 213–15 = AW, pp. 402–403 [n. 18.13–14]); *Ord*. 2.40.un., n. 3 (Wadding, 6:1028 = *WM*, p. 227); *Ord*. 1.17.1.1–2, n. 62 (Vatican, 5:163–64 = *WM*, p. 207); *Ord*. 1.48.un., n. 5 (Vatican, 6:388–89 = *WM*, p. 237). The second of these features makes the action generically good; the third, specifically good.

47. *Quod*. 18, nn. 4, 6 (Wadding, 12:476, 479 = *WM*, pp. 213–17= AW, pp. 402–403 [nn. 18.12, 18.15]).

48. See, for example, in addition to the passages cited in the previous note, *Ord*. 1.17.1.1–2, n. 63 (Vatican, 5:164 = *WM*, p. 207 [note that the Latin text in *WM* is not entirely accurate here]).

49. *Quod*. 18, n. 6 (Wadding, 12:479 = *WM*, p. 215 = AW, p. 403 [n. 18.15]).

50. A different interpretation is suggested by Thomas Williams. Williams argues that the appropriateness of objects, ends, and other circumstances is determined by God's free choice, and that we know this appropriateness "immediately" because the contingent truths of moral law have been "written on our hearts" by God (Rom. 2.15, cited in *Ord*. prol.2.un., n. 108 [Vatican, 1:70]; *Ord*. 2.28.un., n. 8 [Wadding, 6:916]; *Ord*. 3.37.un., n. 14 [Wadding, 7:911 = *WM*, p. 287]); see Williams, "Reason, Morality, and Voluntarism in Duns Scotus: A Pseudo-Problem Dissolved," *The Modern Schoolman*, 74 (1997): 73–94. Prima facie evidence in favor of this sort of reading is a famous passage (*Ord*. 3.19.un., n. 7 [Wadding, 7:417]) in which Scotus states: "Everything other than God is good because God wills it, and

not vice versa." See Williams's stimulating discussion of this in "The Un-mitigated Scotus," *Archiv für Geschichte der Philosophie*, 80 (1998): 162–81. (I am grateful to Prof. Williams for kindly showing me the typescript of this article.) Williams's interpretation of Scotus's discussions of moral goodness elsewhere allows them to be obviously consistent with this passage. But it seems to me that some of the things Scotus says about divine justice do not sit easily with Williams's interpretation. I will point these out below. Further-more, and crucially for my disagreement with Williams, the voluntaristic principle just quoted makes God's willing sufficient for the goodness of everything; but it does not, as it stands, make God's willing something *neces-sary* for goodness. For a further recent attempt to analyze some of these issues, see C. P. Ragland, "Scotus on the Decalogue: What Sort of Voluntarism?" *Vivarium*, 36 (1998): 67–81.

51. *Ord.* 3.37.un., n. 6 (Wadding, 7:898 = *WM*, p. 277); see also *Ord.* prol.5.1–2, nn. 336–39, 344 (Vatican, 1:219–21, 224–25); *Ord.* 4.46.1, n. 3 (Wadding, 10:238 = *WM*, p. 241).

52. *Ord.* 3.27.un., n. 2 (Wadding, 7:645 = *WM*, p. 425).

53. *Ord.* 3.37.un., n. 6 (Wadding, 7:898 = *WM*, p. 277).

54. *Ord.* 4.46.1, n. 3 (Wadding, 10:238 = *WM*, p. 241).

55. *Ord.* 3.37.un., n. 5 (Wadding, 7:898 = *WM*, p. 277).

56. *Ord.* 4.46.1, n. 7 (Wadding, 10:252 = *WM*, p. 247).

57. *Ord.* 4.46.1, n. 7 (Wadding, 10:252 = *WM*, p. 247). According to Scotus, it follows from God's nature as truth that he cannot lie, and that it is necessarily wrong for us to commit perjury; *Ord.* 3.39.un., n. 2 (Wadding, 7:980 = *WM*, p. 505).

58. *Ord.* 4.17.un., n. 3 (Wadding, 9:297 = *WM*, p. 263); see *Ord.* 3.37.un., n. 8 (Wadding, 7:898 = *WM*, p. 279).

59. *Ord.* 3.37.un., n. 8 (Wadding, 7:898 = *WM*, p. 279).

60. *Ord.* 4.46.1, n. 9 (Wadding, 10:252 = *WM*, p. 249).

61. *Ord.* 4.46.1, n. 9 (Wadding, 10:252 = *WM*, p. 249).

62. See *Ord.* 4.46.1, n. 7 (Wadding, 10:252 = *WM*, p. 247), cited above.

63. *Ord.* 4.46.1, n. 8 (Wadding, 10:252 = *WM*, p. 249).

64. *Ord.* 4.46.1, nn. 9, 12 (Wadding, 10:252–53 = *WM*, pp. 249, 253).

65. This claim seems to entail that moral appropriateness is intrinsic somehow to the way creatures are. Given that Scotus sees moral goodness as determined by the appropriateness of an action's circumstances (at least for actions whose objects are creatures), Scotus's account of justice$_2$ seems inconsistent with Williams's reading of Scotus described above, according to which a divine command is necessary for the moral goodness of all such actions.

66. *Ord.* 4.33.1, nn. 2–3 (Wadding, 9:703 = *WM*, pp. 291–93).

67. *Ord.* 4.46.1, nn. 8–9 (Wadding, 10:252 = *WM*, pp. 247–49).

68. *Ord.* 4.46.1, n. 8 (Wadding, 10:252 = *WM*, p. 247).

69. *Ord.* 1.44.un., n. 5 (Vatican, 6:364–65 = *WM*, p. 257).

70. *ST* 2-2.61.2 c (2:300^a).

71. *Ord.* 4.46.1, nn. 4, 12 (Wadding, 10:240, 253 = *WM*, pp. 243, 253); on inequality, see Aristotle, *Eth. Nic.* 5.6 (1134^{b}9–10) cited in *Ord.* 4.46.1, nn. 1, 4 (Wadding, 10:237–38, 240 = *WM*, pp. 239, 243).

72. *Ord.* 3.37.un., n. 4 (Wadding, 7:879 = *WM*, p. 275).

73. *Lect.* 1.39.1–5, nn. 43–44 (Vatican, 17:492–93 = Vos, pp. 104, 106); see also *Ord.* 1.38.un., nn. 5–6 (Vatican, 6:304–305).

74. Thomas V. Morris, "Duty and Divine Goodness," *American Philosophical Quarterly*, 21 (1984): 266, reprinted in Morris, *Anselmian Explorations: Essays in Philosophical Theology*, 37).

75. For further evidence, see *Ord.* 4.46.1. n. 12 (Wadding, 10:253 = *WM*, pp. 253–55).

76. Wolter, *WM*, p. 26.

77. *Rep.* 1.44.2 (MS V, fol. 122va), cited in *WM*, p. 19.

78. *Ord.* 3.38.un., n. 5 (Wadding, 7:919 = *WM*, p. 485).

79. *Ord.* 3.38.un., n. 6 (Wadding, 7:922 = *WM*, p. 487; Wolter's version of the Latin text is defective; for the correct version, see my "Duns Scotus on Goodness, Justice, and What God Can Do," *Journal of Theological Studies*, 48 (1997): 67, n. 61. In my article (p. 69), I claim that lying is intrinsically evil. Scotus looks to be making this sort of claim, but perhaps the weaker claim—that lying can never be in accord with the intrinsic values of things— is more plausible. After all, God can dispense us from the obligation not to lie; and we would presumably want to claim that under such circumstances lying is not morally bad.

80. *Ord.* 3.38.un., n. 6 (Wadding, 7:922 = *WM*, p. 487).

81. *Ord.* 3.37.un., n. 3 (Wadding, 7:879 = *WM*, pp. 273–75); for a corrected version of Wolter's text see my "Duns Scotus on Goodness," 65, n. 56; see also *Ord.* 3.38.un., n. 5 (Wadding, 7:919 = *WM*, p. 485). Scotus's discussion of this case contrasts sharply with that of Aquinas. For Aquinas, it is very important to show how God's command does respect the intrinsic values of things; see *ST* 1-2.100.8 ad 3 (1[2]:462^b).

82. It is false to claim—as I did in "Duns Scotus on Goodness," 70–76—that God could act without right reason. Scotus's claim is that whatever God does reveals his right reason. On this, see in addition to the text noted in note 68 to this chapter, above, *Ord.* 1.10.un., n. 48 (Vatican, 4:359): "The infinite will cannot not be right [*recta*]." Scotus's account, as I am trying to argue here, simply removes most of the significant content from the claim that God acts with right reason. See also chapter 4, section 2, above,

for God's absolute and ordained power; particularly the text cited in note 68, above.

83. *Ord.* 4.14.1, n. 3 (Wadding, 9:7); *Ord.* 2.37.1, n. 6 (Wadding, 6:981); see also *Ord.* 4.14.1, n. 6 (Wadding, 9:9): "There is nothing real, absolute or relative, in someone after the act of sinning, in virtue of which he is called a sinner." An act lacks rectitude if it fails to be elicited in accordance with right reason; see *Lect.* 2.21–2.1–2, n. 5 (Vatican, 19:199).

84. *Ord.* 2.37.1, n. 4 (Wadding, 6:981); see *Comm. Sent.* 2.35.1.1 ad 4 (*Opera Omnia*, 2:823^b). Scotus's rejection of Bonaventure's position assumes (oddly) that rectitude is an essential property of the soul.

85. *Ord.* 2.37.1, n. 4 (Wadding, 6:981); see *ST* 1-2.86.1, 2 (1[2]:391^a–93^b).

86. *Ord.* 4.14.1, n. 6 (Wadding, 9:9); *Ord.* 2.37.2, n. 22 (Wadding, 6:1004).

87. Augustine, *Enarr. in Ps.* 31(II).9 (CCSL, 38:232).

88. *Ord.* 4.14.1, n. 6 (Wadding, 9:9).

89. Norman Powell Williams, *The Ideas of the Fall and of Original Sin: A Historical and Critical Study* (London: Longmans, Green and Co., 1927), 365.

90. For all of this see Williams, *The Ideas of the Fall*, 360–74. For a useful modern discussion, see Christopher Kirwan, *Augustine*, The Arguments of the Philosophers (London and New York: Routledge, 1989), 129–41.

91. Henry, *Quodlib.* 6.11 (*Opera Omnia*, 10:134–36). Scotus, *Lect.* 2.29.un., n. 7 (Vatican, 19:282–83). For the image of "curved rectitude," see, for example, Augustine, *Enarr. in Ps.* 50.15 (CCSL, 38:610).

92. Henry, *Quodlib.* 6.32 (*Opera Omnia*, 10:267–68); Scotus, *Ord.* 2.29.un., n. 2 (Wadding, 6:920).

93. *Ord.* 2.29.un., n. 3 (Wadding, 6:920).

94. *Ord.* 2.29.un., n. 3 (Wadding, 6:920).

95. As we saw in chapter 1, above, Scotus holds that we have a natural desire for the supernatural. But, as we saw there, he also holds that we cannot without the benefit of revelation *know* ourselves to have such a desire.

96. See, for example, *Ord.* 2.29.un., n. 1 (Wadding, 6:919), referring to Dionysius the Pseudo-Areopagite, *De Div. Nom.* 4 (PG 3:725C): "The natural gifts remain whole in the sinner, as is clear from Dionysius; original justice does not remain."

97. *Lect.* 2.29.un., nn. 10–11 (Vatican, 19:284–85); *Ord.* 2.29.un., n. 4 (Wadding, 6:922).

98. *Ord.* 2.29.un., n. 5 (Wadding, 6:923).

99. *ST* 1.97.1 c (1[1]:473^b–74^a); see Scotus, *Ord.* 2.19.un., n. 2 (Wadding, 6:811); *Ord.* 2.29.un., n. 5 (Wadding, 6:923).

100. *Ord.* 2.19.un., n. 2 (Wadding, 6:811).

101. *Ord.* 2.19.un., n. 4 (Wadding, 6:812).

102. *Ord.* 2.19.un., n. 6 (Wadding, 6:812–13).

103. *Ord.* 2.19.un., n. 5 (Wadding, 6:812).

104. On these gifts, see chapter 6, section 3, above.

105. *Ord.* 2.29.un., n. 7 (Wadding, 6:928); *Rep.* 2.29.2, n. 8 (Wadding, 11:381[b]). According to Scotus, venial sin is consistent with original justice. He argues that venial sin consists merely in not pursuing the ultimate goal in the most expeditious manner; *Ord.* 2.21.1, n. 3 (Wadding, 6:832).

106. *Ord.* 2.29.un., n. 7 (Wadding, 6:928); *Rep.* 2.29.2, n. 8 (Wadding, 381[b]).

107. *Ord.* 2.30–32.1–4, n. 19 (Wadding, 6:954–55).

108. *Rep.* 4.1.5, n. 4 (Wadding, 11:571[b]), quoting Peter Lombard, *Sent.* 2.24.1 (3rd ed., 2 vols., Spicilegium Bonaventurianum [Grottaferrata: Collegium Sancti Bonaventurae ad Claras Aquas, 1971–81], 1:450–51); see *Lect.* 2.29.un., n. 15 (Vatican, 19:287); *Lect.* 2.30–2.1–4, nn. 50–53 (Vatican, 19:306–307). Oddly, Scotus never cites this passage from Peter Lombard in the *Ordinatio*.

109. For a full account, see William A. van Roo, *Grace and Original Justice according to St. Thomas*, Analecta Gregoriana, 75 (Rome: Gregorian University, 1955), 127–52, and the texts cited therein.

110. *Ord.* 2.19.un., n. 5 (Wadding, 6:812); *Ord.* 2.29.un., n. 7 (Wadding, 6:928); *Rep.* 2.19.un., n. 6 (Wadding, 11:356[b]).

111. On the nature of Adam's sin, see *Ord.* 2.21.2, n. 2 (Wadding, 6:835), where Scotus notes that Adam's sin was to value his wife above God; on the gravity of the sin, see *Ord.* 2.21.2, n. 3 (Wadding, 6:835–36).

112. *Ord.* 2.30–32.1–4, n. 6 (Wadding, 6:948).

113. *Ord.* 2.30–32.1–4, n. 4 (Wadding, 6:946); see also n. 1 (Wadding, 6:936).

114. *Ord.* 2.30–32.1–4, n. 2 (Wadding, 6:944–45); for problems with this theory, see *Ord.* 2.30–32.1–4, nn. 4–6 (Wadding, 6:946–47).

115. *Ord.* 2.30–32.1–4, n. 6 (Wadding, 6:948).

116. *Ord.* 2.30–32.1–4, n. 8 (Wadding, 6:949); *Lect.* 2.30–32.1–4, nn. 58, 61 (Vatican, 19:309–311). For Anselm's account, see *De Conc. Virg.* 2 (*Opera Omnia*, 2:141–42).

117. *Ord.* 2.30–32.1–4, n. 9 (Wadding, 6:949).

118. *Ord.* 2.30–32.1–4, n. 11 (Wadding, 6:950).

119. *Ord.* 2.30–32.1–4, n. 11 (Wadding, 6:950); see also *Ord.* 4.1.5–6, n. 8 (Wadding, 8:120[a]).

CHAPTER 8

1. *Ord.* 1.41.un., nn. 28–33 (Vatican, 6:328–29).

2. *Ord.* 1.41.un., n. 36 (Vatican, 6:330–31).

3. *Ord.* 1.41.un., n. 40 (Vatican, 6:332). This claim entails a number of further claims, some of which I discuss in chapter 10, section 1, below. Perhaps the most striking is that God's predestination of the blessed is logically prior to his knowledge that Adam, and all human beings after him, sin. So a person's predestination to everlasting life is not in any sense altered by God's knowledge that certain people sin; *Ord.* 2.20.2, n. 2 (Wadding, 6:822). (I discuss the philosophical ramifications of this claim in my "Identity, Origin, and Persistence in Duns Scotus's Physics," section 5.) For a discussion of Scotus on predestination, see Wolfhart Pannenberg, *Die Prädestionationslehre des Duns Skotus in Zusammenhang der scholastischen Lehrentwicklung*, Forschungen zur Kirchen- und Dogmengeschichte, 4 (Göttingen: Vandenhoeck und Ruprecht, 1954).

4. *Ord.* 1.41.un., n. 41 (Vatican, 6:332–33).

5. Scotus is quite clear that this schema is consistent with divine justice. He argues that a person is worthy of salvation only if God wills salvation for this person; see *Ord.* 1.41.un., n. 54 (Vatican, 6:337–38). This is wholly consistent with Scotus's voluntaristic ethical system described in chapter 7, above.

6. Augustine, *De Gen.* 11.22 (CSEL, 28[3/1]:350).

7. *Ord.* 1.41.un., n. 42 (Vatican, 6:332–33).

8. See Calvin, *Inst.* 3.22.11 (*Opera Selecta*, ed. Petrus Barth and others, 5 vols. [Munich: Kaiser, 1926–62], 4:393), where it is expressly stated that God's decision in damning certain people is not made on the basis of their works.

9. *Ord.* 1.41.un., n. 44 (Vatican, 6:333–34).

10. *Ord.* 1.41.un., nn. 45–46 (Vatican, 6:334); I simplify Scotus's account a little here.

11. *Quod.* 17, n. 3 (Wadding, 12:461 = AW, p. 389 [n. 17.6]); see also *Quod.* 17, n. 13 (Wadding, 12:471–72 = AW, pp. 397–98 [n. 17.33]); *Ord* 1.17.1.1–2, nn. 142–44 (Vatican, 5:207–209).

12. According to Scotus, as we shall see in chapter 10, below, Christ's salvific work merits this grace for us.

13. Aquinas, *ST* 1-2.114.1 c (1[2]:565ᵇ–66ᵃ); Bonaventure, *Comm. Sent.* 2.27.2.3 (*Opera Omnia*, 2:667ᵇ–68ᵃ).

14. *Comm. Sent.* 2.27.2.3 (2:667ᵃ–68ᵃ).

15. *Comm. Sent.* 2.27.2.2, 3 (2:664ᵇ–65ᵃ, 667ᵇ–68ᵃ).

16. *Ord.* 1.17.1.1–2, n. 149 (Vatican, 5:210–11). As we shall see in chapter 10, below, Scotus does believe that there is at least one set of human actions that is equal in moral value to the reward assigned to it: Christ's human activity, which merits grace and the remission of sins for some human beings.

17. Thus Scotus sometimes uses 'condign' to mean "equal in value";

see, for example, *Ord*. 3.19.un., n. 8 (Wadding, 7:418); *Ord*. 4.2.1, n. 11 (Wadding, 8:140ª); *Ord*. 4.19.un., n. 12 (Wadding, 9:366). And presumably the point of this—given that human actions are not equal in value to the reward—is that condignly meritorious actions nevertheless have some sort of proportion to their reward. What Scotus does not allow, of course, is that this proportion places God under any sort of obligation.

18. *Ord*. 4.14.2, n. 16 (Wadding, 9:46).

19. *Ord*. 1.17.1.1–2, nn. 131, 144, 148 (Vatican, 5:203, 208–210).

20. Scotus makes the point explicitly at *Ord*. 2.5.1, n. 6 (Wadding, 6:510): A human being cannot demerit at the instant of death, since "He merits, and then impeccability is given to him, so that he cannot place a barrier [to the reception of the reward]."

21. *Ord*. 4.14.2, n. 16 (Wadding, 9:46).

22. *Ord*. 1.17.2.1, nn. 203–204 (Vatican, 5:237).

23. *Ord*. 2.5.1, n. 2 (Wadding, 6:505); *Rep*. 4.2.1, nn. 1, 11 (Wadding, 12:574ª, 577ª).

24. *Ord*. 3.19.un., n. 5 (Wadding, 7:414). In addition, to meriting grace, Christ also merits the remission of sins. I discuss this aspect of Christ's saving work in detail in chapter 10, below. I discuss the process involved in the remission of sins, and its relation to justification, in section 3 of this chapter, below.

25. On demerit, see, for example, *Ord*. 2.5.1, n. 6 (Wadding, 6:510); *Ord*. 2.7.un., nn. 12–13 (Wadding, 6:566–67 = *WM*, pp. 221–25); *Ord*. 4.14.1, n. 4 (Wadding, 9:7). Given Scotus's claim, discussed above, that no sinful act can naturally corrupt a supernatural quality such as charity (I discuss the nature of the habit of charity in section 3 below), Scotus must understand demerit to involve God's deciding to remove the habit whenever we act in a mortally sinful way. Our mortal sins are *occasions* for God's removing the habit of grace. (On non-causal "occasions" for divine activity, see chapter 11, section 1, below.)

26. *Ord*. 3.19.un., n. 8 (Wadding, 7:418).

27. *Ord*. 4.14.2, n. 14 (Wadding, 9:45).

28. *Ord*. 4.14.2, nn. 14–16 (Wadding, 9:45–46).

29. *Ord*. 3.19.un., n. 8 (Wadding, 7:418).

30. *Ord*. 4.14.2, n. 14 (Wadding, 9:45).

31. *Ord*. 4.14.2, n. 14 (Wadding, 9:45).

32. For an account of Scotus's theory of grace, see Werner Dettloff, *Die Lehre von der Acceptatio Divina bei Johannes Duns Scotus mit besonderer Berücksichtigung der Rechtfertigungslehre*, Franziskanische Forschungen, 10 (Dietrich Coelde: Werl, 1954).

33. *Eth. Nic*. 2.5 (1106ª11–12).

34. *Eth. Nic.* 2.2 (1104^a27–$^b3$); also *Eth. Nic.* 2.1 (1103^b21–22).

35. *Cat.* 8 (8^b2–4).

36. For an account of grace as a created quality, see Alister E. McGrath, *Iustitia Dei: A History of the Christian Doctrine of Justification: The Beginnings to the Reformation* (Cambridge: Cambridge University Press, 1986), 100–109.

37. *Quod.* 17, n. 4 (Wadding, 12:461 = AW, p. 390 [n. 7.8]); see *Ord.* 1.17.1.1–2, nn. 106, 129 (Vatican, 5:192, 202–203); *Ord.* 2.37.2, n. 6 (Wadding, 6:993); *Ord.* 3.27.un., n. 19 (Wadding, 7:655 = WM, p. 443). For further references, see AW, p. 390, n. 5.

38. *Ord.* 1.17.1.1–2, n. 150 (Vatican, 5:211); *Ord.* 4.1.1, n. 31 (Wadding, 8:53^a).

39. *Ord.* 1.17.1.1–2, n. 132 (Vatican, 5:204).

40. On this, see above.

41. *Ord.* 2.27.un., nn. 3–4 (Wadding, 6:907); see also *Ord.* 1.17.1.1–2, nn. 126, 135, 137, 154 (Vatican, 5:200–201, 204–205, 207, 212–13); *Quod.* 17, nn. 4–5 (Wadding, 12:461 = AW, pp. 390–91 [nn. 17.8–9]); *Ord.* 2.26.un., n. 3 (Wadding, 6:897–98).

42. *Ord.* 3.34.un., n. 19 (Wadding, 7:744 = WM, p. 371); see also *Ord.* 3.34.un., n. 7 (Wadding, 7:722 = WM, p. 355); *Ord.* 2.6.2, n. 8 (Wadding, 6:539 = WM, p. 469).

43. *Ord.* 2.26.un., n. 6 (Wadding, 6:899).

44. See Aquinas, *De Car.* un.1 c (*Quaestiones Disputatae*, ed. R. M. Spiazzi and others, 2 vols. [Turin and Rome: Marietti, 1949], 2:755^b).

45. *Ord.* 1.17.1.1–2, n. 113 (Vatican, 5:195).

46. *Ord.* 1.17.1.1–2, nn. 114–18 (Vatican, 5:195–97).

47. *Ord.* 1.17.1.1–2, nn. 122–24 (Vatican, 5:199–200).

48. *Ord.* 4.16.2, nn. 6, 9–12 (Wadding, 9:277–79). The remission of original sin is presumably understood likewise: God no longer holds us to be guilty for our lack of the original justice that we are obliged to have. In *Rep.* 4.1.5, n. 6 (Wadding, 11:572$^{a–b}$), Scotus notes that the remission of (original) sin consists in "forgoing (*dimittere*) someone's offense."

49. *Ord.* 4.16.2, nn. 10–12 (Wadding, 9:277–79).

50. *Ord.* 4.14.1, n. 10 (Wadding, 9:19); see also *Ord.* 4.14.1, n. 17 (Wadding, 9:25). Scotus contrasts this voluntary punishment with the involuntary punishment suffered by the damned in hell. This involuntary punishment does not result, of course, in the remission of sin; see *Ord.* 4.14.1, n. 10 (Wadding, 9:19).

51. This voluntary punishment is clearly understood by Scotus to be the same thing as *satisfaction*; see *Ord.* 4.14.1, n. 6 (Wadding, 9:9) for voluntary punishment, and *Ord.* 4.15.1, n. 3 (Wadding, 9:104) for satisfaction defined in much the same way. I discuss satisfaction in more detail in chapter 10, below.

52. *Ord.* 1.17.1.1–2, n. 120 (Vatican, 5:198). The passage Scotus refers to here is *Ord.* 4.16.2, n. 19 (Wadding, 9:288).

53. *Ord.* 3.27.un., n. 19 (Wadding, 7:655 = *WM*, p. 443); *Quod.* 17, nn. 8–9 (Wadding, 12:465 = AW, pp. 393–94 [nn. 17.19–20]).

54. *Ord.* 1.17.1.1–2, nn. 7, 48, 88 (Vatican, 5:142, 158, 181–82).

55. *Ord.* 3.27.un., n. 19 (Wadding, 7:655 = *WM*, p. 443); *Ord.* 1.17.1.1–2, n. 151 (Vatican, 211).

56. *Ord.* 3.27.un., n. 19 (Wadding, 7:655 = *WM*, p. 443). Scotus seems to suppose that the habit of grace achieves these various effects by being a *partial active cause* of a meritorious action (see *Ord.* 1.17.1.1–2, n. 133 [Vatican, 5:158]; Scotus discusses the theory at, for example, *Ord.* 1.17.1.1–2, nn. 32, 158 [Vatican, 5:152, 214–15]). On this theory, the will is the primary cause of the act, and the habit the secondary cause (*Ord.* 1.17.1.1–2, nn. 35–40 [Vatican, 5:153–54]), although the habit is the primary cause of the act's meritoriousness (*Ord.* 1.17.1.1–2, nn. 37, 138–41, 151 [Vatican, 5:153–54, 207, 211]). Sometimes, however, Scotus seems to prefer a rival account, according to which the habit merely *inclines* the will to a meritorious act (see *Quod.* 17, n. 9 [Wadding, 12:466 = AW, p. 394 (n. 17.21)]; Scotus discusses this theory at, for example, *Ord.* 1.17.1.1–2, nn. 48–53 [Vatican, 5:158–60]). On this theory, the habit makes the will more readily receptive of its own action. Scotus explains this receptivity by pinpointing two features in the relationship between a will and its action: an *active* feature—the will *causes* its action—and a *passive* feature—the action belongs to the will, or inheres in the will. Thus, making the will more receptive of its action involves increasing the will's passive capacity to receive its own action.

57. *Ord.* 1.17.1.1–2, n. 160 (Vatican, 5:215); see also *Ord.* 1.17.1.1–2, n. 164 (Vatican, 5:217); *Quod.* 17, n. 13 (Wadding, 12:472 = AW, pp. 397–98 [n. 17.33]).

58. It is less clear whether Scotus believes that God could accept someone without some sort of meritorious action, whether that person's or someone else's (e.g., Christ's). Scotus never claims that God could so save someone. Perhaps he supposes that, as soon as we have the assignment of a reward, we have merit. So a saved person's actions are *eo ipso* meritorious. There seems to me a similar ambiguity in the case of satisfaction, which I will briefly examine in chapter 10, below (see note 22 of that chapter).

59. *Ord.* 1.17.1.1–2, n. 115 (Vatican, 5:196).

60. *ST* 1-2.110.2 c (1[2]:541ᵇ).

61. *Ord.* 1.17.1.1–2, n. 191 (Vatican, 5:229–30).

62. At one point Scotus uses the term 'actual grace', though the sense he gives to it is unrelated to the standard Thomist one. Scotus claims that

actual grace is the moral rectitude exhibited by a meritorious action; *Ord.* 4.14.1, n. 3 (Wadding, 9:7).

CHAPTER 9

1. Council of Chalcedon, *definitio fidei* (Tanner, 1:*86).
2. Constantinople III, *terminus* (Tanner, 1:*126).
3. The medievals used the terms 'suppositum' and 'hypostasis' to refer to a subject of characteristics, irrespective of whether that subject has any psychological properties. To draw attention to the relevant feature of the Chalcedonian definition, Scotus argues that, in terms of the metaphysics involved, there would be no objection to the second person of the Trinity assuming a stone-nature; see *Ord.* 3.2.1, nn. 5–7 (Wadding, 7:65–66). One of his motivations for this is that God's assumption of a created nature cannot in any sense be limited by the created features of that nature. If it were, God's actions would be restricted by a created object.
4. Thomas Aquinas quotes the relevant parts of it in *ST* 3.2.1, sed contra, 3[1]:10[b]–11[a]), and *ST* 3.2.2, sed contra (3[1]:12[b]), and most people after Aquinas would have been acquainted with this part of Thomas's work. On Chalcedon in scholasticism, see the excellent article by Ludwig Ott, "Das Konzil von Chalkedon in der Frühscholastik," in A. Grillmeier and H. Bacht (eds.), *Das Konzil von Chalkedon: Geschichte und Gegenwart*, 3 vols. (Würzburg: Echter-Verlag, 1953), 2:873–922.
5. On this, see chapter 4, above.
6. For the whole discussion, see *ST* 3.17.2 (3[1]:111[a]–12[b]).
7. *ST* 3.2.6 ad 2 (3[1]:19[a–b]).
8. I deal with some of these issues in my "Aquinas on Nature, Hypostasis, and the Metaphysics of the Incarnation," *The Thomist*, 60 (1996): 171–202.
9. For a useful basic introduction to most aspects of Scotus's Christology, see Maria Burger, *Personalität im Horizont absoluter Prädestination: Untersuchungen zur Christologie des Johannes Duns Scotus und ihrer Rezeption in modernen theologischen Ansätzen*, Beiträge zur Geschichte der Philosophie und Theologie des Mittelalters, N. F., 40 (Münster: Aschendorff, 1994). I focus more on some of the metaphysical issues in my "The Doctrine of the Hypostatic Union in the Thought of Duns Scotus" (unpublished doctoral dissertation, Oxford University, 1991).
10. *Ord.* 3.6.1, n. 4 (Wadding, 7:174); see also *Ord.* 3.6.1, n. 5 (Wadding, 7:175).
11. William of Auxerre, *Sum. Aur.* 3.1.3.3 (ed. Jean Ribailler, 4 vols., Spicilegium Bonaventurianum, 16–19 [Paris: Centre National de la Recher-

che Scientifique; Grottaferrata: Collegium Sancti Bonaventurae ad Claras Aquas, 1980–86], 3:20): "One of the natures [viz., the human nature] degenerates into an accident"; see also *Sum. Aur.* 3.1.2 (3:14).

12. See Walter H. Principe, *William of Auxerre's Theology of The Hypostatic Union*, The Theology of the Hypostatic Union in the Early Thirteenth Century, 1; Studies and Texts, 7 (Toronto: Pontifical Institute of Mediaeval Studies, 1963), 94–96 (for William), 96–100 (for the background).

13. See William of Ware's *In Sent.*, 3.1.1 (MS Oxford, Merton College, MS 103, fol. 137va), where he argues that Christ's human nature has the mode of an accident. For an account of William's sophisticated Christology, see my "The Doctrine of the Hypostatic Union," 180–203, 374–92.

14. There were other positions too. I hope later to explore some of these in more detail in a study of the metaphysics of the Incarnation from Aquinas to Scotus, incorporating material from (and I hope wholly superseding) my "The Doctrine of the Hypostatic Union."

15. Scotus holds that the human nature has created existence that it contributes to the divine person (*Ord.* 3.6.1, n. 5 [Wadding, 7:175]): "There is an existence other than the uncreated one that is the proper existence of this *suppositum*."

16. *Ord.* 3.1.1, n. 3 (Wadding, 7:6); see also *Quod.* 19, n. 23 (Wadding, 12:512 = AW, p. 439 [n. 19.83]).

17. In *Quod.* 19, n. 23 (Wadding, 12:512 = AW, pp. 439–40 [n. 19.84]), Scotus says that it would have the mode of an accident without counting as an accident; he earlier rejects the position that Christ's human nature could have the mode of an accident, though it can, presumably, be *like* an accident in the relevant sense (see *Ord.* 3.1.1, n. 5 [Wadding, 7:10]). For the distinction between substance and accident, see my *The Physics of Duns Scotus*, chapter 6.

18. *Ord.* 3.1.1, n. 3 (Wadding, 7:6). Note, however, that the Christ's human nature, according to Scotus, depends in such a way that it can be said to contribute existence to the Word; see *Ord.* 3.6.1, n. 5 (Wadding, 7:175).

19. *Ord.* 3.1.1, n. 3 (Wadding, 7:5–6); *Quod.* 19, n. 2 (Wadding, 12:492 = AW, p. 419 [n. 19.6]).

20. *Ord.* 3.7.2, n. 6 (Wadding, 7:196).

21. *Ord.* 3.1.1, n. 6 (Wadding, 7:12); *Quod.* 19, n. 17 (Wadding, 12:507 = AW, p. 432 [n. 19.55]); also see John of Damascus, *De Fide Orth.* 3.11 (PG, 94:1024A) = 55 (pp. 203–204).

22. Boethius, *De Per.* 3 (p. 85). Scotus does not draw attention to just this difficulty in this context, though he elsewhere argues that on Boethius's definition the human soul would count as a person; see *Ord.* 1.23.un., n. 15 (Vatican, 5:356).

23. *Ord.* 3.1.1, n. 6 (Wadding, 7:12–13); *Quod.* 19, n. 18 (Wadding, 12:507 = AW, p. 433 [n. 19.60]), citing John of Damascus, *De Fide Orth.* 3.6 (PG, 94, 1005B) = 50, p. 188. The aphorism was not, of course, original to John of Damascus.

24. *Ord.* 3.1.1, n. 13 (Wadding, 7:21); *Quod.* 19, n. 25 (Wadding, 12:513 = AW, p. 441 [n. 19.91]).

25. *Quod.* 19, n. 18 (Wadding, 12:508 = AW, p. 433 [n. 19.62]); Scotus offers slightly different argumentation for the same position in *Ord.* 3.1.1, n. 7 (Wadding, 7:12–13).

26. *Ord.* 3.1.1, n. 9 (Wadding, 7:15); *Ord.* 3.5.2, n. 4 (Wadding, 7:132); *Quod.* 19, n. 19 (Wadding, 12:508 = AW, p. 434 [n. 19.63]). This 'negation doctrine' forms part of the tradition that sees Christ's human nature as something like an accident of the Word. The negation doctrine was first formulated by William of Auxerre; see *Sum. Aur.* 3.1.3.8 (3:36–37). Aquinas's definition of 'person' perhaps entails the negation doctrine too; see my "Aquinas on Nature, Hypostasis, and the Metaphysics of the Incarnation," 177, n. 12.

27. Richard of St. Victor, *Trin.* 4.23 (ed. Jean Ribaillier, Textes Philosophiques du Moyen Age, 6 [Paris: J. Vrin, 1958], p. 188); see also Aquinas, *ST* 1.75.4 ad 2 (1[1]:354ᵃ).

28. *Ord.* 3.1.1, n. 9 (Wadding, 7:15); *Quod.* 19, n. 19 (Wadding, 12:508 = AW, p. 434 [n. 19.65]).

29. William of Ockham, *Report.* 3.1 (*OT*, 6:37–38); *Quod. Sept.* 4.7 (*OT*, 9:336 = FK, 1:278). For a worry about Ockham's view, see Alfred J. Freddoso, "Human Nature, Potency, and the Incarnation," *Faith and Philosophy*, 3 (1986): 52, n. 15.

30. *Ord.* 3.5.2, n. 1 (Wadding, 7:122).

31. Scotus is clear that there can be simultaneous multiple incarnations of one divine person; see *Ord.* 3.1.3, n. 2 (7:44).

32. *Ord.* 3.1.1, nn. 9, 12 (Wadding, 7:15–16).

33. *Ord.* 3.1.1, n. 6 (Wadding, 7:12); *Quod.* 19, n. 17 (Wadding, 12:507 = AW, p. 432 [n. 19.55]).

34. On the ontological status of negations, see *Ord.* 1.3.1.1–2, n. 10 (Vatican, 3:5).

35. He should do so, since his position seems open to an obvious objection merely with regard to consistency. Formally distinct properties are, on Scotus's standard account, inseparable. If there is a formal distinction between a human nature and one of its properties, it should be inseparable from this property. So this property cannot be an accident. On this showing, no merely privative properties could be accidental. A point related to this is argued at length in Freddoso, "Human Nature, Potency, and the Incarnation."

36. *Ord.* 3.5.2, n. 5 (Wadding, 7:132).

37. *Quod.* 19, n. 20 (Wadding, 12:509 = AW, p. 435, n. 19.69).

38. See *Ord.* 3.1.1, n. 10 (Wadding, 7:16). On the constitution of the divine persons, see chapter 5, section 3, above.

39. *Ord.* 3.13.4, n. 10 (Wadding, 7:269). Neither does the hypostatic union entail physical incorruptibility. In the tomb, the only reason that Christ's body did not undergo corruption was that God miraculously intervened to prevent it; *Ord.* 3.21.un., nn. 3–5 (Wadding, 7:435–36).

40. *Ord.* 3.2.1, n. 4 (Wadding, 7:62). Scotus here argues against Henry of Ghent, who held that the hypostatic union entailed that Christ's human nature had the beatific vision; see Henry, *Quodlib.* 6.6 (*Opera Omnia*, 10:72). See also *Ord* 3.2.1, n. 2 (Wadding, 7:60–61).

41. *Ord.* 3.12.un., n. 3 (Wadding, 7:254). For the beatific vision as guaranteeing impeccability, see the Appendix, section 3.

42. *Ord.* 3.12.un., n. 3 (Wadding, 7:255).

43. *ST* 3.18.1 ad 4 (3[1]:114ᵇ–15ᵃ).

44. Scotus makes this point by noting that in general the *source* of action is not person but nature; see *Quod.* 8, n. 4 (Wadding, 12:205 = AW, pp. 200–201 [n. 8.8]); *Ord.* 1.12.1, n. 51 (Vatican, 5:54–55); for Christ, see *Rep.* 3.17.1–2, n. 4 (Wadding, 11:484ᵃ). The idea is that the person is just the *subject* of the action, not its driving force. And Scotus is insistent that God cannot have any action in the human will that would compromise its freedom; *Ord.* 3.17.un., n. 5 (Wadding, 7:380).

45. *Rep.* 3.17.1–2, n. 4 (Wadding, 11:484ᵃ); see also *Ord.* 3.17.un., n. 4 (Wadding, 7:380). I discuss the unity of the external actions of the Trinity in chapter 5, section 4, above.

46. *Ord.* 3.13.3, n. 2 (Wadding, 7:260); *Ord.* 3.13.4, nn. 5–14 (Wadding, 7:266–70).

47. *Ord.* 3.13.3, n. 2 (Wadding, 7:260–261); *Ord.* 3.13.4, n. 18 (Wadding, 7:275).

48. *Ord.* 3.14.2, nn. 16–17, (Wadding, 7:296–97); for its knowledge of possibles, see *Ord.* 3.14.2, n. 12 (Wadding, 7:293). This intellectual vision is an instance of intuitive knowledge. I discuss this sort of knowledge briefly in chapter 4, above. Scotus's claim that Christ's human mind sees things "in the Word" is just a way of claiming that he has the beatific vision; see *Ord.* 4.50.3, n. 2 (Wadding, 10:637–38). It does not imply any special cognitive relationship between Christ's human mind and the second person of the Trinity.

49. *Ord.* 3.14.3, n. 4 (Wadding, 7:303); see Augustine, *De Gen.* 4.23 (CSEL, 28[3/1]:122–23); also Scotus, *Ord.* 3.14.2, n. 17 (Wadding, 7:297).

50. *Ord.* 3.14.3, n. 5 (Wadding, 7:303–304). On intuitive knowledge, see chapter 4, section 2, above.

51. *Ord*. 3.14.3, n. 6 (Wadding, 7:305).

52. *Ord*. 3.14.3, n. 6 (Wadding, 7:305).

53. *Ord*. 3.14.3, n. 7 (Wadding, 7:306); see Lk. 2.52, referred to in *Ord*. 3.14.3, n. 8 (Wadding, 7:306).

54. *Ord*. 3.12.un., n. 6 (Wadding, 7:254).

55. *Ord*. 4.49.6, n. 11 (Wadding, 10:455). For impeccability and the beatific vision, see the Appendix, section 3.

56. *Ord*. 3.13.4, n. 8 (Wadding, 7:267).

57. De facto, it is not true that God has given as much knowledge to any other nature (*Ord*. 1.22.un., *textus interpolatus* [Vatican, 5:388]); but presumably he *could*.

58. Heb. 4.15.

59. *Ord*. 3.1.1, n. 18 (Wadding, 7:29).

60. *Ord*. 3.1.4, n. 2 (Wadding, 7:47).

61. *Ord*. 3.1.1, n. 4 (Wadding, 7:7).

62. *Ord*. 3.1.1, n. 18 (Wadding, 7:29).

63. *Ord*. 3.1.1, n. 18 (Wadding, 7:29).

64. See, for example, *Ord*. 3.7.1, n. 3 (Wadding, 7:189); for the expression "communication of properties," see *Ord*. 3.11.1, nn. 3–4 (Wadding, 7:238–39).

65. *Ord*. 3.7.2, n. 9 (Wadding, 7:198).

66. For the discussions, see *Ord*. 3.7.1; *Ord* 3.7.2; *Ord*. 3.7.3; *Ord*. 3.11.1; *Ord*. 3.11.2; *Ord*. 3.11.3); also, for example, *Rep*. 3.17.1–2, n. 4 (Wadding, 11:484[a]), quoted above. For a useful (though not always reliable) discussion of Scotus on the communication of properties, see Allan Bäck, "Scotus on the Consistency of the Incarnation and the Trinity," *Vivarium*, 36 (1998): 87–100.

67. For the most extensive consideration of this sort of problem, see Thomas V. Morris, *The Logic of God Incarnate* (Ithaca, N.Y., and London: Cornell University Press, 1986), chapter 3.

68. *Ord*. 3.11.1, nn. 7–8 (Wadding, 7:240–241).

69. This is of course a perfectly acceptable strategy to adopt; see an analogous contemporary treatment in Thomas Morris's *The Logic of God Incarnate*, 65.

CHAPTER 10

1. *Ord*. 3.7.3, n. 1 (Wadding, 7:199), citing Rom. 1.4 in the Vulgate version: "qui destinatus est Filius Dei."

2. *ST* 3.1.3 c, 3[1]:5[b].

3. In *De Glor*. 13 (CCCM, 29:409–410), Rupert argues from Heb. 2.10.

4. *Sum. Fr. Alex.* 3.1.1.2.2 [23], 4:41ᵃ, 42ᵃ⁻ᵇ.

5. We have already encountered this principle in Scotus's discussion of human predestination in chapter 8, above.

6. *Ord.* 3.7.3, n. 3 (Wadding, 7:202). In this passage, Scotus also proposes a third principle: It is not realistic (*verisimile*) that a decision to bring about a greater good should be made in order to achieve a lesser good. But this seems to be equivalent to (b).

7. *Ord.* 3.7.3, n. 3 (Wadding, 7:202).

8. *Ord.* 3.7.3, nn. 2, 5 (Wadding, 7:199, 204).

9. *Rep.* 3.7.4, n. 4 (Wadding, 12:451ᵃ).

10. *Ord.* 3.7.3, n. 3 (Wadding, 7:202). The fall of Adam is a lesser good than the predestination of human nature to glory.

11. *Ord.* 3.19.un., n. 6 (Wadding, 7:415).

12. In *Ord.* 3.7.3, n. 3 (Wadding, 7:202), Scotus claims that Christ would "perhaps" have come with an impassible, glorified body; in *Rep.* 3.7.4, n. 5 (Wadding, 11:451ᵇ), Scotus claims without qualification that Christ would have come with such a body.

13. Rom. 8.29.

14. Anselm, *CDH* 1.12 and 14 (*Opera Omnia*, 2:69, 72).

15. *CDH* 2.19 (2:130–131).

16. *CDH* 2.14 (2:113–15).

17. *CDH* 2.19 (2:130–131).

18. *CDH* 1.12–13, 16–17, 19–20 (2:69–71, 74–76, 84–88).

19. *Ord.* 3.20.un., n. 3 (Wadding, 7:426).

20. *Ord.* 4.15.1, n. 4 (Wadding, 9:105).

21. *Ord.* 3.20, n. 5 (Wadding, 7:427); see *Ord.* 4.15.1, n. 4 (Wadding, 9:105).

22. We might expect Scotus to take issue with (ii), and claim that God could forgive us without satisfaction. In fact, although Scotus is clear that God could forgive us—if he so chose—in virtue of our own acts of satisfaction without Christ (see note 34, below), he never suggests that God could forgive us without any satisfaction. See also chapter 8, note 58, above.

23. *Ord.* 4.15.1, n. 6 (Wadding, 9:106).

24. *Ord.* 4.15.1, n. 7 (Wadding, 7:107).

25. *Ord.* 4.15.1, n. 6 (Wadding, 9:106). As I shall note below, Scotus is clear that this repayment must be a *voluntary* matter.

26. *Ord.* 3.18.un., n. 4 (Wadding, 7:386); *Quod.* 17, n. 3 (Wadding, 12:461 = AW, pp. 389–90 [n. 17.6]) Note that the reward can be assigned to the one who merits or to another; my prayers can merit a reward for another person, for example (*Ord.* 4.15.1, n. 6 [Wadding, 9:106]).

27. *Ord.* 3.18.un., n. 5 (Wadding, 7:386–87). On the affection for justice, see chapter 7, section 1, above.

28. *Ord.* 3.19.un., n. 5 (Wadding, 7:413); *Ord.* 1.17.1.1–2, n. 192 (Vatican, 5:230).

29. *Ord.* 3.19.un., n. 14 (Wadding, 7:422).

30. In fact, Scotus seems to suggest that the value of Christ's life and death is greater than the reward assigned to it; *Ord.* 3.19.un., n. 12 (Wadding, 7:421).

31. *Ord.* 3.19.un., nn. 7, 14 (Wadding, 7:417–18, 422). In *Rep.* 3.19.un., n. 8 (Wadding, 11:497), Scotus makes it clear that the passion of Christ can only relate to the fixed number of saved on the grounds that the salvation of a certain number is chosen by God prior to the means for this salvation.

32. *Ord.* 4.15.1, n. 5 (Wadding, 8:105–106); *Ord.* 3.18.un., n. 10 (Wadding, 7:390–91); *Ord.* 3.19.un., nn. 10–11, 13 (Wadding, 7:421–22). Scotus claims, as we saw in chapter 8, above, that we are responsible for meriting sanctifying grace and the remission of sins after a fall; but the very first gift of these, made to us by God, is given merely in virtue of the merits of Christ. Note also that the remission of sins includes the remission of original sin. (I discuss the remission of sin in chapter 8, above.)

33. For the term 'justification', see, for example, *Ord.* 1.17.1.1–2, n. 113 (Vatican, 5:195).

34. *Ord.* 3.19.un., n. 8 (Wadding, 7:418); also *Ord.* 3.19.un., n. 5 (Wadding, 7:414) for first grace. Note further that God could give us sanctifying grace without Christ's merits; see *Ord.* 4.15.1, n. 7 (Wadding, 9:107).

35. J. Patout Burns seems to suppose that Scotus rejects a satisfaction theory as a means of interpreting Christ's redemptive work; see "The Concept of Satisfaction in Medieval Redemption Theory," *Theological Studies*, 36 (1975): 302. For a similar assessment, see Douglas Langston, "Scotus's Departure from Anselm's Theory of the Atonement," *Recherches de Théologie Ancienne et Médiévale*, 50 (1983): 227–41.

36. *Ord.* 4.15.1, n. 7 (Wadding, 9: 107).

37. *Ord.* 3.18.un., n. 10 (Wadding, 7:390–391); *Ord.* 3.19.un., nn. 10–11, 13 (Wadding, 7:421–22); for general material on Christ's offering to the Trinity, see also *Ord* 3.20.un, n. 10 (Wadding, 7:430); *Ord.* 4.15.1, nn. 4 and 7 (Wadding, 9:105, 107). See also *Ord.* 4.2.1, n. 7 (Wadding, 8:138[a]–39).

38. *Quod.* 20, n. 1 (Wadding, 12:515 = AW, p. 443 [n. 20.2]). (Note that the text used in AW makes an important correction to the Wadding edition.) See also *Ord.* 3.9.un., n. 13 (Wadding, 7:226).

39. *Rep.* 3.20.un., n. 10 (Wadding, 7:502[a]). For God's ordained power, see chapter 4, section 2, above.

40. See, for example, *Ord.* 3.3.1, n. 5 (Wadding, 7:92); *Rep.* 3.19.un., n. 7 (Wadding, 11:497[a]). There is, however, no hint that Scotus accepts any sort of penal theory of the atonement here. As we saw in chapter 8, above, Scotus associates satisfaction with *voluntary* punishment.

41. *Rep.* 4.15.1, n. 6 (Wadding, 11:719ᵃ).

42. Note that, as we saw in chapter 8, above, our merit here is congruous merit, and the relevant action is attrition.

43. Given that satisfaction is a kind of merit, I think we can be clear that the remission of sins that it earns is dependent upon divine acceptation; there is no suggestion that satisfaction necessitates the remission of sins.

44. See, for example, *CDH* 2.19 (2:130–31).

45. See *Ord.* 3.19.un., n. 4 (Wadding, 7:413), referring to *ST* 3.48.2 ad 3 (3[1]:275ᵇ–76ᵃ).

46. Scotus does not seem to allow any redemptive value to Christ's resurrection and ascension, and as far as I know never discusses these events from a theological viewpoint.

47. The definitive account of the growth of the doctrine in the middle ages is still Jean-François Bonnefoy, *Le ven. Jean Duns Scot docteur de l'immaculée conception: son milieu, sa doctrine, son influence* (Rome: Herder, 1960). A useful and accessible account in English can be found in Allan B. Wolter and Blane O'Neill, *John Duns Scotus: Mary's Architect* (Quincy, Ill.: Franciscan Press, 1993), 56–84.

48. *ST* 1-2.81.3 c (1[2]:374ᵃ), cited in *Ord.* 3.3.1, n. 3 (Wadding, 7:91).

49. *ST* 3.27.2 c (3[1]:154ᵃ), cited in *Ord.* 3.3.1, n. 3 (Wadding, 7:91).

50. *Ord.* 3.3.1, n. 8 (Wadding, 7:93).

51. In *Ord.* 3.3.1, n. 9 (Wadding, 7:94), Scotus makes it clear that the gift of sanctifying grace is sufficient to remove original sin, such that we are no longer held to be guilty for our lack of original justice.

52. *Ord.* 3.3.1, n. 4 (Wadding, 7:92).

53. *Ord.* 3.19.un., nn. 10–11 (Wadding, 7:421).

54. Even setting aside the questions of divine timelessness discussed in chapter 4, above, this sort of divine action does not involve any sort of backward causation. God rewards me on the basis of God's (past) infallible expectation of my (present or future) actions.

55. *Ord.* 3.3.1, nn. 5–7 (Wadding, 7:92).

56. *Ord.* 3.3.1, n. 9 (Wadding, 7:95).

CHAPTER 11

1. *Ord.* 4.1.3, n. 2 (Wadding, 8:69ᵃ).

2. Heb. 9.11–15.

3. *Ord.* 4.2.1, n. 2 (Wadding, 8:134ᵃ–35ᵃ).

4. *Ord.* 4.2.1, n. 3 (Wadding, 8:135ᵃ–36ᵃ).

5. *Ord.* 4.2.1, nn. 4–5 (Wadding, 8:137ᵃ–38ᵃ). Contrary to Scotus's claim,

of course, the number and identity of the sacraments did not become fixed until the middle of the twelfth century. Peter Lombard is perhaps one of the best-known early defenders of the seven sacraments as we now have them; see *Sent*. 4.2.1.1 (3rd ed., 2 vols., Spicilegium Bonaventurianum [Grottaferrata: Collegium Sancti Bonaventurae ad Claras Aquas, 1971–81], 2:239).

6. *Ord*. 4.1.2, n. 9 (Wadding, 8:61ᵃ).

7. *Comm. Sent*. 4.1.1.un.1 ad 1 (*Opera Omnia*, 4:12ᵇ).

8. *ST* 3.62.1 c (3[1]:348ᵇ–49ᵃ).

9. *ST* 3.62.4 (3[1]:351ᵃ⁻ᵇ).

10. *ST* 3.62.4 ad 1 (3[1]:351ᵇ).

11. *Ord*. 4.1.1, nn. 26–27, 31, 34 (Wadding, 8:47ᵃ–49, 52ᵃ–53ᵃ, 55); *Ord*. 4.1.4–5, n. 15 (Wadding, 8:89ᵃ).

12. *Ord*. 4.1.4–5, n. 8 (Wadding, 8:89ᵃ).

13. *Ord*. 4.1.4–5, n. 8 (Wadding, 8:89ᵃ).

14. *Ord*. 4.1.4–5, n. 4 (Wadding, 8:81ᵃ). I discuss Scotus's argument in *The Physics of Duns Scotus*, appendix.

15. *Ord*. 4.1.4–5, n. 4 (Wadding, 8:82ᵃ).

16. *Ord*. 4.1.4–5, n. 12 (Wadding, 94ᵃ–95ᵃ); *Ord*. 4.2.1, n. 6 (Wadding, 8:138ᵃ).

17. *Ord*. 4.1.4–5, n. 12 (Wadding, 8:94ᵃ). Scotus is happy to call this sort of occasion an instrumental cause. But he is careful to distinguish this use of 'instrumental cause' from Aquinas's; see *Ord*. 4.1.4–5, n. 13 (Wadding, 95ᵃ).

18. *Ord*. 4.1.4–5, n. 16 (Wadding, 8:105ᵃ).

19. As we saw in chapter 7, above, God's truthfulness entails that he cannot lie; *Ord*. 3.39.un., n. 2 (Wadding, 7:980 = *WM*, p. 505). Presumably the same divine truthfulness entails that God cannot break a promise.

20. *Ord*. 4.13.1, n. 40 (Wadding, 8:808). This does not compromise the *ex opere operato* aspect of the sacraments. In the case of the Eucharist the content of God's covenant, as revealed by Jesus, and reported in 1 Cor. 11.26 (cited in *Ord*. 4.13.2, n. 4 [Wadding, 8:810]), includes a promise to convert the bread and wine into the body and blood of Christ.

21. *Ord*. 4.2.1, nn. 6, 9 (Wadding, 8:138, 139ᵃ).

22. *Ord*. 4.2.1, n. 9 (Wadding, 8:140ᵃ).

23. *Ord*. 4.7.3 (Wadding, 8:400); *Ord*. 4.1.2, n. 10 (Wadding, 8:62ᵃ).

24. *Ord*. 4.1.6, n. 10 (Wadding, 8:125ᵃ); *Ord*. 4.19.un., nn. 23, 32 (Wadding, 8:382, 386).

25. *Ord*. 4.1.6, n. 13 (Wadding, 8:128ᵃ).

26. *Ord*. 4.4.1, n. 2 (Wadding, 8:219); *Ord*. 4.4.2, n. 3 (Wadding, 8:272); *Rep*. 4.1.5, n. 2 (Wadding, 11:570ᵇ). I discuss the remission of original sin in chapter 8, above.

27. *Ord.* 4.4.5, n. 9 (Wadding, 8:248). I discuss the process of the remission of actual sin in chapter 8, above.

28. *Ord.* 4.7.3 (Wadding, 8:399).

29. *Ord.* 4.4.5, n. 3 (Wadding, 8:242); *Ord.* 4.6.7, n. 3 (Wadding, 8:332). As we saw in chapter 10, above, these effects are caused by the merits of Christ.

30. *Ord.* 4.2.1, n. 3 (Wadding, 8:136ᵃ).

31. *Ord.* 4.4.4, n. 6 (Wadding, 8:239).

32. *Ord.* 4.6.1, n. 3 (Wadding, 8:302).

33. *Ord.* 4.14.4, n. 2 (Wadding, 9:81). As we saw in chapter 8, above, the effects of confession are brought about in virtue of our own congruous merits gained through the act of attrition.

34. *Ord.* 4.8.3, n. 2 (Wadding, 8:445).

35. *Ord.* 4.6.10, n. 13 (Wadding, 8:360); see also *Ord.* 4.6.9, n. 3 (Wadding, 8:340).

36. *Ord.* 4.6.9, n. 3 (Wadding, 8:340).

37. *Ord.* 4.6.9, n. 3 (Wadding, 8:340); in *Ord.* 4.6.10, n. 13 (Wadding, 8:360) and *Ord.* 4.6.9, n. 18 (Wadding, 8:345), Scotus refers to character as a 'configurative sign' in so far as it places those who have it under an obligation to Christ. The idea, I think, is that we receive the sacraments through the merits of Christ; so our receiving them places us under some sort of obligation to him.

38. *Ord.* 4.6.9, nn. 3, 15 (Wadding, 8:340, 344); *Ord.* 4.6.10, nn. 3, 13 (Wadding, 8:351, 360).

39. *Script. Sent.* 4.4.1.1 (4:147–52), discussed in *Ord.* 4.6.10, n. 2 (Wadding, 8:351).

40. *Script. Sent.* 4.4.1.3 (4:156, 159), discussed in *Ord.* 4.6.11, n. 2 (Wadding, 8:369–70).

41. *Script. Sent.* 4.4.1.1 ad 4 (4:152).

42. *Ord.* 4.6.10, n. 3 (Wadding, 8:351–52).

43. *Ord.* 4.6.11, n. 4 (Wadding, 8:371).

44. *Ord.* 4.6.11, n. 4 (Wadding, 8:371); see also *Ord.* 4.6.9, n. 18 (Wadding, 8:345).

45. *Ord.* 4.6.10, n. 12 (Wadding, 8:359). This priestly character seems to be distinct from priestly power. According to Scotus, God gives a priest certain (presumably natural) powers in virtue of which he can be an appropriate occasion for a divine activity (*Ord.* 4.6.10, n. 8 [Wadding, 8:354]). Scotus likens priestly power to judicial power. A judge's legal powers are relative to the real powers of some authority. Priestly power is like this. It is relative to some authority—in this case God—capable of actually bringing about the

relevant effect; *Ord.* 4.6.10, n. 7 (Wadding, 8:354); *Ord.* 4.13.1, n. 40 (Wadding, 8:808). (It is not clear to me why Scotus should think of this priestly function in terms of a *power* at all.) As we shall see below, the priest also has some active powers delegated to him by the Church. Such powers cannot, of course, be *supernatural* powers, for reasons we examined in section 1 of this chapter.

46. Lateran IV, const. 1 (Tanner, 1:*230).

47. *Cat.* 4 (1^{b}25–27).

48. For a thorough account of Scotus on transubstantiation, see D. Burr, "Scotus and Transubstantiation," *Mediaeval Studies*, 34 (1972): 336–60. See also Marilyn McCord Adams, "Aristotle and the Sacrament of the Altar," in Richard Bosley and Martin Tweedale (eds.), *Aristotle and his Medieval Interpreters*, *Canadian Journal of Philosophy*, supplementary vol. 17 (1991): 222–35.

49. *ST* 3.75.4 c (3[1]:450$^{a–b}$); *Quod.* 10, n. 3 (Wadding, 12:241 = AW, p. 237 [n. 10.4]); *Ord.* 4.11.1, nn. 2, 10 (Wadding, 8:586, 590).

50. *ST* 3.75.2 c (3[1]:448$^{a–b}$).

51. *Quod.* 10, n. 20 (Wadding, 12:255 = AW, p. 251 [n. 10.54]); *Ord.* 4.10.1, n. 8 (Wadding, 8:499).

52. *Quod.* 10, n. 11 (Wadding, 12:249 = AW, p. 245 [n. 10.32]); *Ord.* 4.10.1, n. 9 (Wadding, 8:501).

53. *Ph.* 4.2 (209^{a}31–^{b}1); see *Ord.* 2.2.2.1–2, nn. 219–20 (Vatican, 7:254–55); *Ord.* 4.10.1, n. 16 (Wadding, 8:506). I discuss these texts in detail in *The Physics of Duns Scotus*, chapter 11, section 1.

54. *Ord.* 4.10.1, nn. 9–11; *Ord.* 4.10.2, n. 11 (Wadding, 8:513); I discuss Scotus's arguments in *The Physics of Duns Scotus*, chapter 11, section 2.

55. *Ord.* 4.10.1, n. 9 (Wadding, 8:501); *Quod.* 10, n. 11 (Wadding, 12:249 = AW, p. 245 [n. 10.32]).

56. *Ord.* 4.11.3, nn. 3, 14 (Wadding, 605, 618).

57. *Ord.* 4.11.3, nn. 4, 14 (Wadding, 605, 618).

58. *Ord.* 4.11.3, n. 5 (Wadding, 8:606).

59. *Ord.* 4.11.3, nn. 13, 15 (Wadding, 8:616–19). On Scotus's de facto acceptance of a two-source theory of revelation, see chapter 1, above.

60. *Ord.* 4.12.1, n. 9 (Wadding, 8:717); Scotus refers to *Metaph.* 5.30 (1025^{a}19–21) and *Metaph.* 7.5 (1030^{b}20–21).

61. The whole discussion is in *Ord.* 4.10.1, n. 9 (Wadding, 8:717). I give a detailed account of Scotus's argument in *The Physics of Duns Scotus*, chapter 6, section 2.

62. For the arguments, see *Ord.* 2.3.1.4, nn. 89–92 (Vatican, 7:434–36 = Spade, pp. 80–81), discussed in *The Physics of Duns Scotus*, chapter 6, sec-

tion 2. Scotus's account might seem to blur the distinction between substances and accidents; for his attempt to give an account of this distinction, see *Ord*. 4.11.3, nn. 43–44 (Wadding, 8:647–48), and my discussion in *The Physics of Duns Scotus*, chapter 6, section 2.

63. *ST* 3.77.1 ad 3 (3[1]:465ᵃ).

64. *Ord*. 4.12.2, n. 15 (Wadding, 8:734); see my discussion in *The Physics of Duns Scotus*, chapter 6, n. 28. Scotus refers to *Cat*. 5 (5ᵇ2–3): "A white object is often called large because the surface it covers is large."

65. *ST*. 3.76.4 ad 1 (3[1]:459ᵃ).

66. Aquinas uses this concomitance claim to try to explain how two bodies could exist in the same place. See *ST* 3.76.4 ad 2 (3[1]:459ᵃ).

67. *ST* 3.76.1 ad 1 (3[1]:456ᵇ).

68. *ST* 3.76.2 c (3[1]:457ᵃ).

69. *Ord*. 4.10.1, n. 13 (Wadding, 8:503–504).

70. *Ord*. 4.10.1, n. 12 (Wadding, 8:503).

71. I discuss what this sort of presence would be like in *The Physics of Duns Scotus*, chapter 11, section 2. Scotus has an (unsound) philosophical argument in favor of the possibility of such presence; see *Ord*. 4.12.1, n. 15 (Wadding, 7:505–506). I discuss the argument in *The Physics of Duns Scotus*, chapter 11, section 2.

72. *Quod*. 11, n. 15 (Wadding, 12:271 = AW, p. 268 [n. 11.44]); see also *Ord*. 4.10.2, nn. 3–4 (Wadding, 8:528–29). I discuss these arguments in *The Physics of Duns Scotus*, chapter 11. See also *Ord*. 4.49.16, nn. 17–19 (Wadding, 10:620–21), which I discuss in chapter 6, above.

73. *Ord*. 4.10.4, n. 10, nn. 12–13 (Wadding, 8:540–41); *Ord*. 4.11.3, nn. 28, 31 (Wadding, 8:630, 632). Scotus suggests that the claim that the soul is present only concomitantly means that its presence with the body is not absolutely necessary (*Ord*. 4.10.4 n. 4 [Wadding, 8:533]). As far as I can tell, Scotus never suggests that Christ's divinity is present in any special way at all in the Eucharist.

74. Session 22, c. 1 (Tanner: 2:*733).

75. *Quod*. 20, n. 22 (Wadding, 12:529 = AW, p. 460 [n. 20.48]); *Quod*. 20, n. 34 (Wadding, 12:535 = AW, p. 468 [n. 20.71]).

76. *Quod*. 20, n. 22 (Wadding, 12:529 = AW, p. 460 [n. 20.48]).

77. *Quod*. 20, nn. 1–2 (Wadding, 12:514–15 = AW, p. 443 [n. 20.2–3]).

78. *Quod*. 20, n. 22 (Wadding, 12:529 = AW, p. 460 [n. 20.48]).

79. *Quod*. 20, n. 22 (Wadding, 12:529 = AW, p. 460 [n. 20.48]), citing Heb. 9.25: "Not that Christ might offer himself there again and again."

80. *Quod*. 20, n. 22 (Wadding, 12:529 = AW, p. 460 [n. 20.48]).

81. *Quod.* 20, n. 2 (Wadding, 12:515 = AW, p. 443-44 [n. 20.3]);
Quod. 20, n. 21 (Wadding, 12:529 = AW, p. 459 [n. 20.47]).

82. *Quod.* 20, n. 14 (Wadding, 12:525 = AW, p. 454 [n. 20.33]).

APPENDIX

1. *Rep.* prol.3.1 (*PW*, pp. 10-12 = FW, pp. 23-27).

2. See, in particular, *Cat.* 4 (1ᵇ25-28).

3. *Metaph.* 3.3 (998ᵇ20-27).

4. For some of the earliest developments, see Allan B. Wolter, *The Transcendentals*, 1-3.

5. *Ord.* 1.8.1.3, n. 115 (Vatican, 4:206-207 = *PW*, p. 3). On the transcendentals in Scotus's thought, see Wolter, *The Transcendentals*; Duns Scotus, *Contingency and Freedom: Lectura I 39*, ed. A. Vos Jaczn. and others, The New Synthese Historical Library, 42 (Dordrecht, Boston and London: Kluwer, 1994), 99-101; Duns Scotus, *Sur la connaissance de Dieu et l'univocité de l'étant*, ed. and trans. Olivier Boulnois, Epiméthée (Paris: Presses Universitaires de France, 1988), 54-63.

6. On being as the subject of the other transcendental attributes, see *Ord.* 1.8.1.3, n. 114 (Vatican, 4:206 = *PW*, p. 3). For the transcendentals as the proper study of metaphysics, see *In Metaph.* prol, n. 18 (Wadding, 4:506ᵇ-507ᵃ = *PW*, p. 2 = FW, p. 21); for (equivalently) being as the subject of metaphysics, see *Rep.* prol.3.1 (*PW*, pp. 10-12 = FW, pp. 23-27). For a different and probably earlier account, see, for example, *In Metaph.* 1.1, nn. 40-41 (Wadding, 4:519ᵇ-20ᵃ). For an exhaustive discussion of Scotus's account of being, see Ludger Honnefelder, *Ens Inquantum Ens: Der Begriff der Seienden als solchen als Gegenstand der Metaphysik nach der Lehre des Johannes Duns Scotus*, BGPTM, N. F., 16 (Münster: Aschendorff, 1979).

7. *Ord.* 1.8.1.3, n. 115 (Vatican, 4:206-207).

8. See Bonaventure, *De Myst. Trin.* 1.1 (*Opera Omnia*, 5:46ᵇ-47ᵇ).

9. For the first three of the disjunctions, see *Ord.* 1.8.1.3, n. 115 (Vatican, 4:207); for the whole list, see Wolter, *The Transcendentals*, 138, and his excellent discussion on pages 138-61. Clearly, the set of possible disjunctive attributes coextensive with being is infinite. But most of them presumably can be classified in terms of Aristotle's categories. Blue-or-not-blue, for example, will be (broadly speaking) covered under the category of quality. The significance of Scotus's list lies in the *choice* of disjunctive attributes.

10. See Wolter, *The Transcendentals*, 11.

11. *Rep.* prol.3.1 (*PW*, pp. 11-12 = FW, pp. 25-27).

12. Wolter, *The Transcendentals*, 177–84. Wolter summarizes the basic method employed in Scotus's natural theology on page 130: for each of the disjunctive transcendentals, we can infer that, if the less perfect of the pair is instantiated, the more perfect is as well; see *Lect.* 1.39.1–5, n. 39 (Vatican, 17:490–491 = Vos, p. 96). How Scotus goes about drawing these inferences is the subject of chapters 2–3 herein.

13. For Scotus's formal distinction, see usefully *Ord.* 1.8.1.4, n. 193 (Vatican, 4:261–62). For a thorough discussion, see Maurice J. Grajewski, *The Formal Distinction of Duns Scotus: A Study in Metaphysics*, The Catholic University of America Philosophical Series, 90 (Washington, D. C.: Catholic University of America, 1944). For a more rigorous presentation, see the account by Marilyn McCord Adams, "Universals in the Early Fourteenth Century," in Kretzmann, Kenny, and Pinborg (eds.), *The Cambridge History of Later Medieval Philosophy*, 412–17.

14. See in particular *Quod.* 3, n. 15 (Wadding, 12:81; AW, pp. 73–74 [n. 3.46]) for the *sufficiency* of inseparability for real identity; and *Ord.* 2.1.4–5, n. 200 (Vatican, 7:101) for the *necessity* of inseparability for real identity.

15. For the relevance of Scotus's formal distinction to his account of individuation, see *Ord.* 2.3.1.1, n. 32 (Vatican, 7:403 = Spade, pp. 63–64); *Ord.* 2.3.1.5–6, nn. 179–80, 192 (Vatican, 7:479, 486 = Spade, pp. 104, 108). On Scotus's account of individuation in general, see *Ord.* 2.3.1 passim (Vatican, 7:391–516 = Spade, pp. 57–113); also Marilyn McCord Adams, "Universals in the Early Fourteenth Century," 412–17; Tamar M. Rudavsky, "The Doctrine of Individuation in Duns Scotus," *Franziskanische Studien*, 59 (1977): 320–77, 62 (1980): 62–83; Allan B. Wolter, "John Duns Scotus," in Jorge J. E. Gracia (ed.), *Individuation in Scholasticism: The Later Middle Ages and the Counter-Reformation 1150–1650* (Albany, N.Y.: State University of New York, 1994), 271–98; Woosuk Park, "The Problem of Individuation for Scotus: A Principle of Indivisibility or a Principle of Distinction?" *Franciscan Studies*, 48 (1988): 105–123.

16. *Ord.* 1.1.1.2, nn. 34, 54 (Vatican, 2:23, 38–39).

17. *Ord.* 1.1.1.2, n. 42 (Vatican, 2:26–27).

18. *Ord.* 1.1.2.1, nn. 64–73 (Vatican, 2:48–56); *Ord.* 1.1.2.2, n.178 (Vatican, 2:116–17). Elsewhere Scotus makes it clear that, whatever the status of beatific enjoyment, blessedness itself is an operation, since it is what joins us to God (*Ord.* 4.49.7, n. 3 [Wadding, 10:479]).

19. See Benedict XII, *Benedictus Deus* (DS, nn. 1000–1001).

20. *ST* 1-2.10.2 c (1[2]:58^b).

21. *Ord.* 1.1.2.2, nn. 136–40,149 (Vatican, 2:91–95, 100).

22. *Ord.* 1.1.2.2, n. 175 (Vatican, 2:115).

23. *Ord.* 4.49.6, n. 11 (Wadding, 10:455).

24. *Ord.* 4.49.6, n. 11 (Wadding, 10:455). See also *Ord.* 1.1.2.2., n. 81 (Vatican, 2:61).

25. *Ord.* 1.1.2.2, n. 175 (Vatican, 2:115).

26. Douglas C. Langston, *God's Willing Knowledge: The Influence of Scotus's Analysis of Omniscience* (University Park, Pa., and London: Pennsylvania State University Press, 1986), 41, referring to Scotus, *Ord.* 4.49.6, n. 15 (Wadding, 10:457).

27. Langston, God's Willing Knowledge, 42.

28. *Quod.* 16, n. 8 (Wadding, 12:454 = AW, p. 378 [n. 16.32]). As William Frank points out, the text in both Wadding and AW is mistaken; see the accessible summary of Frank's discovery in *WM*, pp. 14–15. AW should read "Action that has to do with the ultimate end is the most perfect. But *firmness* pertains to the perfection of such an action" (alteration italicized).

29. See Douglas C. Langston, "Did Scotus Embrace Anselm's Notion of Freedom?" *Medieval Philosophy and Theology*, 5 (1996): 154–55, arguing against Frank's proposed identification of steadfastness with freedom.

30. *Ord.* 4.29.un., n. 6 (Wadding, 9:618 = *WM*, pp. 175–77), citing *Eth. Nic.* 3.1 (1110ᵃ13).

BIBLIOGRAPHY

MANUSCRIPTS

Assisi, Biblioteca Communale, MS 137 (Duns Scotus, *Ordinatio*). [*Ord.*]
Oxford, Merton College, MS 103 (William of Ware, *In Sententias*). [*In Sent.*]
Vienna, Österreichische Nationalbibliothek, MS 1453 (Duns Scotus, *Reportatio Parisiensis* 1). [contains book 1 of *Rep.*]

PRINTED PRIMARY SOURCES

Anselm, *Opera Omnia*, ed. Franciscus Salesius Schmitt, 6 vols. (Edinburgh: Thomas Nelson and Sons, 1946–61). [contains *CDH*, *De Casu Diab.*, *De Conc. Virg.*, *Monol.*, and *Pros.*]
Aquinas, Thomas, *Opera Omnia*, ed. Roberto Busa, 7 vols. (Stuttgart and Bad Constatt: Fromann and Holzburg, 1980). [contains *Script. Sent.* 4.44]
——, *Quaestiones Disputatae*, ed. R. M. Spiazzi and others, 2 vols. (Turin and Rome: Marietti, 1949). [contains *De Car.*]
——, *Quaestiones Quodlibetales*, ed. R. M. Spiazzi (Turin and Rome: Marietti, 1949). [*Quae. Quod.*]
——, *Scriptum super Libros Sententiarum*, ed. P. Mandonnet and M. F. Moos, 4 vols. (Paris: Lethielleux, 1929–47). [*Script. Sent.*]
——, *Summa Theologiae*, ed. Petrus Caramello, 3 vols. (Turin and Rome: Marietti, 1952–56). [*ST*]

Aristotle, *Opera*, ed. Immanuel Bekker, 5 vols. (Berlin: Georgius Reimer, 1831). [contains *An. post.*, *Cael.*, *Cat.*, *De an.*, *Eth. Nic.*, *Int.*, *Metaph.*, *Ph.*, *Soph. el.*, and *Top.*]

Augustine, *Contra Maximinum*, PL, 42 (Paris: J.-P. Migne, 1865). [*Contra. Max.*]

————, *De Civitate Dei*, 2 vols., CCSL 47–8 (Turnhout: Brepols, 1955). [*De Civ. Dei*]

————, *De Diversis Quaestionibus Octoginta Tribus*, ed. Almut Mutzenbecher, CCSL, 44A (Turnhout: Brepols, 1975). [*De Div. Qu.*]

————, *De Genesi ad Litteram*, CSEL, 28(3/1) (Prague and Vienna: F. Tempsky; Leipzig: G. Freytag, 1894). [*De Gen.*]

————, *De Trinitate*, ed. W. J. Mountain, 2 vols., CCSL, 50 (Turnhout: Brepols, 1968). [*De Trin.*]

————, *Enarrationes in Psalmos*, 3 vols., CCSL, 38–40 (Turnhout: Brepols, 1956). [*Enarr. in Ps.*]

Basil of Caesarea, *Lettres*, ed. Yves Courtonne, 3 vols., Collections des Universités de France (Paris: Les Belles Lettres, 1957). [*Ep.*]

Boethius, *The Theological Tractates. The Consolation of Philosophy*, ed. H. F. Stewart, E. K. Rand, and S. J. Tester, Loeb Classical Library (Cambridge: Harvard University Press; London: Heinemann, 1978). [contains *De Per.*]

Bonaventure, *Opera Omnia*, 10 vols. (Quaracchi: Collegium Sancti Bonaventurae, 1882–1902). [contains *De Myst. Trin.* and *Comm. Sent.*]

Calvin, John, *Opera Selecta*, ed. Petrus Barth and others, 5 vols. (Munich: Kaiser, 1926–62). [contains *Inst.*]

Cartularium Universitatis Parisiensis, ed. H. Denifle and E. Chatelain, 4 vols. (Paris: Delalain, 1889–97).

Denzinger, Henricus, and Adolfus Schönmetzer (eds.), *Enchiridion Symbolorum, Definitionum et Declarationum de Rebus Fidei et Morum*, 36th ed. (Barcelona, Freiburg, and Rome: Herder, 1976). [DS]

Dionysius the Pseudo-Areopagite, *De Divinis Nomibus*, PG 3 (Paris: J.-P. Migne, 1857). [*De Div. Nom.*]

Duns Scotus, John, *Contingency and Freedom: Lectura I 39*, ed. and trans. A. Vos Jaczn. and others, The New Synthese Historical Library, 42 (Dordrecht, Boston, and London: Kluwer, 1994). [Vos]

————, *De Primo Principio*, ed. and trans. Allan B. Wolter (Chicago: Franciscan Herald Press, 1982). [*DPP*]

————, *Duns Scotus, Metaphysician*, ed. and trans. William A. Frank and Allan B. Wolter, Purdue University Press Series in the History of Philosophy (West Lafayette, Ind.: Purdue University Press, 1995). [FW]

————, "Duns Scotus on the Necessity of Revealed Knowledge" [*Ordinatio*, prol.1.un.], trans. Allan B. Wolter, *Franciscan Studies*, 11 (1951): 231–72. [*WFS*]

———, *Duns Scotus on the Will and Morality*, ed. and trans. Allan B. Wolter (Washington, D.C.: The Catholic University of America Press, 1986). [*WM*]

———, "Duns Scotus's Parisian Proof for the Existence of God," ed. and trans. Allan B. Wolter and Marilyn McCord Adams, *Franciscan Studies*, 42 (1982): 248–321. [WA]

———, *God and Creatures: The Quodlibetal Questions*, ed. and trans. Felix Alluntis and Allan B. Wolter (Princeton, N.J., and London: Princeton University Press, 1975). [AW]

———, *Opera Omnia*, ed. C Balić and others (Vatican City: Typis Polyglottis Vaticanis, 1950–). [Vatican; contains *Lect.*, *Ord.*, 1–2.3]

———, *Opera Omnia*, ed. Luke Wadding, 12 vols. (Lyons: Durand, 1639). [Wadding; contains *Add. Mag.*, *In Metaph.*, *Ord.* 2.4–4.50, *Quod.*, *Rep.*, and *Super Praed.*]

———, *Philosophical Writings: A Selection*, ed. and trans. Allan B. Wolter (Indianapolis, Ill., and Cambridge: Hackett, 1987). [*PW*]

———, *Sur la connaissance de Dieu et l'univocité de l'étant*, ed. and trans. Olivier Boulnois, Epiméthée (Paris: Presses Universitaires de France, 1988).

Henry of Ghent, *Opera Omnia*, ed. R. Macken and others, Ancient and Medieval Philosophy, De Wulf-Mansion Centre, Series 2 (Leuven: Leuven University Press; Leiden: E. J. Brill, 1979–). [contains *Quodlib.* 1–2, 6–7, 9, 10, 12–13]

———, *Quodlibeta*, 2 vols. (Paris, 1518). [contains *Quodlib.* 3–5, 8, 11, 14–15]

———, *Summa Quaestionum Ordinariarium*, 2 vols. (Paris, 1520). [*SQ*]

John of Damascus, *De Fide Orthodoxa*, PG, 94 (Paris: J.-P. Migne, 1864). [*De Fide Orth.*]

———, *De Fide Orthodoxa: Versions of Burgundio and Cerbanus*, ed. Eligius M. Buytaert, Franciscan Institute Publications: Text Series, 8 (St. Bonaventure, N. Y.: The Franciscan Institute; Louvain: E. Nauwelaerts; Paderborn: F. Schöningh, 1955). [*De Fide Orth.*]

Lombard, Peter, *Sententiae in Quatuor Libris Distinctae*, 3rd ed., 2 vols., Spicilegium Bonaventurianum (Grottaferrata: Collegium Sancti Bonaventurae ad Claras Aquas, 1971–81). [*Sent.*]

Major, John, *Historia Maioris Britanniae tam Angliae tam Scotiae* (Paris, 1521).

Richard of St. Victor, *De Trinitate*, ed. Jean Ribaillier, Textes Philosophiques du Moyen Age, 6 (Paris: J. Vrin, 1958). [*De Trin.*]

Rupert of Deutz, *De Gloria et honore filii hominis super Mattheum*, ed. Hrabanus Haacke, CCCM, 29 (Turnhout: Brepols, 1979). [*De Glor.*]

Spade, Paul Vincent (ed. and trans.), *Five Texts on the Mediaeval Problem of Universals: Porphyry, Boethius, Abelard, Duns Scotus, Ockham* (Indianapolis, Ind., and Cambridge: Hackett, 1994). [Spade]

Summa Fratris Alexandri, 4 vols. (Quaracchi: Collegium Sancti Bonaventurae, 1924–48). [*Sum. Fr. Alex.*]

Tanner, Norman (ed.), *Decrees of the Ecumenical Councils*, 2 vols. (London: Sheed and Ward; Washington, D. C.: Georgetown University Press, 1990). [Tanner]

William of Auxerre, *Summa Aurea*, ed. Jean Ribailler, 4 vols., Spicilegium Bonaventurianum, 16–19 (Paris: Centre National de la Recherche Scientifique; Grottaferrata: Collegium Sancti Bonaventuae ad Claras Aquas, 1980–86). [*Sum. Aur.*]

William of Ockham, *Opera Theologica*, ed. Iuvenalis Lalor and others, 10 vols. (St. Bonaventure, N.Y.: St. Bonaventure University, 1967–86). [*OT*; contains *Quod. Sept.* and *Report.*]

———, *Quodlibetal Questions*, trans. Alfred J. Freddoso and Francis E. Kelley, Yale Library of Medieval Philosophy, 2 vols. (New Haven and London: Yale University Press, 1991). [FK; *Quod. Sept.*]

SECONDARY SOURCES

Adams, Marilyn McCord, "Universals in the Early Fourteenth Century," in Norman Kretzmann, Anthony Kenny, and Jan Pinborg (eds.), *The Cambridge History of Later Medieval Philosophy*, 411–29.

———, "Aristotle and the Sacrament of the Altar," in Richard Bosley and Martin Tweedale (eds.), *Aristotle and his Medieval Interpreters, Canadian Journal of Philosophy*, supplementary vol. 17 (1991): 195–249.

———, "The Resurrection of the Body According to Three Medieval Aristotelians: Thomas Aquinas, John Duns Scotus, William Ockham," *Philosophical Topics*, 20 (1992): 1–33.

Adams, Robert Merrihew, "A Modified Divine Command Theory of Ethical Wrongness," in his *The Virtue of Faith and Other Essays in Philosophical Theology*, 97–122.

———, *The Virtue of Faith and Other Essays in Philosophical Theology* (New York and Oxford: Oxford University Press, 1987).

Alston, William, "Aquinas on Theological Predication," in Eleonore Stump (ed.), *Reasoned Faith: Essays in Philosophical Theology in Honor of Norman Kretzmann* (Ithaca, N.Y., and London: Cornell University Press, 1993), 145–78.

Bäck, Allan, "Scotus on the Consistency of the Incarnation and Trinity," *Vivarium*, 36 (1998): 83–107.

Bąk, F., "Scoti schola numerosior est omnibus aliis simul sumptis," *Franciscan Studies*, 16 (1956): 144–65.

Balić, C., "Life and Works of Duns Scotus," in John K. Ryan and Bernardine Bonansea (eds.), *John Duns Scotus, 1265–1965*, Studies in Philosophy and the History of Philosophy, 3 (Washington, D.C.: Catholic University of America Press, 1965), 1–27.

Bartel, T. W., "Could there be More than One Lord?" *Faith and Philosophy*, 11 (1994): 357–78.

Boler, John, "Transcending the Natural: Duns Scotus on the Two Affections of the Will," *American Catholic Philosophical Quarterly*, 67 (1993): 109–26.

Bonnefoy, Jean-François, *Le ven. Jean Duns Scot docteur de l'immaculée conception: son milieu, sa doctrine, son influence* (Rome: Herder, 1960).

Brampton, C. K., "Duns Scotus at Oxford, 1288–1301," *Franciscan Studies*, 24 (1964), 5–20.

Brown, Patterson, "Infinite Causal Regression," *Philosophical Review*, 75 (1966): 510–25, reprinted in Anthony Kenny (ed.), *Aquinas: A Collection of Critical Essays*, Modern Studies in Philosophy (London and Melbourne: Macmillan, 1969), 214–36.

Brown, Stephen F., "Scotus's Method in Theology," in Leonardo Sileo (ed.), *Via Scoti*, 1:229–43.

Burger, Maria, *Personalität im Horizont absoluter Prädestination: Untersuchungen zur Christologie des Johannes Duns Scotus und ihrer Rezeption in modernen theologischen Ansätzen*, Beiträge zur Geschichte der Philosophie und Theologie des Mittelalters, N. F., 40 (Münster: Aschendorff, 1994).

Burns, J. Patout, "The Concept of Satisfaction in Medieval Redemption Theory," *Theological Studies*, 36 (1975): 285–304.

Burr, D., "Scotus and Transubstantiation," *Mediaeval Studies*, 34 (1972): 336–60.

Castañeda, H.-N., "Omniscience and Indexical Reference," *Journal of Philosophy*, 64 (1967): 203–10.

Catania, Francis J., "John Duns Scotus on *Ens Infinitum*," *American Catholic Philosophical Quarterly*, 67 (1993): 37–54.

Courtenay, William J., "Scotus at Paris," in Leonardo Sileo (ed.), *Via Scoti*, 1:149–64.

Craig, William Lane, *The Kalām Cosmological Argument*, Library of Philosophy and Religion (London and Basingstoke: Macmillan, 1979).

———, *The Cosmological Argument from Plato to Leibniz*, Library of Philosophy and Religion (London and Basingstoke: Macmillan, 1980).

Cross, Richard, "The Doctrine of the Hypostatic Union in the Thought of

Duns Scotus" (unpublished doctoral dissertation, Oxford University, 1991).

———, "Aquinas on Nature, Hypostasis, and the Metaphysics of the Incarnation," *The Thomist*, 60 (1996): 171–202.

———, "Duns Scotus on Eternity and Timelessness," *Faith and Philosophy*, 14 (1997): 3–25.

———, "Duns Scotus on Goodness, Justice, and What God Can Do," *Journal of Theological Studies*, 48 (1997): 48–76.

———, "Is Aquinas's Attempt to Prove the Indestructibility of the Soul Successful?" *British Journal for the History of Philosophy*, 5 (1997): 1–20.

———, *The Physics of Duns Scotus: The Scientific Context of a Theological Vision* (Oxford: Clarendon Press, 1998).

———, "Identity, Origin, and Persistence in Duns Scotus's Physics," *History of Philosophy Quarterly*, 16 (1999): 1–19.

Dettloff, Werner, *Die Lehre von der Acceptatio Divina bei Johannes Duns Scotus mit besonderer Berücksichtigung der Rechtfertigungslehre*, Franziskanische Forschungen, 10 (Dietrich Coelde: Werl, 1954).

Dumont, Stephen D., "The Univocal Concept of Being in the Fourteenth Century: I. John Duns Scotus and William of Alnwick," *Mediaeval Studies*, 49 (1987): 1–75.

———, "Theology as a Practical Science and Duns Scotus's Distinction between Intuitive and Abstractive Cognition," *Speculum*, 64 (1989): 579–99.

———, "The Question on Individuation in Scotus's 'Quaestiones super Metaphysicam,'" in Leonardo Sileo (ed.), *Via Scoti*, 1:193–227.

Finkenzeller, Josef, *Offenbarung und Theologie nach der Lehre des Johannes Duns Scotus: eine historische und systematische Untersuchung*, BGPTM, 38(5) (Münster: Aschendorff, 1961).

Frank, William A., "Duns Scotus on Autonomous Freedom and Divine Co-Causality," *Medieval Philosophy and Theology*, 2 (1992): 142–164.

Frank, William A., and Allan B. Wolter (ed. and trans.), *Duns Scotus, Metaphysician*, Purdue University Press Series in the History of Philosophy (West Lafayette, Ind.: Purdue University Press, 1995).

Freddoso, Alfred J., "Human Nature, Potency, and the Incarnation," *Faith and Philosophy*, 3 (1986): 27–53.

Grajewski, Maurice J., *The Formal Distinction of Duns Scotus: A Study in Metaphysics*, The Catholic University of America Philosophical Series, 90 (Washington, D.C.: Catholic University of America, 1944).

Hilbert, David, "On the Infinite," in *Philosophy of Mathematics*, ed. Paul Benacerraf and Hilary Putnam (Englewood Cliffs, N.J.: Prentice-Hall, 1964).

Honnefelder, Ludger, *Ens Inquantum Ens: Der Begriff der Seienden als solchen als Gegenstand der Metaphysik nach der Lehre des Johannes Duns Scotus*, BGPTM, N. F., 16 (Münster: Aschendorff, 1979).

Honnefelder, Ludger, Rega Wood, and Mechthild Dreyer (eds.), *John Duns Scotus: Metaphysics and Ethics*, STGM, 53 (Leiden, New York, and Cologne: E. J. Brill, 1996).

Hughes, Christopher, *On a Complex Theory of a Simple God: An Investigation in Aquinas's Philosophical Theology*, Cornell Studies in the Philosophy of Religion (Ithaca, N.Y., and London: Cornell University Press, 1989).

———, "Aquinas on Continuity and Identity," *Medieval Philosophy and Theology*, 6 (1997): 93–108.

Hughes, Gerard J., *The Philosophical Assessment of Theology: Essays in Honor of Frederick C. Copleston* (Tunbridge Wells: Search Press; Washington, D. C.: Georgetown University Press, 1987).

Ingham, Mary Elizabeth, "John Duns Scotus: An Integrated Vision," in Kenan B. Osborne (ed.), *The History of Franciscan Theology* (St. Bonaventure, N.Y.: The Franciscan Institute, 1994), 185–230.

Jenkins, John I., *Knowledge and Faith in Thomas Aquinas* (Cambridge: Cambridge University Press, 1997).

King, Peter, "Duns Scotus on the Common Nature and the Individual Differentia," *Philosophical Topics*, 20 (1992): 51–76.

———, "Duns Scotus on the Reality of Self-Change," in Mary Louise Gill and James G. Lennox (eds.), *Self-Motion from Aristotle to Newton* (Princeton, N.J.: Princeton University Press, 1994), 229–90.

Kirwan, Christopher, *Augustine*, The Arguments of the Philosophers (London and New York: Routledge, 1989).

Knuuttila, Simo, "Modal Logic," in Norman Kretzmann, Anthony Kenny, and Jan Pinborg (eds.), *The Cambridge History of Later Medieval Philosophy*, 342–57.

———, *Modalities in Medieval Philosophy*, Topics in Medieval Philosophy (London and New York: Routledge, 1993).

———, "Duns Scotus and the Foundations of Logical Modalities," in Ludger Honnefelder, Rega Wood, and Mechthild Dreyer (eds.), *John Duns Scotus*, 127–43.

Kretzmann, Norman, "Omniscience and Immutability," *Journal of Philosophy*, 63 (1966): 409–21.

———, *The Metaphysics of Theism: Aquinas's Natural Theology in "Summa Contra Gentiles" I* (Oxford: Clarendon Press, 1997).

Kretzmann, Norman, Anthony Kenny, and Jan Pinborg (eds.), *The Cambridge History of Later Medieval Philosophy* (Cambridge: Cambridge University Press, 1982).

Langston, Douglas, C., "Scotus and Ockham on the Univocal Concept of Being," *Franciscan Studies*, 39 (1979): 105–29.

———, "Scotus's Departure from Anselm's Theory of the Atonement," *Recherches de Théologie Ancienne et Médiévale*, 50 (1983): 227–41.

———, *God's Willing Knowledge: The Influence of Scotus's Analysis of Omniscience* (University Park, Pa., and London: Pennsylvania State University Press, 1986).

———, "Did Scotus Embrace Anselm's Notion of Freedom?" *Medieval Philosophy and Theology*, 5 (1996): 145–59.

Lee, Sukjae, "Scotus on the Will: The Rational Power and the Two Affections," *Vivarium*, 36 (1998): 40–54.

Lobkowicz, Nicholas, *Theory and Practice: The History of a Concept from Aristotle to Marx* (Notre Dame: University of Notre Dame Press, 1967).

Lonergan, Bernard J., *Verbum: Word and Idea in Aquinas*, ed. David B. Burrell (London: Darton, Longman, and Todd, 1968).

Magrini, Aegidius, *Ioannis Duns Scoti doctrina de scientifica theologiae natura*, Studia Antoniana, 5 (Rome: Antonianum, 1952).

Mann, William E., "Divine Simplicity," *Religious Studies*, 18 (1982): 451–71.

———, "Duns Scotus, Demonstration, and Doctrine," *Faith and Philosophy*, 9 (1992): 436–62.

Marenbon, John, *Later Medieval Philosophy (1150–1350): An Introduction* (London and New York: Routledge, 1987).

McGrath, Alister E., *Iustitia Dei: A History of the Christian Doctrine of Justification: The Beginnings to the Reformation* (Cambridge: Cambridge University Press, 1986).

Moonan, Lawrence, *Divine Power: The Medieval Power Distinction up to Its Adoption by Albert, Bonaventure, and Aquinas* (Oxford: Clarendon Press, 1994).

Moore, A. W., *The Infinite*, Problems of Philosophy: Their Past and their Present (London and New York: Routledge, 1990).

Morris, Thomas V., "Duty and Divine Goodness," *American Philosophical Quarterly*, 21 (1984): 261–68.

———, "The God of Abraham, Isaac, and Anselm," *Faith and Philosophy*, 1 (1984): 177–87.

———, *The Logic of God Incarnate* (Ithaca, N.Y., and London: Cornell University Press, 1986).

———, *Anselmian Explorations: Essays in Philosophical Theology* (Notre Dame: University of Notre Dame Press, 1987).

Noone, Timothy B., "Scotus's Critique of the Thomistic Theory of Individuation and the Dating of the 'Quaestiones in Libros Metaphysicorum,' VII q. 13," in Leonardo Sileo (ed.), *Via Scoti*, 1:391–406.

O'Connor, Timothy, "Scotus's Argument for the Existence of a First Effi-
cient Cause," *International Journal for Philosophy of Religion*, 33 (1993):
17–32.
————, "From First Efficient Cause to God: Scotus on the Identification
Stage of the Cosmological Argument," in Ludger Honnefelder, Rega
Wood, and Mechthild Dreyer (eds.), *John Duns Scotus*, 435–54.
Ott, Ludwig, "Das Konzil von Chalkedon in der Frühscholastik," in *Das
Konzil von Chalkedon: Geschichte und Gegenwart*, ed. A. Grillmeier and
H. Bacht, 3 vols. (Würzburg: Echter-Verlag, 1953), 2:873–922.
Panaccio, Claude, "From Mental Word to Mental Language," *Philosophi-
cal Topics*, 20 (1992): 125–47.
Pannenberg, Wolfhart, *Die Prädestinationslehre des Duns Skotus in Zusam-
menhang der scholastischen Lehrentwicklung*, Forschungen zur Kirchen-
und Dogmengeschichte, 4 (Göttingen: Vandenhoeck und Ruprecht,
1954).
Park, Woosuk, "The Problem of Individuation for Scotus: A Principle of
Indivisibility or a Principle of Distinction?" *Franciscan Studies*, 48 (1988):
105–23.
Pasnau, Robert, *Theories of Cognition in the Later Middle Ages* (Cambridge:
Cambridge University Press, 1997).
Perler, Dominik, "What Am I Thinking About? John Duns Scotus and Peter
Aureol on Intentional Objects," *Vivarium*, 32 (1994): 72–89.
Pernoud, M. A., "The Theory of the *Potentia Dei* according to Aquinas,
Scotus, and Ockham," *Antonianum*, 47 (1972): 69–95.
Principe, Walter H., *William of Auxerre's Theology of The Hypostatic Union*,
The Theology of the Hypostatic Union in the Early Thirteenth Cen-
tury, 1; Studies and Texts, 7 (Toronto: Pontifical Institute of Mediae-
val Studies, 1963).
Quinton, Anthony, "British Philosophy," in P. Edwards (ed.), *The Encyclo-
pedia of Philosophy*, 8 vols. (London: Collier-Macmillan, 1965), 1:369–96.
Ragland, C. P., "Scotus on the Decalogue: What Sort of Voluntarism?"
Vivarium, 36 (1998): 67–81.
Randi, Eugenio, "A Scotist Way of Distinguishing between God's Absolute
and Ordained Powers," in Anne Hudson and Michael Wilks (eds.),
From Ockham to Wyclif, Studies in Church History: Subsidia, 5 (Oxford:
Basil Blackwell, 1987), 43–50.
Roo, William A. van, *Grace and Original Justice according to St. Thomas*,
Analecta Gregoriana, 75 (Rome: Gregorian University, 1955).
Rudavsky, Tamar M., "The Doctrine of Individuation in Duns Scotus,"
Franziskanische Studien, 59 (1977): 320–77; 62 (1980): 62–83.
Schmaus, Michael, *Die Liber Propugnatorius des Thomas Anglicus und die*

Lehrunterschiede zwischen Thomas von Aquin und Duns Scotus. II. Teil: Die Trinitarischen Lehrdifferenzen. Erste Band: Systematische Darstellung und historische Würdigung, BGPTM, 29(1) (Münster: Aschendorff, 1930), 482–550.

Schönberger, Rolf, "*Negationes non summe amamus*: Duns Scotus's Auseinandersetzung mit der negativen Theologie," in Ludger Honnefelder, Rega Wood, and Mechthild Dreyer (eds.), *John Duns Scotus*, 475–96.

Seeberg, Reinhold, *Die Theologie des Johannes Duns Scotus: Eine dogmengeschichtliche Untersuchung*, Studien zur Geschichte der Theologie und der Kirche, 5 (Leipzig: Dieterich'sche Verlags-Buchhandlung, 1900).

Sileo, Leonardo (ed.), *Via Scoti: Methodologica ad mentem Joannis Duns Scoti*, Atti del Congresso Scotistico Internazionale, Roma, 9–11 Marzo 1993, 2 vols. (Rome: Antonianum, 1995).

Swinburne, Richard, *The Existence of God*, 2nd ed. (Oxford: Clarendon Press, 1991).

———, *The Christian God* (Oxford: Clarendon Press, 1994).

Thomas, Janice, "Univocity and Understanding God's Nature," in Gerald H. Hughes (ed.), *The Philosophical Assessment of Theology*, 85–100.

Torrell, Jean-Pierre, *Saint Thomas Aquinas. Volume 1: The Person and His Work*, trans. Robert Royal (Washington, D.C.: Catholic University of America Press, 1996).

Veuthey, Léon, *Jean Duns Scot: pensée théologique* (Paris: Éditions Franciscaines, 1967).

Vooght, Paul de, *Les sources da la doctrine chrétienne d'après les théologiens du XIVe siècle et du début du XVe avec le texte intégrale des XII premières questions de la Summa inédite de Gérard de Bologne († 1317)* (Paris: Desclée de Brouwer, 1954).

Vos Jaczn., Antonie, *Johannes Duns Scotus*, Kerkhistorische Monografieën (Leiden: J. J. Groen en Zoon, 1994).

Wainwright, William J., "Monotheism," in Robert Audi and William J. Wainwright (eds.), *Rationality, Religious Belief, and Moral Commitment: New Essays in the Philosophy of Religion* (Ithaca, N.Y., and London: Cornell University Press, 1986), 289–314.

Wass, Meldon C., *The Infinite God and the Summa Fratris Alexandri* (Chicago: Franciscan Herald Press, 1964).

Wetter, Friedrich, *Die Trinitätslehre des Johannes Duns Scotus*, BGPTM, 41(5) (Münster: Aschendorff, 1967).

Williams, Norman Powell, *The Ideas of the Fall and of Original Sin: A Historical and Critical Study* (London: Longmans, Green, 1927).

Williams, Thomas, "How Scotus Separates Morality from Happiness," *American Catholic Philosophical Quarterly*, 69 (1995): 425–45.

————, "Reason, Morality, and Voluntarism in Duns Scotus: A Pseudo-Problem Dissolved," *The Modern Schoolman*, 74 (1997): 73–94.

————, "The Unmitigated Scotus," *Archiv für Geschichte der Philosophie*, 80 (1998): 162–81.

Wippel, John F., *Metaphysical Themes in Thomas Aquinas*, Studies in Philosophy and the History of Philosophy, 10 (Washington, D.C.: Catholic University of America Press, 1984).

Wolter, Allan B., *The Transcendentals and their Function in the Metaphysics of Duns Scotus*, Franciscan Institute Publications, Philosophy Series, 3 (St. Bonaventure, N.Y.: The Franciscan Institute, 1946).

————, "Duns Scotus on the Existence and Nature of God," *Proceedings of the American Catholic Philosophical Association*, 28 (1954): 94–121.

————, "Duns Scotus on Intuition, Memory, and Our Knowledge of Individuals," in his *Philosophical Theology of John Duns Scotus*, 98–122.

————, *The Philosophical Theology of John Duns Scotus*, ed. Marilyn McCord Adams (Ithaca, N.Y., and London: Cornell University Press, 1990).

————, "Scotus's Paris Lectures on God's Knowledge of Future Events," in his *The Philosophical Theology of John Duns Scotus*, 285–333.

————, "Reflections on the Life and Works of Scotus," *American Catholic Philosophical Quarterly*, 67 (1993): 1–36.

————, "John Duns Scotus," in Jorge J. E. Gracia (ed.), *Individuation in Scholasticism: The Later Middle Ages and the Counter-Reformation 1150–1650* (Albany, N.Y.: State University of New York, 1994), 271–298.

————, "Duns Scotus at Oxford," in Leonardo Sileo (ed.), *Via Scoti*, 1:183–91.

————, "Reflections about Scotus's Early Works," in Ludger Honnefelder, Rega Wood, and Mechthild Dreyer (eds.), *John Duns Scotus*, 37–57.

Wolter, Allan B., and Marilyn McCord Adams, "Memory and Intuition: A Focal Debate in Fourteenth Century Cognitive Psychology," *Franciscan Studies*, 53 (1993): 175–230.

Wolter, Allan B., and Blane O'Neill, *John Duns Scotus: Mary's Architect* (Quincy, Ill.: Franciscan Press, 1993).

Wood, Rega, "Scotus's Argument for the Existence of God," *Franciscan Studies*, 47 (1987): 257–77.

Zavalloni, Roberto, *Richard de Mediavilla et la controverse sur la pluralité des formes*, Philosophes Médiévaux, 2 (Louvain: L'Institut Supérieur de Philosophie, 1951).

INDEX LOCORUM

ALEXANDER OF HALES, SCHOOL OF

Summa Fratris Alexandri
1.2.3 c   157 n. 27
3.1.1.2.2   204 n. 4

ANSELM

Cur Deus Homo
1.12–13   204 n. 18
1.12   204 n. 14
1.14   204 n. 14
1.16–17   204 n. 18
1.19–20   204 n. 18
2.14   204 n. 16
2.19   204 nn. 15, 17; 206 n. 44

De Casu Diaboli
4   188 n. 21

De Conceptu Virginali
2   194 n. 116

Monologion
15   166 n. 3, 167 n. 5

Proslogion
3   164 n. 26

AQUINAS, THOMAS

Quaestio Disputata de Caritate
un.1 c   197 n. 44

Quaestiones Quodlibetales
3.2.2   184 n. 7
4.5.un.   184 n. 7

Scriptum super Libros Sententiarum
4.4.1.1   208 n. 39
4.4.1.1 ad 4   208 n. 41
4.4.1.3   208 n. 40
4.44.1.1.2 ad 3   184 n. 5, 186 n. 44

Summa Theologiae
1.1.1 c   159 n. 45
1.1.4 c   158 n. 35
1.1.8 c   159 n. 43
1.2.2 ad 1   157 n. 29
1.2.3 c   160 n. 2
1.3–26   160 n. 2
1.3 introductory passage   172 n. 68
1.3   164 n. 33
1.3.1–3   165 n. 54
1.3.4   166 n. 54
1.3.5 c   171 n. 53
1.3.6–7   165 n. 64
1.7.1–2   164 n. 33
1.7.1 c   169 n. 38
1.10.2   165 n. 54
1.11.3 c   164 n. 33, 182 n. 59
1.13.4 c   165 n. 54, 172 n. 66
1.13.5 c   167 n. 17, 168 n. 23
1.15.1   175 n. 21
1.25.3   155 n. 6

1.36.2 c   180 n. 24
1.46.2   162 n. 13
1.46.2 ad 7   161 n. 5
1.50.2 c   183 n. 2
1.51.3   185 n. 20
1.75.4 ad 2   201 n. 27
1.75.6 c   186 n. 26
1.76.1 c   184 n. 26
1.76.1 ad 6   184 n. 27
1.76.3 c   183 n. 3
1.76.4 c   183 n. 3
1.76.4 ad 2   185 n. 17
1.77.1 ad 5   187 n. 1
1.82.1 c   187 n. 7
1.83.1 c   187 n. 11
1.89.1 c   185 n. 22
1.97.1 c   193 n. 99
1-2.2.8   187 n. 9
1-2.10.2 c   212 n. 20
1-2.77.2 ad 4   187 n. 8
1-2.81.3 c   206 n. 48
1-2.86.1   193 n. 85
1-2.86.2   193 n. 85
1-2.94.2 c   190 n. 41
1-2.110.2 c   198 n. 60
1-2.100.8 ad 3   192 n. 81
1-2.114.11 c   195 n. 13
2-2.1.4 c   157 n. 27
2-2.1.5 c   157 n. 27
2-2.47.1–2   187 n. 10
2-2.61.2 c   192 n. 70
3.1.3 c   203 n. 2
3.2.1 sed contra   199 n. 4
3.2.2 sed contra   199 n. 4
3.2.6 ad 2   199 n. 6
3.17.2   199 n. 6
3.18.1 ad 4   202 n. 43
3.37.2 c   206 n. 49
3.48.3 ad 2   206 n. 45
3.62.1 c   207 n. 8
3.62.4   207 n. 9
3.62.4 ad 1   207 n. 10
3.75.2 c   209 n. 50
3.75.4 c   209 n. 49
3.76.1 ad 1   210 n. 67
3.76.2 c   210 n. 68
3.76.4 ad 1   210 n. 65

3.76.4 ad 2   210 n. 66
3.77.1 ad 3   210 n. 63

ARISTOTLE

Analytica posteriora
1.2 (71^b9–12)   158 n. 33
1.5 (74^b5–39)   162 n. 15
1.13 (78^a22–$^b23$)   163 n. 16

Categoriae
4 (1^b25–28)   211 n. 2
4 (1^b25–27)   209 n. 47
5 (5^b2–3)   210 n. 64
8 (8^b2–4)   197 n. 35

De anima
2.2 (413^b29–31)   186 n. 29

De caelo
2.3 (286^a18)   186 n. 42

De interpretatione
1 (16^a3–9)   174 n. 14

Ethica Nicomachea
1.1 (1094^a3–5)   164 n. 25
2.1 (1103^b21–22)   197 n. 34
2.2 (1104^a27–$b3$)   197 n. 34
2.5 (1106^a11–12)   196 n. 33
3.1 (1110^a13)   213 n. 30
5.6 (1134^b9–10)   192 n. 71
6.1 (1139^a11–15)   158 n. 34

Physica
3.6 (207^a7–9)   170 n. 43
4.2 (209^a31–$^b1$)   209 n. 53

Metaphysica
3.3 (998^b20–27)   211 n. 3
5.30 (1025^a19–21)   209 n. 60
7.5 (1030^b20–21)   209 n. 60
9.2 (1046^b1–4)   187 n. 13

Topica
1.4 (101^b15–28)   169 n. 35

AUGUSTINE

Contra Maximinum
2.10.2   183 n. 72

AUGUSTINE (*continued*)
  De Civitate Dei
  18.23   160 n. 51
  22.20   186 n. 45

  De Diversis Quaestionibus
  46   175 n. 21

  De Genesi ad Litteram
  4.23   202 n. 49
  11.22   195 n. 6

  De Trinitate
  1.7   183 n. 72
  2.3   183 n. 72
  5.4   180 n. 30
  5.6   180 nn. 31, 32
  5.15   179 n. 18, 183 n. 72
  6.7   179 n. 14
  7.10   172 n. 62, 182 n. 58
  9.8–16   179 n. 4
  10.13–19   179 n. 4
  15.8   167 n. 8
  15.27   179 nn. 13, 18

  Enarrationes in Psalmos
  31(II).9   193 n. 87
  50.15   193 n. 91

BASIL OF CAESAREA
  Epistulae
  38   178 n. 1

BOETHIUS
  De Persona et Duabus Naturis
  3   181 n. 53, 200 n. 22

BONAVENTURE
  *Commentaria in Quatuor Libros
    Sententiarum*
  1.35.un.1   175 n. 26
  1.35.un.3   175 n. 26
  1.35.un.4   175 n. 26
  2.1.1.1.2   162 n. 13
  2.27.2.2   195 n. 15
  2.27.2.3   195 nn. 13, 14
  2.35.1.1 ad 4   193 n. 84

  3.25.1.2 arg. 6 and ad 6   159 n. 47
  4.1.1.un.1 ad 1   207 n. 7

  De Mysterio Trinitatis
  1.1   211 n. 8

CALVIN, JOHN
  Christianae Religionis Institutio
  3.22.11   195 n. 8

DIONYSIUS THE PSEUDO–AREOPAGITE
  De Divinis Nominibus
  4   193 n. 96

DUNS SCOTUS, JOHN
  Additiones Magnae
  1.36.4, nn. 26–27   175 n. 20

  De Primo Principio
  3.5   162 nn. 17, 18
  3.6   161 n. 9
  3.7   163 n. 19
  3.8   161 n. 10
  3.11   161 n. 6
  3.13   162 n. 12, 164 n. 23
  3.14   162 n. 13
  3.19   163 n. 20
  3.20   163 n. 21
  3.24–26   164 n. 32
  3.29   164 n. 24
  3.31–32   164 n. 30
  3.35–37   164 n. 27
  3.43–62   164 n. 32
  4.4   165 n. 52
  4.14   173 n. 6
  4.15   173 nn. 2, 3, 5
  4.22   172 n. 1
  4.26   173 n. 4
  4.48   164 n. 35
  4.63   165 n. 38
  4.64   165 n. 39
  4.65   164 n. 28
  4.66   165 n. 37
  4.67–72   165 n. 36
  4.75   165 n. 51
  4.76   166 n. 55
  4.80   166 n. 56

4.85   175 n. 22
4.86   154 n. 6
4.88   165 n. 41
4.91   165 n. 45

Lectura
prol.4.1–2, n. 133 *(WM, p. 1–227)*
    158 n. 38
prol.4.1–2, n. 163 *(WM, p. 137)*
    159 n. 40
prol.4.1–2, n. 164 *(WM, p. 137)*
    158 n. 37; 159 nn. 39, 41
1.2.1, nn. 38–135   160 n. 3
1.2.2.1–4, n. 165   156 n. 21
1.2.2.1–4, n. 185   156 n. 21
1.2.2.1–4, n. 239   180 nn. 28, 29
1.2.2.1–4, n. 242   156 n. 21
1.3.1.1–2, n. 113   168 n. 25
1.8.1.3, nn. 103–4   170 n. 41
1.26.un., n. 17   180 n. 35
1.26.un., n. 29   180 n. 38
1.26.un., n. 34   180 n. 39
1.26.un., n. 59   180 n. 37
1.26.un., n. 66   180 n. 34
1.26.un., n. 68   180 n. 40
1.26.un., n. 75   180 n. 41
1.39.1–5, nn. 20–21   175 n. 22
1.39.1–5, n. 39   212 n. 12
1.39.1–5, n. 40   188 n. 16
1.39.1–5, nn. 43–44   176 n. 38, 192
    n. 73
1.39.1–5, n. 46   177 n. 61
1.39.1–5, nn. 49–51   177 n. 64
1.39.1–5, nn. 51–52   188 n. 14
1.39.1–5, nn. 53–54   177 n. 63
1.39.1–5, n. 53   177 n. 62
1.39.1–5, n. 62   174 n. 19, 176 n. 39,
    177 n. 65
1.39.1–5, n. 64   176 n. 42
1.39.1–5, n. 65   176 n. 43
1.39.1–5, n. 73   177 n. 50
1.43.un., n. 15   174 n. 18
1.44.un., n. 10   177 n. 67
2.1.1, n. 48   182 n. 59
2.21–22.1–2, n. 4   193 n. 83
2.21–22.1–2, n. 29   190 n. 43
2.25.un., n. 28   190 n. 37
2.25.un., n. 35   187 n. 12

2.25.un., n. 37   187 n. 12
2.25.un., n. 55   187 n. 5, 190 n. 38
2.25.un., n. 58   190 n. 39
2.25.un., n. 68   187 n. 5
2.25.un., nn. 69–70   189 n. 36
2.29.un., n. 7   193 n. 91
2.29.un., nn. 10–11   193 n. 97
2.29.un., n. 15   194 n. 108
2.30–32.1–4, nn. 50–53   194
    n. 108
2.30–32.1–4, n. 58   194 n. 116
2.30–32.1–4, n. 61   194 n. 116

Ordinatio
[Vatican edition]
prol.1.un., n. 5   159 nn. 44, 46
prol.1.un., n. 12   159 n. 48
prol.1.un., nn. 13–15   160 n. 50
prol.1.un., nn. 54–55   159 n. 47
prol.1.un., n. 71   160 n. 50
prol.2.un., nn. 101–119   160 n. 51
prol.2.un., n. 108   190 n. 50
prol.2.un., n. 110   160 n. 52
prol.2.un., n. 112   155 n. 8
prol.2.un., n. 120   159 n. 47
prol.2.un., n. 123   157 n. 24
prol.3.1–3, n. 141   156 n. 17
prol.3.1–3, n. 151   156 n. 18
prol.3.1–3, n. 154   156 n. 16
prol.3.1–3, nn. 167–68   156 n. 18
prol.3.1–3, nn. 170–71   156 n. 18
prol.3.1–3, nn. 200–201   156 n. 16
prol.3.1–3, nn. 204   157 n. 24
prol.3.1–3, nn. 205   157 n. 27
prol.3.1–3, nn. 207   157 n. 24
prol.4.1–2, nn. 208–212   157 n. 32
prol.4.1–2, n. 208   158 n. 33
prol.4.1–2, n. 214   157 n. 28
prol.5.1–2, n. 227   158 n. 37
prol.5.1–2, n. 228   158 n. 37
prol.5.1–2, nn. 236–37   159 n. 41
prol.5.1–2, nn. 270–302   158 n. 35
prol.5.1–2, n. 303   158 n. 36
prol.5.1–2, n. 304   158 n. 36
prol.5.1–2, n. 310   159 n. 40
prol.5.1–2, n. 313   158 n. 35
prol.5.1–2, n. 314   157 n. 32, 159
    n. 39

DUNS SCOTUS, *Ordinatio*
[Vatican edition] (*continued*)
prol.5.1–2, n. 332   157 n. 32, 159 n. 39
prol.5.1–2, nn. 336–39   191 n. 51
prol.5.1–2, n. 344   191 n. 51
prol.5.1–2, n. 352   159 n. 42
1.1.1.2, n. 34   212 n. 16
1.1.1.2, n. 42   212 n. 17
1.1.1.2, n. 54   212 n. 16
1.1.2.1, nn. 64–73   212 n. 18
1.1.2.2, n. 81   213 n. 24
1.1.2.2, n. 92   188 n. 18
1.1.2.2, n. 93   188 n. 17
1.1.2.2, nn. 136–40   212 n. 21
1.1.2.2, n. 149   212 n. 21
1.1.2.2, n. 175   212 n. 22, 213 n. 25
1.1.2.2, n. 178   188 n. 18
1.2.1, nn. 39–190   160 n. 3
1.2.1.1–2, nn. 15–19   164 n. 29
1.2.1.1–2, n. 28   164 n. 29
1.2.1.1–2, nn. 35–36   164 n. 29
1.2.1.1–2, n. 43 (*PW*, p. 39)   161 nn. 9, 10
1.2.1.1–2, nn. 48–51 (*PW*, pp. 40–41)   161 n. 6
1.2.1.1–2, n. 50 (*PW*, p. 41)   164 n. 31
1.2.1.1–2, n. 53 (*PW*, p. 41)   161 n. 11, 164 n. 23
1.2.1.1–2, n. 53 (*PW*, pp. 41–42)   162 n. 12
1.2.1.1–2, n. 54 (*PW*, p. 43)   162 n. 13
1.2.1.1–2, n. 56 (*PW*, p. 44)   162 n. 14; 163 nn. 17, 18, 19
1.2.1.1–2, n. 58 (*PW*, p. 46)   163 n. 20
1.2.1.1–2, n. 59 (*PW*, p. 47)   163 n. 21
1.2.1.1–2, n. 60 (*PW*, p. 47)   164 n. 24
1.2.1.1–2, n. 61 (*PW*, pp. 47–48)   164 nn. 30, 31
1.2.1.1–2, n. 64 (*PW*, p. 48)   164 n. 27
1.2.1.1–2, n. 65 (*PW*, pp. 48–49)   164 n. 31
1.2.1.1–2, nn. 68–69 (*PW*, p. 49)   164 n. 31

1.2.1.1–2, nn. 70–73 (*PW*, pp. 49–52)   164 n. 32
1.2.1.1–2, n. 78 (*PW*, p. 53)   173 n. 6
1.2.1.1–2, n. 79 (*PW*, pp. 53–54)   173 n. 2
1.2.1.1–2, n. 80 (*PW*, p. 54)   173 n. 3
1.2.1.1–2, n. 81 (*PW*, p. 54)   173 n. 5
1.2.1.1–2, n. 95 (*PW*, p. 58)   175 n. 25
1.2.1.1–2, nn. 98–104 (*PW*, pp. 58–60)   176 n. 40
1.2.1.1–2, n. 98 (*PW*, p. 58)   176 n. 37
1.2.1.1–2, n. 109 (*PW*, p. 61)   175 n. 20
1.2.1.1–2, nn. 111–24 (*PW*, pp. 64–68)   165 n. 36
1.2.1.1–2, nn. 125–29 (*PW*, pp. 68–69)   164 n. 35
1.2.1.1–2, n. 130 (*PW*, pp. 70–71)   165 n. 37
1.2.1.1–2, n. 131 (*PW*, p. 71)   165 n. 38
1.2.1.1–2, n. 132 (*PW*, p. 71)   165 n. 39
1.2.1.1–2, n. 138 (*PW*, pp. 73–74)   164 n. 28
1.2.1.1–2, nn. 140–41 (*PW*, p. 74)   164 n. 34
1.2.1.1–2, n. 142 (*PW*, p. 75)   170 n. 41
1.2.1.1–2, n. 143 (*PW*, p. 75)   170 n. 40
1.2.1.3, nn. 172–73 (*PW*, p. 87)   165 n. 45
1.2.1.3, n. 180 (*PW*, p. 90)   165 n. 48
1.2.1.3, n. 181 (*PW*, p. 90)   165 nn. 49, 50
1.2.2.1–4, n. 196   178 n. 70
1.2.2.1–4, nn. 221–22   156 n. 21
1.2.2.1–4, n. 222   180 nn. 28, 29
1.2.2.1–4, n. 226   156 n. 21
1.2.2.1–4, n. 233   180 n. 27
1.2.2.1–4, n. 235   180 n. 27
1.2.2.1–4, nn. 238–39   156 n. 21
1.2.2.1–4, n. 239   180 n. 26
1.2.2.1–4, n. 262   178 n. 70
1.2.2.1–4, n. 291   179 n. 7

1.2.2.1–4, nn. 292–94   179 n. 6
1.2.2.1–4, nn. 301–302   156 n. 21
1.2.2.1–4, n. 310   174 n. 15
1.2.2.1–4, nn. 311–12   179 n. 9
1.2.2.1–4, n. 312   179 n. 6
1.2.2.1–4, n. 320   179 n. 7
1.2.2.1–4, n. 321   179 n. 9
1.2.2.1–4, n. 323   174 n. 16
1.2.2.1–4, nn. 325–26   174 n. 17
1.2.2.1–4, n. 367   182 n. 63
1.2.2.1–4, nn. 379–80   181 n. 56
1.2.2.1–4, n. 381   181 n. 55; 182
   nn. 58, 59
1.2.2.1–4, nn. 382–84   166 n. 4
1.2.2.1–4, n. 385   182 n. 63
1.2.2.1–4, nn. 386–87   182 n. 62
1.2.2.1–4, n. 387   182 n. 61
1.2.2.1–4, n. 388   182 n. 64
1.2.2.1–4, n. 389   182 n. 65
1.2.2.1–4, n. 391   182 n. 65
1.2.2.1–4, n. 393   182 n. 65
1.2.2.1–4, n. 394   175 nn. 23, 35
1.2.2.1–4, nn. 396–408   182 n. 65
1.2.2.1–4, n. 398   182 n. 65
1.2.2.1–4, n. 400   171 n. 59
1.2.2.1–4, n. 403   182 n. 65
1.2.2.1–4, n. 412   182 n. 62
1.2.2.1–4, n. 415   182 nn. 66, 68
1.2.2.1–4, nn. 417–18   182 n. 67
1.2.2.1–4, n. 417   182 n. 66
1.2.2.1–4, n. 421   182 n. 69
1.2.2.1–4, n. 437   181 n. 54
1.3.1.1–2, n. 10 (PW, p. 14)   167
   n. 11, 201 n. 34
1.3.1.1–2, n. 20 (PW, p. 18)   167
   n. 12
1.3.1.1–2, textus interpolatus (PW,
   p. 19)   168 n. 21
1.3.1.1–2, n. 26 (PW, p. 19)   168
   n. 20, 169 n. 32
1.3.1.1–2, n. 26 (PW, p. 20)   168 n. 27
1.3.1.1–2, nn. 27–28 (PW, p. 20)
   168 n. 23
1.3.1.1–2, n. 35 (PW, p. 22)   168 n. 26
1.3.1.1–2, n. 38 (PW, p. 24)   166 n. 24
1.3.1.1–2, n. 39 (PW, p. 25)   167
   n. 7, 169 n. 31

1.3.1.1–2, n. 40 (PW, p. 25)   168 n. 24
1.3.1.1–2, nn. 56–57 (PW, pp. 25–
   26)   156 n. 19
1.3.1.1–2, n. 58 (PW, p. 27)   169
   nn. 32, 36; 170 nn. 49, 52
1.3.1.1–2, n. 59 (PW, p. 27)   165 n. 40
1.3.1.3, n. 135   167 n. 9
1.3.1.4, n. 268   175 n. 33
1.3.1.4, n. 269   174 n. 19
1.3.1.4, n. 277   173 n. 11, 175 n. 32
1.3.2.un., n. 301   182 n. 70
1.3.3.1, n. 349   173 n. 12
1.3.3.1, n. 352   173 nn. 11, 12
1.3.3.1, n. 354   173 n. 11
1.3.3.1, n. 360   173 n. 11
1.3.3.1, n. 367   174 n. 13
1.3.3.1, n. 370   173 nn. 11, 12
1.3.3.1, nn. 394–97   174 n. 15
1.3.3.2, n. 471   185 n. 20
1.3.3.2, nn. 487–89   174 n. 15
1.3.3.2, n. 494   174 n. 15
1.3.3.2, n. 496   161 n. 5
1.3.3.2, n. 500   175 n. 24
1.3.3.2, n. 502   185 n. 20
1.3.3.4, n. 580   179 n. 4
1.3.3.4, n. 583   179 n. 4
1.3.3.4, nn. 483–86   179 n. 4
1.3.3.4, nn. 601–604   174 n. 17
1.4.1.un., n. 1   153 n. 4
1.5.1.un., n. 10   181 n. 53
1.5.2.un., n. 117   182 n. 63
1.5.2.un., n. 135   182 n. 62
1.6.un., n. 14   174 n. 17
1.7.1, n. 27   178 n. 70
1.8.1.1, n. 7   166 n. 58
1.8.1.1, n. 15   166 n. 56
1.8.1.1, n. 16   165 n. 52
1.8.1.1, n. 17   166 n. 55
1.8.1.1, n. 19   166 n. 55
1.8.1.1, n. 22   166 n. 4
1.8.1.3, n. 67   168 n. 24
1.8.1.3, n. 82   169 n. 33
1.8.1.3, n. 95   171 n. 58
1.8.1.3, n. 97   172 n. 62
1.8.1.3, n. 101   171 n. 53
1.8.1.3, n. 108   171 n. 53
1.8.1.3, n. 113   169 n. 30

DUNS SCOTUS, *Ordinatio*
  [Vatican edition] (*continued*)
    1.8.1.3, n. 114   211 n. 6
    1.8.1.3, n. 115   211 nn. 5, 7, 9
    1.8.1.3, n. 120   169 n. 35
    1.8.1.3, n. 122   172 n. 62
    1.8.1.3, n. 127   169 n. 35
    1.8.1.3, n. 134   172 n. 62
    1.8.1.3, nn. 138–40   170 n. 52
    1.8.1.3, n. 139   169 n. 34
    1.8.1.3, n. 148   171 n. 53
    1.8.1.3, n. 153   169 n. 35
    1.8.1.4, n. 167   166 n. 4; 167 nn. 4, 10
    1.8.1.4, n. 192   171 nn. 54, 57
    1.8.1.4, n. 193   171 n. 55, 212 n. 13
    1.8.1.4, n. 198   172 n. 62
    1.8.1.4, n. 200   172 n. 65
    1.8.1.4, n. 202   171 n. 60
    1.8.1.4, n. 209   171 n. 58
    1.8.1.4, n. 210   171 n. 61
    1.8.1.4, n. 214   172 n. 64
    1.8.1.4, nn. 219–20   171 n. 53
    1.8.2.un., n. 229   173 n. 7
    1.8.2.un., nn. 275–77   173 n. 9
    1.8.2.un., nn. 281–82   173 n. 3
    1.8.2.un., n. 294   178 n. 71
    1.8.2.un., n. 297   178 n. 72
    1.9.un., n. 7   179 n. 3
    1.9.un., n. 11   177 n. 48
    1.10.un., n. 9   180 nn. 27, 28
    1.10.un., n. 10   192 n. 82
    1.10.un., n. 62   175 n. 23, 179 n. 11
    1.11.1, n. 9   179 n. 19
    1.11.1, n. 10   180 n. 20
    1.11.1, n. 11   181 n. 21
    1.11.1, nn. 15–16   179 n. 11
    1.11.1, n. 20   157 n. 25
    1.11.2, nn. 40–41   181 n. 47
    1.11.2, n. 40   180 n. 25
    1.11.2, n. 45   181 n. 47
    1.11.2, n. 49   180 n. 35
    1.12.1, n. 1   179 n. 14
    1.12.1, n. 19   179 n. 21
    1.12.1, n. 20   179 n. 16
    1.12.1, n. 36   180 n. 22
    1.12.1, n. 37   179 n. 16
    1.12.1, n. 48   179 n. 17

    1.12.1, n. 41   202 n. 44
    1.12.2, n. 60   180 n. 23
    1.13.un., n. 39   179 n. 15
    1.13.un., n. 83   177 n. 48
    1.17.1.1–2, n. 2   198 n. 54
    1.17.1.1–2, n. 32   198 n. 56
    1.17.1.1–2, nn. 35–40   198 n. 56
    1.17.1.1–2, n. 37   198 n. 56
    1.17.1.1–2, nn. 48–53   198 n. 56
    1.17.1.1–2, n. 48   198 n. 54
    1.17.1.1–2, n. 62 (*WM*, p. 207)   190 n. 46
    1.17.1.1–2, n. 63 (*WM*, p. 207)   190 n. 48
    1.17.1.1–2, n. 88   198 n. 54
    1.17.1.1–2, n. 106   197 n. 37
    1.17.1.1–2, n. 113   197 n. 45, 205 n. 33
    1.17.1.1–2, nn. 114–18   197 n. 46
    1.17.1.1–2, n. 115   198 n. 59
    1.17.1.1–2, n. 120   198 n. 52
    1.17.1.1–2, nn. 122–24   197 n. 47
    1.17.1.1–2, n. 126   197 n. 41
    1.17.1.1–2, n. 129   197 n. 37
    1.17.1.1–2, n. 131   196 n. 19
    1.17.1.1–2, n. 132   197 n. 39
    1.17.1.1–2, n. 133   198 n. 56
    1.17.1.1–2, n. 135   197 n. 41
    1.17.1.1–2, n. 137   197 n. 41
    1.17.1.1–2, nn. 138–41   198 n. 56
    1.17.1.1–2, nn. 142–44   195 n. 11
    1.17.1.1–2, n. 144   196 n. 19
    1.17.1.1–2, n. 148   196 n. 19
    1.17.1.1–2, n. 149   195 n. 16
    1.17.1.1–2, n. 150   197 n. 38
    1.17.1.1–2, n. 151   198 nn. 55, 56
    1.17.1.1–2, n. 154   197 n. 41
    1.17.1.1–2, n. 158   198 n. 56
    1.17.1.1–2, n. 160   198 n. 57
    1.17.1.1–2, n. 164   198 n. 57
    1.17.1.1–2, n. 161   198 n. 61
    1.17.1.1–2, n. 192   205 n. 28
    1.17.2.1, nn. 203–204   196 n. 22
    1.19.2, n. 42   183 n. 71
    1.19.2, n. 54   183 n. 71
    1.19.2, n. 67   183 n. 71
    1.22.un., textus interpolatus
      (5:388)   203 n. 57

1.23.un., n. 15   181 n. 53, 200 n. 22
1.24.un., n. 70   182 n. 70
1.26.un., n. 1   181 n. 47
1.26.un., n. 10   181 n. 48
1.26.un., n. 24   180 n. 35
1.26.un., n. 26   180 n. 36
1.26.un., n. 38   180 n. 38
1.26.un., n. 45   180 n. 39
1.26.un., n. 47   180 n. 39
1.26.un., n. 49   181 n. 47
1.26.un., n. 64   182 n. 62
1.26.un., n. 80   180 n. 37
1.26.un., n. 82   180 n. 37, 182 n. 63
1.26.un., n. 48   180 n. 40
1.26.un., n. 93   180 n. 41
1.26.un., textus interpolatus (5:49–
    50)   181 n. 44
1.26.un., textus interpolatus
    (5:50)   182 n. 63
1.27.1–3, n. 20   174 n. 15
1.27.1–3, n. 51   174 n. 16
1.27.1–3, n. 64   179 nn. 7, 9
1.27.1–3, n. 71   179 n. 9
1.27.1–3, n. 78   174 n. 15, 179 n. 6
1.27.1–3, nn. 85–86   179 n. 6
1.27.1–3, n. 95   179 n. 5
1.28.1–2, nn. 19–20   181 n. 48
1.28.1–2, n. 27   181 n. 48
1.28.1–2, n. 30   181 n. 48
1.28.1–2, n. 44   181 n. 51
1.28.1–2, nn. 45–46   181 n. 47
1.28.3, n. 55   181 n. 47
1.28.3, n. 90   181 n. 49
1.28.3, n. 93   181 n. 47
1.30.1–2, n. 41   177 n. 50
1.30.1–2, n. 42   177 n. 51
1.30.1–2, n. 50   171 n. 60, 173 n. 7
1.30.1–2, n. 51   173 nn. 8, 10
1.30.1–2, nn. 56–57   175 n. 33
1.32.1–2, n. 23   174 n. 15
1.32.1–2, nn. 24–25   179 n. 6
1.35.un., nn. 9–11   175 n. 26
1.35.un., n. 14   175 nn. 23, 35
1.35.un., n. 15   175 n. 28
1.35.un., n. 32   175 nn. 23, 31, 35
1.35.un., nn. 38–40   174 n. 18
1.35.un., n. 49   175 nn. 23, 35

1.36.un., n. 1   175 n. 20
1.36.un., n. 2   175 n. 27
1.36.un., nn. 4–5   175 n. 27
1.36.un., n. 13   175 n. 29
1.36.un., n. 15   175 n. 30
1.36.un., n. 19   175 n. 33
1.36.un., n. 39–40   175 n. 33
1.36.un., n. 39   188 n. 19
1.36.un., nn. 45–46   173 n. 11
1.36.un., nn. 60–63   174 n. 18
1.38.un., nn. 5–6   176 n. 38, 192
    n. 73
1.38.un., n. 10   174 n. 19
1.41.un., nn. 28–33   194 n. 1
1.41.un., n. 36   194 n. 2
1.41.un., n. 40   195 n. 3
1.41.un., n. 41   195 n. 4
1.41.un., n. 42   195 n. 7
1.41.un., n. 44   195 n. 9
1.41.un., nn. 45–46   195 n. 10
1.41.un., n. 54   195 n. 5
1.42.un., nn. 8–9   165 n. 43
1.42.un., n. 9   177 n. 55
1.42.un., n. 10   177 n. 59
1.42.un., n. 16   156 n. 21
1.43.un., n. 14   174 n. 19
1.43.un., n. 16   174 n. 19
1.44.un., n. 5 (WM, p. 357)   191 n. 69
1.48.un., n. 5 (WM, p. 237)   190 n. 46
2.1.1, n. 6   183 n. 74
2.1.1, n. 8   183 n. 75
2.1.1, n. 18   183 n. 76
2.1.1, n. 19   183 n. 77
2.1.1, n. 40   179 n. 7
2.1.2, n. 85   178 n. 72
2.1.2, n. 86   178 n. 71
2.1.3, n. 154   162 n. 13
2.1.3, n. 155   177 n. 48
2.1.3, n. 156   162 n. 13
2.1.4–5, n. 200   212 n. 14
2.1.6, n. 316   187 n. 2
2.2.1.1, n. 63   162 n. 13
2.2.2.1–2, nn. 219–20   209 n. 53
2.3.1   212 n. 15
2.3.1.1, n. 32   212 n. 15
2.3.1.4, nn. 89–92   209 n. 62
2.3.1.5–6, nn. 179–80   212 n. 15

DUNS SCOTUS, *Ordinatio*

[Vatican edition] (*continued*)

2.3.1.5–6, n. 192   212 n. 15

2.3.1.5–6, n. 191   175 n. 20

2.3.1.7, n. 227   182 n. 63

2.3.2.3, n. 395   175 n. 34

[Wadding edition]

2.5.1, n. 2   196 n. 23

2.5.1, n. 6   196 nn. 20, 25

2.6.2, n. 8 (*WM*, pp. 469–73)   188 n. 21

2.6.2, n. 8 (*WM*, pp. 469–71)   189 n. 23

2.6.2, n. 8 (*WM*, p. 471)   197 n. 42

2.6.2, n. 8 (*WM*, p. 471)   189 n. 27

2.6.2, n. 9 (*WM*, pp. 471–73)   189 n. 28

2.6.2, n. 9 (*WM*, p. 471)   189 n. 30

2.6.2, n. 11 (*WM*, p. 475)   187 n. 12

2.6.2, n. 11 (*WM*, p. 477)   188 n. 22

2.7.un., nn. 12–13 (*WM*, pp. 221–25)   196 n. 25

2.8.un., n. 2   185 n. 18

2.8.un., nn. 4–5   185 n. 21

2.8.un., n. 4   185 n. 20

2.16.un., n. 8   187 n. 4

2.16.un., nn. 15–16   187 nn. 2, 3

2.16.un., n. 18   187 n. 2

2.16.un., n. 20   179 n. 4

2.19.un., n. 2   193 nn. 99, 100

2.19.un., n. 4   193 n. 101

2.19.un., n. 5   194 nn. 103, 110

2.19.un., n. 6   194 n. 102

2.20.2, n. 2   195 n. 3

2.21.1, n. 3   194 n. 105

2.21.2, n. 2   194 n. 111

2.21.2, n. 3   194 n. 111

2.26.un., n. 3   197 n. 41

2.26.un., n. 6   197 n. 43

2.27.un., nn. 3–4   197 n. 41

2.28.un., n. 8   190 n. 50

2.29.un., n. 1   193 n. 96

2.29.un., n. 2   193 n. 92

2.29.un., n. 3   193 nn. 93, 94

2.29.un., n. 4   193 n. 97

2.29.un., n. 5   193 nn. 98, 99

2.29.un., n. 7   194 nn. 105, 106, 110

2.30–32.1–4, n. 1   194 n. 113

2.30–32.1–4, n. 2   194 n. 114

2.30–32.1–4, nn. 4–6   194 n. 114

2.30–32.1–4, n. 4   194 n. 113

2.30–32.1–4, n. 6   194 nn. 112, 115

2.30–32.1–4, n. 8   194 n. 116

2.30–32.1–4, n. 9   194 n. 117

2.30–32.1–4, n. 11   194 nn. 118, 119

2.30–32.1–4, n. 19   194 n. 107

2.37.2, n. 3   176 n. 39

2.37.2, n. 4   193 nn. 84, 85

2.37.2, n. 6   192 n. 83, 197 n. 37

2.37.2, n. 7   176 n. 44

2.37.2, n. 22   193 n. 86

2.40.un., n. 3 (*WM*, p. 227)   190 nn. 45, 46

2.42.1–4, nn. 10–11 (*WM*, pp. 173–75)   187 n. 6

2.43.2, n. 2 (*WM*, p. 479)   189 n. 34

3.1.1, n. 3   200 nn. 16, 18, 19

3.1.1, n. 5   200 n. 17

3.1.1, n. 6   200 nn. 20, 21; 201 nn. 23, 33

3.1.1, n. 7   201 n. 25

3.1.1, n. 9   201 nn. 26, 28, 32

3.1.1, n. 10   202, n. 38

3.1.1, n. 12   210 n. 32

3.1.1, n. 13   201 n. 24

3.1.1, n. 18   203 nn. 59, 62, 63

3.1.3, n. 2   201 n. 31

3.1.4, n. 2   203 n. 61

[MS A]

3.1.5   181 nn. 43, 44

[Wadding edition]

3.2.1, n. 2   202 n. 40

3.2.1, n. 4   202 n. 40

3.2.1, nn. 5–7   199 n. 3

3.2.2, nn. 7–11   184 n. 10

3.3.1, n. 3   206 nn. 49, 50

3.3.1, n. 4   206 n. 52

3.3.1, nn. 5–7   206 n. 55

3.3.1, n. 5   205 n. 41

3.3.1, n. 9   206 nn. 51, 56

3.5.2, n. 1   201 n. 30

3.5.2, n. 4   201 n. 26

3.5.2, n. 5   201 n. 36

3.6.1, n. 4   199 n. 10

3.6.1, n. 5   199 n. 10; 200 nn. 15, 18
3.7.1   203 n. 66
3.7.1, n. 3   203 n. 64
3.7.2   203 n. 66
3.7.2, n. 9   203 n. 65
3.7.3   203 n. 66
3.7.3, n. 1   203 n. 1
3.7.3, n. 2   204 n. 8
3.7.3, n. 3   204 nn. 6, 7, 10, 12
3.7.3, n. 5   204 n. 8
3.9.un., n. 13   205 n. 38
3.11.1   203 n. 66
3.11.1, nn. 3–4   203 n. 64
3.11.1, nn. 7–8   203 n. 68
3.11.2   203 n. 66
3.11.3   203 n. 66
3.12.un., n. 3   202 nn. 41, 42
3.12.un., n. 6   203 n. 54
3.13.3, n. 2   202 nn. 46, 47
3.13.4, nn. 5–13   202 n. 46
3.13.4, n. 8   203 n. 56
3.13.4, n. 10   202 n. 39
3.14.2, n. 12   202 n. 48
3.14.2, nn. 16–17   202 n. 48
3.14.2, n. 17   202 n. 49
3.14.3, n. 4   202 n. 49
3.14.3, n. 5   202 n. 50
3.14.3, n. 5   173 n. 12
3.14.3, n. 6   203 nn. 51, 52
3.14.3, n. 7   203, n. 53
3.14.3, n. 8   203 n. 53
3.17.un., n. 4   202 n. 45
3.17.un., n. 5   202 n. 44
3.18.un., n. 4   204 n. 26
3.18.un., n. 5   204 n. 27
3.18.un., n. 10   205 nn. 32, 37
3.19.un., n. 4   206 n. 45
3.19.un., n. 5   196 n. 24; 205 nn. 28, 34
3.19.un., n. 7   190 n. 50, 205 n. 31
3.19.un., n. 8   196 nn. 17, 26, 29; 205 n. 34
3.19.un., nn. 10–11   205 nn. 32, 37; 206 n. 53
3.19.un., n. 12   205 n. 30
3.19.un., n. 13   205 n. 32
3.19.un., n. 14   205 nn. 29, 31

3.20.un., n. 3   204 n. 19
3.20.un., n. 5   204 n. 21
3.21.un., nn. 3–5   202 n. 39
3.24.un., n. 4   157 n. 28
3.24.un., n. 7   157 n. 27
3.24.un., n. 13   158 n. 33
3.24.un., n. 16   157 n. 28
3.24.un., n. 17   157 n. 32, 158 n. 33
3.26.un., nn. 17–18 (*WM*, pp. 179–81)   188 n. 21
3.26.un., n. 17 (*WM*, p. 179)   189 n. 27
3.27.un., n. 2 (*WM*, p. 425)   191 n. 52
3.27.un., n. 19 (*WM*, p. 443)   197 n. 37; 198 nn. 53, 55, 56
3.34.un., n. 7 (*WM*, p. 355)   197 n. 42
3.34.un., n. 19 (*WM*, p. 371)   197 n. 42
3.37.un., n. 3 (*WM*, pp. 273–75)   192 n. 81
3.37.un., n. 4 (*WM*, p. 275)   192 n. 72
3.37.un., n. 5 (*WM*, p. 277)   191 n. 55
3.37.un., n. 6 (*WM*, p. 277)   191 nn. 51, 52
3.37.un., n. 8 (*WM*, p. 279)   191 n. 59
3.37.un., n. 14 (*WM*, p. 287)   190 n. 50
3.38.un., n. 5 (*WM*, p. 485)   192 nn. 78, 81
3.38.un., n. 6 (*WM*, p. 487)   192 nn. 79, 80
3.39.un., n. 2 (*WM*, p. 505)   191 n. 57, 207 n. 19
4.1.1, nn. 26–27   177 n. 52, 207 n. 11
4.1.1, n. 27   185 n. 25
4.1.1, n. 30   185 n. 24
4.1.1, n. 31   197 n. 38, 207 n. 11
4.1.1, n. 34   107 n. 11
4.1.2, n. 9   207 n. 6
4.1.2, n. 10   207 n. 23
4.1.3, n. 2   206 n. 1
4.1.4–5, n. 4   207 nn. 14, 15
4.1.4–5, n. 8   207 nn. 12, 13
4.1.4–5, n. 12   207 nn. 16, 17
4.1.4–5, n. 16   207 n. 18
4.1.5–6, n. 8   194 n. 119
4.1.6, n. 10   207 n. 24
4.1.6, n. 13   207 n. 25
4.2.1, n. 2   206 n. 3
4.2.1, n. 3   206 n. 4, 208 n. 30

DUNS SCOTUS, *Ordinatio*
[Wadding edition] (*continued*)
4.2.1, nn. 4–5   206 n. 5
4.2.1, n. 6   207 nn. 16, 21
4.2.1, n. 7   205 n. 37
4.2.1, n. 9   207 nn. 21, 22
4.2.1, n. 11   195 n. 17
4.4.1, n. 2   207 n. 26
4.4.2, n. 3   207 n. 26
4.4.4, n. 6   208 n. 31
4.4.5, n. 3   208 n. 29
4.4.5, n. 9   208 n. 27
4.6.1, n. 3   208 n. 32
4.6.7, n. 3   208 n. 29
4.6.9, n. 3   208 nn. 35, 36, 37, 38
4.6.9, n. 13   157 n. 27
4.6.9, n. 14   157 n. 26
4.6.9, n. 15   208 n. 38
4.6.9, n. 18   208 nn. 37, 44
4.6.10, n. 2   208 n. 39
4.6.10, n. 3   208 nn. 38, 42
4.6.10, n. 7   209 n. 45
4.6.10, n. 8   208 n. 45
4.6.10, n. 12   208 n. 45
4.6.10, n. 13   208 nn. 35, 37, 38
4.6.11, n. 2   208 n. 40
4.6.11, n. 4   208 nn. 43, 44
4.7.3   207 n. 23, 208 n. 28
4.8.3, n. 2   208 n. 34
4.10.1, n. 8   209 n. 51
4.10.1, nn. 9–11   209 n. 54
4.10.1, n. 9   209 nn. 52, 55, 61
4.10.1, n. 10   210 n. 70
4.10.1, n. 13   210 n. 69
4.10.1, n. 16   209 n. 53
4.10.2, nn. 3–4   210 n. 72
4.10.4, n. 4   210 n. 73
4.10.4, n. 10   210 n. 73
4.10.4, nn. 12–13   210 n. 73
4.10.7, n. 3   185 n. 20
4.11.1, n. 2   209 n. 49
4.11.1, n. 10   209 n. 49
4.11.3, n. 3   209 n. 56
4.11.3, n. 4   209 n. 57
4.11.3, n. 5   209 n. 58
4.11.3, n. 13   157 n. 26, 209 n. 59
4.11.3, n. 14   209 nn. 56, 57

4.11.3, n. 15   209 n. 59
4.11.3, n. 28   184 n. 7
4.11.3, n. 31   184 n. 7
4.11.3, nn. 43–44   210 n. 62
4.11.3, n. 46   166 n. 54, 183 n. 3, 184 n. 9
4.11.3, n. 50   183 n. 3
4.11.3, n. 54   184 n. 6
4.12.1, n. 9   209 n. 60
4.12.1, n. 15   210 n. 71
4.12.2, n. 15   210 n. 64
4.13.1, n. 37   177 n. 53
4.13.1, n. 40   207 n. 20, 209 n. 45
4.13.2, n. 4   207 n. 20
4.14.1, n. 3   193 n. 83, 199 n. 62
4.14.1, n. 4   196 n. 25
4.14.1, n. 6   193 nn. 83, 86, 88; 197 n. 51
4.14.1, n. 10   197 n. 50
4.14.1, n. 17   197 n. 50
4.14.2, nn. 14–16   196 n. 28
4.14.2, n. 14   196 nn. 27, 30, 31
4.14.2, n. 16   196 nn. 18, 21
4.14.4, n. 2   208 n. 33
4.15.1, n. 3   197 n. 51
4.15.1, n. 4   204 nn. 20, 21; 205 n. 37
4.15.1, n. 5   205 n. 32
4.15.1, n. 6   204 nn. 23, 25, 26
4.15.1, n. 7   204 n. 24; 205 nn. 34, 36, 37
4.16.2, n. 6   197 n. 48
4.16.2, nn. 9–12   197 n. 48
4.16.2, nn. 10–12   197 n. 49
4.16.2, n. 19   198 n. 52
4.17.un., n. 3 (*WM*, p. 263)   191 n. 58
4.17.un., nn. 4–5 (*WM*, p. 265)   190 n. 42
4.19.un., n. 12   196 n. 17
4.19.un., n. 23   207 n. 24
4.19.un., n. 32   207 n. 24
4.29.un., n. 30 (*WM*, pp. 175–77)   213 n. 30
4.33.1, nn. 2–3 (*WM*, pp. 291–93)   191 n. 66
4.43.1, n. 3   186 nn. 45, 46
4.43.1, n. 4   186 n. 47, 187 n. 50
4.43.1, n. 11   186, n. 35

4.43.2, n. 6 (*PW*, p. 139)   185
    nn. 18, 19
4.43.2, n. 7 (*PW*, p. 139)   184 n. 14
4.43.2, n. 7 (*PW*, p. 140)   184 n. 14
4.43.2, n. 10 (*PW*, p. 141)   184 n. 12
4.43.2, n. 10 (*PW*, p. 142)   184 n. 13
4.43.2, n. 12 (*PW*, pp. 143–44)   185
    n. 15
4.43.2, n. 12 (*PW*, pp. 144–45)   185
    n. 16
4.43.2, n. 13 (*PW*, p. 145)   186 n. 30
4.43.2, n. 16 (*PW*, p. 148–49)   186
    n. 28
4.43.2, n. 17 (*PW*, p. 149)   186 n. 31
4.43.2, n. 23 (*PW*, p. 154)   186 n. 33
4.43.2, n. 24 (*PW*, p. 154)   186 n. 42
4.43.2, n. 24 (*PW*, p. 155)   186
    nn. 41, 43
4.43.3, nn. 9–13   186 n. 36
4.43.3, n. 11   186 n. 38
4.43.3, n. 20   186 n. 37
4.43.3, nn. 21–22   186 n. 39
4.43.3, n. 22   186 n. 40
4.43.4, n. 5   186 n. 40
4.44.1, nn. 16–17   187 n. 48
4.45.2, n. 12   185 n. 23
4.45.3   173 n. 11
4.46.1, n. 1 (*WM*, p. 239)   192 n. 71
4.46.1, n. 3 (*WM*, p. 241)   191
    nn. 51, 54
4.46.1, n. 4 (*WM*, p. 243)   192 n. 71
4.46.1, n. 7 (*WM*, p. 247)   191 nn. 56,
    57, 62
4.46.1, nn. 8–9 (*WM*, pp. 247–49)
    191 n. 67
4.46.1, n. 8 (*WM*, p. 249)   191 nn. 63,
    68
4.46.1, n. 9 (*WM*, p. 249)   191 nn. 60,
    61, 64
4.46.1, n. 12 (*WM*, p. 253)   191 n. 64,
    192 n. 71
4.46.1, n. 12 (*WM*, pp. 253–55)   192
    n. 75
4.49.6, n. 11   203 n. 55, 212 n. 23,
    213 n. 24
4.49.6, n. 15   213 n. 26
4.49.7, n. 3   212 n. 18

4.49.9–10, nn. 2–3 (*WM*, pp. 183–
    87)   188 nn. 23, 25
4.49.9–10, n. 3 (*WM*, pp. 185–
    87)   189 n. 29
4.49.9–10, n. 3 (*WM*, p. 185)   188 n. 26
4.49.9–10, n. 5 (*WM*, p. 189)   187
    n. 5, 188 n. 24
4.49.9–10, n. 6 (*WM*, p. 191)   189 n. 32
4.49.9–10, nn. 8–9 (*WM*, p. 193)
    189 n. 35
4.49.13, n. 9   187 n. 57
4.49.14, n. 4   187 n. 52
4.49.14, n. 11   187 n. 53
4.49.15, nn. 2–3   187 n. 54
4.49.16, nn. 17–19   210 n. 72
4.49.16, n. 17   187 n. 55
4.49.16, n. 19   187 n. 56
4.50.3, n. 2   202 n. 48

Quaestiones super libros
    Metaphysicorum
prol., n. 18 (*PW*, p. 2)   211 n. 6
1.1, nn. 40–41   211 n. 6
2.6, n. 2   169 n. 39
4.1, n. 12   169 n. 32
9.15, n. 2 (*WM*, p. 147)   187 n. 14,
    188 n. 15
9.15, n. 4 (*WM*, p. 151)   188 nn. 15, 19
9.15, n. 5 (*WM*, p. 153)   188 n. 16
9.15, n. 5 (*WM*, pp. 153–55)   188 n. 20
9.15, n. 6 (*WM*, p. 155)   187 n. 12
9.15, nn. 12–13 (*WM*, pp. 167–69)
    188 n. 14

Quaestiones super Praedicamenta
4, n. 7   169 n. 32

Quodlibetum
1, n. 3   182 n. 58
1, nn. 5–6   179 n. 10
1, n. 7   181 n. 45
1, n. 8   166 n. 4, 167 n. 5, 173 n. 10
1, n. 9   183 n. 77
1, nn. 19–20   179 n. 9
1, n. 22   179 n. 9
1, nn. 23–24   181 n. 46
1, n. 24   182 n. 58
2, n. 1   181 n. 47

DUNS SCOTUS,
Quodlibetum (continued)
2, n. 8   179 n. 9
2, n. 25   156 n. 21
2, nn. 28–29   179 n. 8
2, n. 30   176 n. 41
3, n. 6   181 n. 44
3, n. 10   182 n. 64
3, n. 15   212 n. 14
3, n. 17   181 n. 58
3, n. 18   180 n. 32
4, n. 2   181 n. 45
4, n. 25   181 n. 47
4, n. 32   180 n. 32
5, n. 2   170 nn. 43, 44, 47, 50
5, nn. 5–6   182 n. 66
5, n. 7   179 n. 15
5, n. 13   166 n. 4, 167 n. 10
5, n. 17   182 n. 66
5, n. 18   182 n. 66
6, n. 14   167 n. 6, 177 n. 48
7, n. 4   165 n. 43, 177 n. 55
7, n. 10   157 n. 32, 158 n. 33
7, n. 19   177 nn. 55, 56, 57, 58
7, n. 20   177 n. 59
7, n. 23   177 n. 60
7, n. 32   165 n. 43
8, n. 3   183 n. 72
8, nn. 4–5   183 n. 77
8, n. 4   202 n. 44
8, n. 6   156 n. 21
8, n. 7   183 n. 77
8, n. 15   183 n. 77
8, n. 20   183 n. 77
8, n. 21   156 n. 21
9, n. 10   185 n. 14
9, n. 11   185 nn. 15, 20
9, n. 12   186 n. 32
10, n. 3   209 n. 49
10, n. 11   209 nn. 52, 55
10, n. 20   209 n. 51
11, n. 15   210 n. 72
13, nn. 3–4   174 n. 17
13, n. 5   174 n. 17
13, n. 8   175 n. 24
13, n. 10   175 n. 24
14, n. 9   156 n. 21

14, n. 10   175 n. 24
14, n. 14   175 n. 35; 179 nn. 5, 9
14, n. 16   156 n. 22
15, n. 2   174 n. 17
15, n. 7   174 n. 15
15, n. 8   174 n. 15
15, n. 9   174 n. 15
15, n. 20   174 n. 15
15, n. 24   174 n. 15
16, n. 8   213 n. 28
17, n. 3   195 n. 11, 204 n. 26
17, n. 4   197 n. 37
17, nn. 8–9   198 n. 53
17, n. 9   198 n. 56
17, n. 13   195 n. 11, 198 n. 57
18, n. 4 (*WM*, p. 213)   190 n. 47
18, nn. 5–6 (*WM*, pp. 213–15)   190 n. 46
18, n. 6 (*WM*, p. 215)   190 n. 49
18, n. 6 (*WM*, p. 217)   190 n. 47
19, n. 2   200 n. 19
19, n. 17   200 n. 21, 201 n. 33
19, n. 18   201 nn. 23, 25
19, n. 19   201 nn. 26, 28
19, 20   202 n. 37
19, n. 23   200 nn. 16, 17
19, n. 25   201 n. 24
20, nn. 1–2   210 n. 77
20, n. 1   205 n. 38
20, n. 2   211 n. 81
20, n. 14   211 n. 82
20, n. 20   210 n. 75
20, n. 21   211 n. 81
20, n. 22   210 nn. 76, 78, 79, 80
20, n. 34   210 n. 75

Reportatio Parisiensis
[ed. in Scotus, *PW*]
prol.3.1 (*PW*, pp. 10–12)   211 nn. 1, 6
prol.3.1 (*PW*, pp. 11–12)   211 n. 11
[ed. Wolter and Adams]
1.2.1   160 n. 3
1.2.1.1–2, n. 12   161 nn. 9, 10
1.2.1.1–2, nn. 17–20   161 n. 6
1.2.1.1–2, n. 21   161 n. 11, 162 n. 12
1.2.1.1–2, n. 27   161 n. 13
1.2.1.1–2, n. 28   161 n. 14; 162 nn. 17, 18

1.2.1.1–2, n. 29   163 nn. 20, 21; 164 n. 23
1.2.1.1–2, n. 30   164 n. 27
1.2.1.1–2, n. 31   164 n. 30
1.2.1.1–2, nn. 36–40   164 n. 32
1.2.1.3, nn. 64–88   165 n. 36
1.2.1.3, nn. 69–70   164 n. 35
1.2.1.3, n. 71   165 n. 38
1.2.1.3, n. 73   164 nn. 28, 165 n. 39
1.2.1.3, n. 75   165 n. 37
1.2.2.un., nn. 100–101   165 n. 48
1.2.2.un., n. 102   165 nn. 49, 50
[MS V]
1.26.2   181 n. 46
1.38   176 nn. 39, 42, 45
1.44.2   192 n. 77
[Wadding edition]
2.19.un., n. 6   194 n. 110
2.29.2, n. 8   194 nn. 105, 106
3.7.4, n. 4   204 n. 9
3.7.4, n. 5   204 n. 12
3.17.1–2, n. 4   202 nn. 44, 45
3.19.un., n. 7   205 n. 40
3.19.un., n. 8   205 n. 31
3.20.un., n. 10   205 n. 39
4.1.5, n. 2   207 n. 26
4.1.5, n. 4   194 n. 108
4.1.5, n. 6   197 n. 48
4.2.1, n. 1   196 n. 23
4.2.1, n. 11   196 n. 23
4.15.1, n. 6   206 n. 41

HENRY OF GHENT

Quodlibeta
6.2   183 n. 73
6.6   202 n. 40
6.11   193 n. 91
6.32   193 n. 92
8.2   176 n. 42

Summa Quaestionum Ordinariarium
6.1   157 n. 27
21.2   167 n. 14
21.2 c   167 n. 12
21.2 ad 3   167 nn. 13, 15
21.4   175 n. 27
53.10   183 n. 72

JOHN OF DAMASCUS

De Fide Orthodoxa
1.8   182 n. 71
1.9   172 n. 62
1.14   182 n. 71
3.6   201 n. 23
3.11   200 n. 21
4.18   182 n. 71

LOMBARD, PETER

Sententiae in Quatuor Libros Distinctae
2.24.1   194 n. 108
4.2.1.1   207 n. 5

RICHARD OF ST. VICTOR

De Trinitate
4.23   201 n. 27

RUPERT OF DEUTZ

De Gloria et honore filii hominis super Mattheum
13   203 n. 3

WILLIAM OF AUXERRE

Summa Aurea
3.1.2   200 n. 11
3.1.3.3   199 n. 11
3.1.3.8   201 n. 26

WILLIAM OF OCKHAM

Quodlibeta septem
1.10   184 n. 11
2.3 ad 3   159 n. 43
4.7   201 n. 29

Reportatio
3.1   201 n. 29

WILLIAM OF WARE

In Sententias
3.1.1   200 n. 13

GENERAL INDEX

abstractive cognition. *See* cognition
acceptation. *See* grace; merit
accident
  categories of, 139
  individuation of, 142
  relation of a. to substance, 115–17
  separated a. and Eucharist, 142–43
Adams, Marilyn McCord, 173 n. 11;
    186 n. 36; 209 n. 48; 212 nn. 12, 15
Adams, Robert, 190 n. 40
adultery, 94–95
affection for beneficial, 87–89
  and fall of Satan, 88
  and sin, 88
affection for justice, 87–89
  in Christ, 130
  and freedom, 87–88, 189 n. 27
  and happiness, 88–89
Albert the Great, on theology as
    science, 36
Alexander of Hales, school of, on
    motive for Incarnation, 127–28
Alnwick, William of. *See* William of
    Alnwick
Alston, William, 36, 168 n. 22, 172 n. 67
analogy
  of being, 45
  of concepts, 35

  defined, 33
  requires univocity, 37–38
  of terms, 35
anamnesis. *See* Eucharist
angel, can affect human body, 185 n. 18
Anselm
  on affections of will, 87
  on divine perfections, 32
  on existence of God, 24
  on original sin, 99
  on redemption, 129–30
apophatic theology, 45, 167 n. 11
Aquinas, Thomas, 4
  on actual grace, 111
  on analogy, 35, 168 n. 23, 172 n. 66
  on apophatic theology, 45
  on body's identity, 79–80
  on Christ's impeccability, 122–24
  on Christ's presence in Eucharist,
    143
  on conclusion of arguments for
    God's existence, 160 n. 2
  on concomitance, 143
  on distinction between essence and
    existence, 166 n. 54
  and Duns Scotus, 5
  on eternity of world, 162 n. 13
  on *filioque*, 64

on freedom, 85
on God's incommunicability, 182
    n. 60
on God's ineffability, 39
on God's infinity, 26, 42
on God's pure actuality, 171 n. 53
on God's simplicity, 26, 29, 44–45,
    165 n. 54
on God's unicity, 26
on grace and original justice, 98–99
on happiness, 84
on human action, 84–85, 86
on hypostatic union, 114
on impeccability, 150
on impossibility of infinite regress of
    causes, 18–19
on incorruptibility of soul, 8, 77
on infinity as relational concept, 39–
    40
on logical possibility, 155 n. 6
on motive for Incarnation, 127
on necessity of revelation, 159 n. 45
on powers of soul, 83
on resurrection of the body, 79
on sacramental causality, 136
on separated accidents, 142
on sin, 95
on theological method, 167 n. 11
on theology, 8, 157 n. 29, 158 n. 35,
    159 n. 43
on transubstantiation, 140–41
on unity of body and soul, 75–76,
    77, 81
on unity of substantial form, 74, 184
    n. 7
Arianism, 65
Aristotle
on accidents, 139, 142
on extension, 142–43
on goals, 87
on human action, 86
on incorruptibility of soul, 78
on intellect, 49
on matter and form, 73–74
on mental language, 49
on requirements for proof, 20, 158
    n. 33, 162 n. 16

on science, 9
on sensation, 76
on virtue as habits, 107
attrition, 106–7
Augustine
on creation, 80
on divine action and the Trinity, 70
on divine essence and substance, 172
    n. 62
on *filioque*, 63–64
on sin, 96
on Trinity, 61–65, 179 n. 4

Bäck, Allan, 203 n. 66
Bak, F., 153 n. 1
Balić, C., 153 n. 2
Baptism
effect of, 138
and justification, 130
and sacramental character, 139
Bartel, T. W., 165 n. 42
Basil of Caesarea, 61, 78 n. 1
being
analogy of, 45
univocity of, 168 n. 18
See also existence (*esse*);
    transcendentals
belief and knowledge incompatible, 8
Benedict XII, Pope, 212 n. 19
Bible
credibility of, 12
as a source of revelation, 7
body. *See* forms, plurality of;
    resurrection of body; soul
Boethius
and Christology, 113
on person, 118, 181 n. 53, 200 n. 22
Boler, John, 189 n. 27
Bonaventure, 4
on divine ideas, 50
and Duns Scotus, 5
on impossibility of eternity of world,
    162 n. 13
on merit, 104–105
on possibility of salvation without
    revelation, 159 n. 47
on sacramental causality, 136

Bonaventure (*continued*)
on sin, 95
on theology as affective science, 158
n. 36
Bonnefoy, Jean-François, 206 n. 47
Boulnois, Olivier, 211 n. 5
Brampton, C. K., 153 n. 2
Bridlington, Philip, 4
Brown, Patterson, 161 nn. 7, 12
Brown, Stephen F., 158 n. 32
Burger, Maria, 199 n. 9
Burns, J. Patout, 205 n. 25
Burr, David, 209 n. 48

Calvin, John on predestination, 102,
195 n. 8
Cantor, Georg, 57
Castañeda, H.-N., 177 n. 49
Catania, Francis J., 169 n. 37, 170
n. 42
causal concurrence, 47–48; 53–54; 56–
57; 176 nn. 45, 46
See also causation; cause
causation
nature of, 16–18, 136–37, 161 n. 4
See also cause
cause
accidentally ordered, 16–18, 161
n. 8, 162 n. 13
essentially ordered, 16–17; 161 nn. 7,
12; 162 n. 13; 165 n. 46
final c., 23
impossibility of infinite regress, 18–
19, 161 n. 12
instrumental, 56, 136
and logical possibility, 60
See also causal concurrence;
causation; God
cause, primary and secondary. *See*
causal concurrence
Chalcedon, Council of, 113
character, sacramental. *See*
sacramental character
charity. *See* grace
choice at an instant. *See* power for
opposites, synchronic; will,
freedom of

Christ
and affection for justice, 130
ascension of, 206 n. 46
and communication of properties,
125
dead body of, 74, 184 n. 7, 202 n. 39
descent into Hell, 8
and Eucharistic presence, 143–44,
210 n. 73
and Eucharistic sacrifice, 144–45
and Fall of Adam, 127–29
grace of, 122–23
human nature of C. and existence,
200 nn. 15, 18
human nature of C. individual
substance, 117–18
human nature of C. like accident,
115–17, 200 n. 18
human nature of C. not person,
118–21, 201 n. 26
impeccability of, 122–24
knowledge of, 122–24, 202 n. 48
merits of, 129–32; 138; 195 n. 16;
205 nn. 30, 31
and multiple incarnations, 210 n. 31
predestination of, 127–29
resurrection of, 206 n. 46
and satisfaction, 131
as second person of Trinity, 113–14
two natures of, 113
two wills of, 113
See also union, hypostatic
Church as a source of revelation, 7–8,
142
cognition
abstractive, 36–37
in Christ, 123–24
intuitive, 50, 123, 175 n. 24
See also knowledge
Condemnation of 1277, 74, 184 n. 7
confession
effect of, 138
and merit, 106–107
obligation for, 90
See also attrition; contrition
confirmation, and character, 138–39
Constantinople, Third Council of, 113

consubstantiation, 5, 141
contrition
  defined, 106–107
  and penance, 109
Courtenay, William J., 153 n. 2
Craig, William Lane, 160 n. 3, 170
  n. 44
creation
  proper to God, 77
  identical with conservation, 162 n. 13
Cross, Richard, 156 n. 15; 160 n. 53; 167
  n. 6; 171 n. 52; 177 nn. 48, 50; 183
  nn. 1, 2, 3; 184 nn. 6, 8, 10; 185
  n. 25; 186 nn. 26, 36, 47; 187 nn. 49,
  55; 192 nn. 79, 81, 82; 199 nn. 8, 9,
  200 nn. 13, 14; 209 nn. 53, 54, 61,
  62; 210 nn. 64, 71, 72

damnation, and predestination, 102–
  103
decalogue, 91–93
Dettloff, Werner, 196 n. 32
Dumont, Stephen, 155 n. 15, 158 n. 32,
  168 n. 18
Duns Scotus, John
  and Aquinas, 5
  and Bonaventure, 5
  and Franciscan theology, 5
  and Henry of Ghent, 5
  life of, 3–4
  and the Reformers, 5
  and William of Ockham, 5
  works of, 4, 6, 155 nn. 8–15

equivocation
  defined, 33
  harmful results of, 35–37
essence-existence distinction
  denied, 166 n. 54
  See also existence (esse)
essentialism, 174 n. 18
  and Christology, 115
eternity of world
  impossible according to
    Bonaventure, 162 n. 13
  possibility of, 162 n. 13
  possibility of in Aquinas, 162 n. 13

ethics, 89–95
  divine command theories of, 89–90,
    95, 190 n. 50
  natural law theories of, 90
Eucharist
  and anamnesis, 144
  causes of, 137
  effects of, 138
  and presence of Christ, 143–44
  as sacrifice, 144–45
  See also transubstantiation
existence (esse)
  and concrete parts, 115
  and hypostatic union, 114; 200
    nn. 15, 18
  See also being; essence-existence
    distinction

Father, divine
  and divine infinity, 63
  and divine memory, 62
  and procession of Holy Spirit, 64
  and procession of Son, 62
  See also person; Trinity
filioque. See Holy Spirit; Trinity
Finkenzeller, Josef, 157 n. 26
first agent, proof for existence of, 16–
  23, 25–26
  modal version, 19–23
  non-modal version, 16–19
  See also God
forgiveness, and satisfaction, 204
  n. 22
form, substantial, 69–70, 149
  as individual, 69
  See also forms, plurality of
formal distinction
  defined, 149
  and definition of person, 120–21,
    201 n. 35
  and divine attributes, 43
  and divine substance and attributes,
    43–45
  and God's simplicity, 43
  and individuation, 69–70, 149
  and infinity of divine attributes, 42,
    170 n. 52

formal distinction (*continued*)
  and the soul's powers, 83–84
  and Trinity, 69–70
forms, plurality of, 74
  and unity of body, 74–75
  See also form, substantial
Freddoso, Alfred J., 201 nn. 29, 35
freewill. *See* will, freedom of
Frank, William A., 34; 41; 53–54; 161
  n. 7; 176 nn. 39, 45, 46; 177 n. 47

Giles of Rome, 154 n. 5
  on theology as science, 158 n. 36
God
  absolute and ordained power of, 59,
    177 n. 68, 193 n. 82
  attributes of, 38–39, 43–45
  essence of, 7, 63
  existence of not known a priori, 164
    n. 29
  as first agent, 15–23
  formal distinction in, 42–45, 170
    n. 52
  freedom of, 52, 57–60, 93–94
  goodness of, 52
  ideas in, 50, 175 n. 22
  immutability of, 48, 173 n. 7
  indivisibility of, 69–69
  ineffability of, 39
  infinite power of, 27–28, 56–57
  infinity of, 26, 30, 32, 41–42, 63
  intellect of, 48, 62, 167 n. 7
  justice of, 91–93, 95, 192 n. 82
  knowledge of, 7, 48–50
  knowledge of contingent truths, 51–
    53
  knowledge of future contingents,
    53–55
  knowledge of G. and divine Word,
    62
  knowledge of necessary truths, 50–
    51
  knowledge of temporal truths, 55
  maximal excellence of, 23–26
  memory of, 62
  moral restrictions on power, 91, 191
    n. 57

necessity of, 21, 24, 48, 163 nn. 19–
    20, 173 n. 7
  not in genus, 171 n. 53
  not related to creatures, 48, 173 n. 10
  as object of *theologia in se*, 156 n. 16
  obligations of, 91, 94
  omnipotence of, 27–29, 56–57
  perfection of, 31–32
  as primary cause, 47–48, 53–54, 56
  pure actuality of, 171 n. 53
  self-knowledge of, 50, 51
  self-love of, 50
  simplicity of, 26, 29–30, 41–45, 48,
    171 n. 60, 173 n. 7
  substance of, 43–44, 172 n. 62
  timeless action of, 57–60, 62, 109,
    178 n. 72
  timelessness of, 55
  as ultimate goal of activity, 23, 25–26
  unconditioned, 48, 53, 90, 93–94,
    111, 155 n. 6
  unicity of, 26–29
  well-ordered actions of, 101–102,
    128, 204 n. 6
  will of, 47–48, 63, 64–65, 167 n. 7
  See also first agent, proof for
    existence of; Trinity; vision,
    beatific
Godfrey of Fontaines, 154 n. 5
Gonsalvus of Spain on theology as
  science, 158 n. 36
goodness, moral, 91, 190 n. 46, 191 n. 65
grace
  actual, 111
  and charity, 108
  and Christ's merit, 196 n. 24, 205 n. 34
  as habit, 108, 110–11
  and justice, 108
  and justification, 105–106
  and merit, 103
  and original justice, 98–99
  and remission of original sin, 206
    n. 51
  and remission of sins, 109–110
  See also Christ, grace of
Grajewski, Maurice, 212 n. 12
Gregory of Nazianzus, 61

Gregory of Nyssa, 61, 178 n. 1
Grosseteste, Robert, 63

habit, 107–108
    as active cause, 198 n. 56
    of grace, 108, 110–11
happiness
    and affections of will, 88–89
    as goal of action, 84
Henry of Ghent, 4
    on analogy, 34–35, 168 n. 23
    on Christ's beatific vision, 202 n. 40
    on divine action and the Trinity,
        70–71
    on divine ideas, 50
    and Duns Scotus, 5
    on essence-existence distinction, 50–
        51
    on God's ineffability, 39
    on God's knowledge of his own
        decisions, 52
    on perichoresis, 183 n. 71
    on sin, 96–97
Hilbert, David, 170 n. 44
Holy Spirit
    as communion, 63
    and divine infinity, 63
    as love, 63
    procession of, 36, 62–63
    See also person; Trinity
Honnefelder, Ludger, 211 n. 6
Hughes, Christopher, 166 n. 54
Hughes, Gerard J., 168 n. 19

immaculate conception of Mary, 5
impeccability
    of Christ, 122
    and freedom, 149–51
    and vision of God, 149
Incarnation, motive for, 127–29
individuation, 6, 69
    of accidents, 142
    and formal distinction, 149
    primacy of matter in, 80
infinity
    as intrinsic degree, 40–41
    as intrinsic mode, 42

mathematical properties of, 30
    See also God
Ingham, Mary Elizabeth, 154 n. 6
intellect
    as natural power, 85
    as power of soul, 83–84
    relation to will, 84, 86–87, 89, 190 n. 39
intellect, active. See intelligence
intellect, passive. See memory
intelligence, 49, 174 n. 16
intelligible objects, 49, 173 n. 12
    and production of mental word, 62
intelligible species. See intelligible
        objects
intrinsic mode, 40–42, 171 n. 53
    formally distinct from its subject, 42
intuitive cognition. See cognition

Jenkins, John I., 158 n. 32
Jesus. See Christ; Son, divine
John Duns Scotus. See Duns Scotus, John
John of Damascus, 182 n. 71
    Christology of, 113, 115
justice
    commutative and distributive, 93
    and divine command, 191 n. 65
    and merit, 104
    and right reason, 94–95
    virtue of, 108
    See also grace
justice, original
    and bodily incorruptibility, 97–98
    effect of, 97, 99
    and grace, 98–99
    as natural rectitude, 96–97
    as supernatural gift, 97
    and venial sin, 194 n. 105
justification
    and baptism, 130
    caused by merits of Christ, 129–30,
        205 n. 32
    and confession, 106
    and grace, 105, 110–11
    and merit, 105–106
    term used by Scotus, 205 n. 33
    types of, 92–93
    See also grace; justice

Kilwardby, Robert
  on plurality of forms, 184 n. 7
King, Peter, 170 n. 52, 188 n. 15
Kirwan, Christopher, 193 n. 90
knowledge, 48–49, 174 n. 15
  and belief, 8
  and body, 76–77
  immateriality of, 75; 184 nn. 11, 14,
    15
  and procession of Son, 62
  See also cognition
Knuuttila, Simo, 59–60, 175 n. 36, 178
  n. 70
Kretzmann, Norman, 167 n. 11, 177
  n. 49

Langston, Douglas C., 151; 168 n. 18;
  205 n. 35; 213 nn. 26, 27, 29
Lateran, Fourth Council of the, 68,
  139, 180 n. 34
Lee, Sukjae, 189 n. 27
Leibniz, 5, 60
Lobkowicz, Nicholas, 159 n. 42
Lombard, Peter, 4
  on grace and original justice, 98
  on sacraments, 207 n. 5
Lonergan, Bernard, 174 n. 14
lying, 94, 192 n. 79
Lyons, Council of, 180 n. 34

McGrath, Alister, 197 n. 36
Magrini, Aegidius, 158 n. 32
Major, John, 3, 153 n. 3
Mann, William E., 159 n. 49, 160 n. 50,
  171 n. 56
Marenbon, John, 173 n. 11, 174 n. 14
marriage, goals of, 92–93
Marx, Karl, on praxis, 159 n. 42
matter, 69–70
  in individuation, 80
memory, 49; 174 nn. 15, 16
  and production of mental word, 62
  See also remembering
merit
  and attrition, 106
  condign and congruous, 104–105,
    106, 195 n. 17
  and confession, 106
  and contrition, 106
  and demerit, 196 n. 25
  and divine acceptation, 103, 198
    n. 58
  and grace, 103, 105–106
  and justice, 104
  and justification, 105–106
  and Pelagianism, 106–107
  and predestination, 107
  and reward, 103, 129–30, 204 n. 26
  See also Christ; satisfaction
metaphysics
  independent of theology, 13
  object of, 8, 15, 147
  and proof of God's existence, 8, 15,
    147
  scope of, 8
  subject of, 147–48, 157 n. 30, 211
    n. 6
modalism, 61
monophysitism, 114
Moonan, Lawrence, 177 n. 66, 178
  n. 69
Moore, A. W., 166 n. 57
Morris, Thomas V., 94; 166 n. 2; 192
  n. 74; 203 nn. 67, 69

natural law, 91–92
  See also ethics
negations, ontological status of, 201
  n. 34
Nestorianism, 117–18, 120
Noone, Timothy, 155 n. 15

occasionalism, 57, 136–37
O'Connor, Timothy, 22; 163 n. 20; 164
  nn. 23, 34
O'Neill, Blane, 206 n. 47
ordination, 139
Ott, Ludwig, 199 n. 4

pact between God and creatures
  and divine reliability, 207 n. 19
  and power of God, 178 n. 68
  and sacraments, 137
Panaccio, Claude, 174 n. 14

Pannenberg, Wolfhart, 195 n. 3
Park, Woosuk, 212 n. 15
Pasnau, Robert, 174 n. 14
penance, and punishment, 109
perichoresis. *See* Trinity
Perler, Dominik, 174 n. 13
Pernoud, M. A., 178 n. 68
person
    Boethius's definition and divine p.,
        181 n. 53
    and Christ's human nature, 118–19
    constitution of divine p., 65–67
    defined, 66–67
    divine p. includes essence and
        property, 69–70
    divine p. and infinity, 63
    divine p. instance of divine essence,
        64–65, 68–69
    and formal distinction, 120–21, 201
        n. 35
    and possession of causal powers,
        122–23
    not univocal, 121
    and two-fold negation, 119–21, 201
        n. 26
Peter Lombard. *See* Lombard, Peter
possibility, logical, 59–60; 155 n. 6; 178
    nn. 69, 70
possible worlds, 5
power, causal
    free vs. natural, 85–88
    nature of, 161 n. 4
    and self-motion, 85–86
    subject of, 83–84, 122–23, 202 n. 44
power, legal, 208 n. 45
power for opposites, synchronic
    and freedom of will, 187 n. 14
    and God's action, 155 n. 6
    nature of, 57–58
    and theology, 154 n. 6
    See also will, freedom of
praxis, Scotus and Marx contrasted,
    159 n. 42
predestination
    and damnation, 102–103
    and Fall of Adam, 195 n. 3
    and foreseen merits, 101–102

and merit, 107
and salvation, 101–103
See also Christ, predestination of;
    grace; justification
Principe, Walter H., 200 n. 12
punishment
    and penance, 109
    voluntary and involuntary, 199 nn.
        50, 51
    See also satisfaction
pure perfections, 31–32, 38–39, 47,
    148, 172 n. 1
    See also transcendentals

Quinton, Anthony, 90, 190 n. 44

Ragland, C. P., 191 n. 51
Randi, Eugenio, 177 n. 68
redemption
    and debt-payment, 133
    of Mary, 132–33
    and merit, 129–30
    and merit of Christ, 195 n. 16
    and satisfaction, 129–31
    See also justification; predestination;
        salvation
remembering, 173 n. 11
    in Christ, 123
resurrection of body
    cannot be proved, 79–80
    identity of resurrected body, 80
    and natural agency, 78–79
    properties of resurrected body, 80–81
revelation
    as abstractive understanding of
        divine essence, 158 n. 32
    credibility of, 12
    impossibility of according to the
        "philosophers," 11
    necessity of in Aquinas and others,
        10
    not required for salvation, 11
    required for human action, 11–12,
        160 n. 50
    sources of, 7–8, 157 n. 26
Richard of St. Victor
    on disembodied soul, 120

right. *See* justice

Robert Grosseteste. *See* Grosseteste, Robert

Robert Kilwardby. *See* Kilwardby, Robert

Roo, William A. van, 194 n. 109

Rudavsky, Tamar M., 212 n. 15

Rupert of Deutz, 127

sacramental character, 8, 138–39, 208 n. 37

sacraments
  as causes, 136–37
  correspond to nature, 135
  defined, 135–36
  effects of, 138
  as *ex opere operato*, 207 n. 20
  number of, 135
  and Old Testament ceremonies, 138
  powers of minister of, 5, 137–39, 208 n. 45

sacrifice. *See* Eucharist

salvation
  and Christ's merits, 129–30
  willed by God, 101–103

satisfaction, 129–30, 197 n. 51
  and Christ's human nature, 131
  and merit, 131
  and punishment, 205 n. 40
  and remission of sin, 131, 206 n. 43

Schmaus, Michael, 180 n. 42

Schönberger, Rolf, 167 n. 11

science, nature of, 8–9, 158 n. 33
  in Aristotle, 9
  See also theology

science, theoretical and practical distinguished, 9–10, 159 n. 42

Scotus, John Duns. *See* Duns Scotus, John

Seeberg, Reinhold, 154 n. 6

sensation. *See* soul

sin, actual
  and act, 95
  as debt, 129
  explained, 88
  finitude of, 130
  forensic account of, 95–96

and guilt, 95–96
  and ignorance, 88
  and punishment, 95–96, 109–110
  venial, 194 n. 105

sin, original
  and concupiscence, 96, 99
  and Mary, 132–33
  as offense, 133
  and original guilt, 96
  and original justice, 99–100
  See also justice, original

sin, remission of, 5
  and Christ's merit, 129–30, 196 n. 24, 205 n. 32
  and grace, 109–110
  and original sin, 131, 197 n. 48, 205 n. 34, 206 n. 51
  and punishment, 109–110
  and satisfaction, 131, 206 n. 43

Son, divine
  and divine infinity, 62
  and divine will, 63–64
  generation of, 62
  and God's knowledge, 62, 179 n. 5
  personal property of, 64
  procession of, 36, 62
  and mental word, 62
  See also Christ; person; Trinity

soul
  and body, 68–69, 75–76
  created directly, 77, 185 n. 25
  and extension, 68–69
  immateriality of, 75, 184 n. 15
  incorruptibility of, 8, 73, 77–78
  and its powers, 83–84
  not person, 119–20
  and sensation, 76, 184 n. 14

sufficient reason, principle of, 20–21

Swinburne, Richard, 162 n. 12, 165 n. 47

synchronic contingency. *See* power for opposites, synchronic

theologia in se, 7
  object of, 156 n. 16
  as science, 157 n. 32
  See also theology

theologia nostra, 7
  See also theology
theology
  of blessed, 157 n. 32
  coherence of, 10, 159 n. 42
  and philosophy, 7–8, 154 n. 6
  as practical science, 9–10, 159 n. 42
  of prophets and apostles, 157 n. 32
  as science, generally, 8–9; 157 nn. 28,
    32; 158 n. 33
  scope of, 7–8, 157 n. 28
  sources of, 7–8, 157 n. 26
  See also theologia in se; *theologia
    nostra*
Thomas Aquinas. *See* Aquinas,
  Thomas
Thomas, Janice, 168 n. 28
Torrell, Jean-Pierre, 184 n. 7
transcendentals, 167–68, 211 n. 9, 212
  n. 12
  common to God and creatures, 39,
    169 n. 35
  and essential properties, 44
  and God's attributes, 32, 38
  and God's existence, 21, 23
  subject of metaphysics, 157 n. 30
transubstantiation, 5, 8, 73
  and accidents, 142–43
  as conversion of substance, 140–42
  defined, 139
  and place of Christ's body, 140–41
  and real presence, 141, 143–44
  See also Eucharist
Trent, Council of, 144
Trinity, 61
  absolute-property theory of,
    65–67
  analogies for, 62, 179 n. 4
  and divine action, 70–71
  and divine simplicity, 66
  and divine unity, 67–70
  and formal distinction, 69–70
  and Incarnation, 124–25
  and indivisibility of essence, 68–69
  and natural reason, 7, 156 n. 21
  notional vs. essential acts in, 62–64,
    179 n. 10

  and number, 182 n. 70
  and perichoresis, 182 n. 71
  processions in, 62–65
  relation theory of, 65–67
  and relations of origin, 64
  social models for, 61
  and tritheism, 61
  See also Father, divine; Holy Spirit;
    person; Son, divine

union, hypostatic, 114–17
  and accidental whole, 114–15
  cause of, 124–25
  and concrete whole, 114–15
  contingency of, 118–19
  and God's unconditioned nature,
    117
  See also Christ
univocity
  of being, 168 n. 18
  of concepts, 168 n. 18
  defined, 33
  and definition of person, 121
  and divine simplicity, 43–44
  and equivocation, 34–35
  necessary for analogy, 37–38
  of terms, 168 n. 18
  and Trinitarian relations, 66

Veuthey, Léon, 154 n. 6
virtue
  as habit, 107–108
  theological, 108
  See also grace
vision, beatific
  active vs. passive, 149
  caused by Christ's merits,
    129–30
  cognitive vs. appetitive, 149
  as goal of human action, 11–12, 85,
    189 n. 28
  and impeccability, 133, 149–51
  and intuitive cognition of divine
    essence, 124, 158 n. 32
  See also happiness
Vooght, Paul de, 156 n. 23
Vos Jaczn., Antonie, 154 n. 6

Wainwright, William J., 165 nn. 42, 47
Ware, William of. *See* William of Ware
Wass, Meldon C., 170 n. 41
Wetter, Friedrich, 178 n. 2, 181 n. 46
will
    and intellect, 84, 86–87, 89, 190 n. 39
    as power of soul, 83–84
will, freedom of
    and affection for justice, 86–89, 189 n. 27
    and coercion, 151
    defended, 86
    and determinism, 150–51, 188 n. 15
    and God's causal concurrence, 47–48; 53–54; 176 nn. 45, 46
    and immateriality of soul, 75
    nature of, 6, 57–58
    See also power for opposites, synchronic
William of Alnwick, 6
William of Auxerre
    on hypostatic union, 115
    on negation theory of person, 201 n. 26

William of Ockham
    and Duns Scotus, 5
    on immateriality of knowledge, 184 n. 11
    on negation theory of person, 120
    on philosophical incoherence of Trinity, 159 n. 42
William of Ware, 154 n. 5
    on Christ's human nature, 200 n. 13
    on theology as science, 158 n. 36
Williams, Norman Powell, 193 nn. 89, 90
Williams, Thomas, 188 n. 22, 190 n. 50
Wippel, John F., 175 n. 30
Wolter, Allan B., 34; 41; 53–54; 94–95; 153 n. 2; 155 n. 15; 161 n. 3; 170 n. 52; 173 n. 11; 174 n. 12; 176 nn. 39, 42, 43, 44, 45; 182 n. 58; 206 n. 47; 211 nn. 4, 9, 10; 212 nn. 12, 15
Wood, Rega, 160 n. 3
Word, divine. *See* Christ; Son, divine
word, mental, 49, 174 nn. 15, 17

Zavalloni, Roberto, 184 n. 8